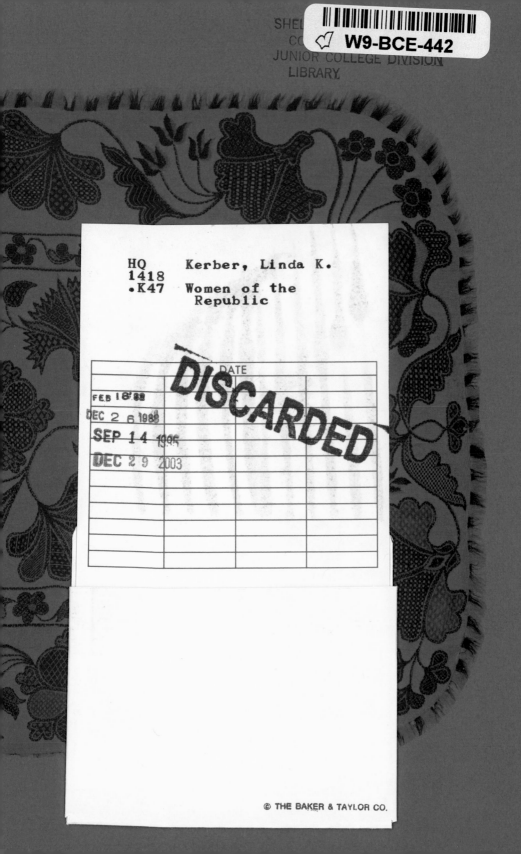

Women of the Republic

LINDA K. KERBER

Women of the Republic

INTELLECT AND IDEOLOGY

IN REVOLUTIONARY AMERICA

PUBLISHED FOR THE INSTITUTE OF

EARLY AMERICAN HISTORY AND CULTURE

WILLIAMSBURG, VIRGINIA

BY THE UNIVERSITY OF NORTH CAROLINA PRESS

CHAPEL HILL

The Institute of Early American
History and Culture
is sponsored jointly by
The College of William and Mary and
The Colonial Williamsburg Foundation.

Manufactured in the United States of America
Cloth edition, ISBN 0-8078-1440-7
Paper edition, ISBN 0-8078-4065-3
Library of Congress Catalog Card Number 79-28683

Library of Congress Cataloging in Publication Data

Kerber, Linda K
    Women of the Republic.

    Includes index.
    1. Women—United States—History. 2. United
States—History—Revolution, 1775–1783. I. Title.
HQ1418.K47   305.4'2'0973   79-28683
ISBN 0-8078-1440-7
ISBN 0-8078-4065-3 pbk.

FOR

Justin Seth Kerber and

Ross Jeremy Kerber

Contents

Illustrations

Preface

Women of the Republic began as an essay to honor the memory of Richard Hofstadter. I intended to write a brief account of Americans' response to Mary Wollstonecraft's explosive *Vindication of the Rights of Woman*, a simple report on the passage of political ideas across the Atlantic. But it quickly became apparent to me that some American women and men had begun to wrestle with Wollstonecraft's major issues —the place of women in the political system, and the extent to which women's independence and intelligence ought to be encouraged—long before the *Vindication* arrived in America. When the Philadelphian Elizabeth Drinker, a conservative Quaker, read the radical *Vindication*, she observed calmly, "In very many of her sentiments, she ... *speaks my mind.*"

The Revolutionary era is one of the most exciting periods in the American past, a time of innovation and risk taking in political theory and practice, a period of spiritual revival and social change. American women shared in the turmoil of their times, and many thought hard about their place in the new republic. Their testimony endures in letters and diaries, court records, petitions to legislatures, pamphlets, and books. With the notable exception of Mary Sumner Benson, historians have not read these records with sufficient care. Libraries have often cataloged women's papers as "family miscellany" or "Letters from Ladies"; writers have been content to draw upon them as a source of local color or charming anecdote. The "real" story of the Revolutionary years has been thought to lie in accounts of battles or constitutional conventions—events from which women were necessarily absent—and women's work has been treated as service to men, women's words treated as trivial.

This book assumes that women's work and women's words did make a difference, and that our understanding of the general contours of the American past will be more accurate if we assess women's experience as carefully as we do men's experience. The early Republic does look different when seen through women's eyes. The Revolutionary army turns out to have been dependent on women for nursing, cooking, and cleanliness. Both patriot and tory forces could recruit men not because cheerful women waved them off to war, but because those same women bravely stayed on alone, keeping family farms and mills in operation, fending off squatters, and protecting the family property by their heavy labor, often at grave physical risk. Political theory appears less radical and more conservative when measured against the conscious refusal of constitution makers to recognize women's presence in the Republic and to change women's status. And the catalog of significant American literature is enriched by the addition of essays, memoirs, and fiction written by women that have awaited careful evaluation.

When in 1848 Elizabeth Cady Stanton came to write the Declaration of Sentiments for the New York Women's Rights Convention in Seneca Falls, she shaped it as a direct echo in form and substance of the Declaration of Independence. This did not represent a failure of imagination—Stanton would show in the course of a long career that she could write forcefully in her own voice. Rather, it was a conscious effort to make a political point. There had been a blind spot in the Revolutionary vision. The promises of the Revolution had not been explored for what they might mean to women. The obvious way to make this point was to write a parallel declaration; to ask what the Declaration of Independence might have been like had women's private and public demands been included.

The paired female images of so many engravings of the Revolutionary era that show both Minerva, emblem of force and intelligence, and Columbia, surrounded by emblems of domestic work and prosperity, suggest the difficulty of merging the two themes. A synthesis was needed that would facilitate women's entry into politics without denying women's commitment to domesticity. The search for this synthesis has permeated women's history in America from the time of the Revolution to our own; this book explores the early stages of that search. I hope it will be clear that I have treated women's history both as a subject to be studied for its own intrinsic interest, and as a strategy by which we can test long-accepted generalizations about the past.

It is a pleasure, at last, to thank the archivists, librarians, and curators of manuscripts and prints who welcomed me to their institutions and introduced me to the rare materials under their care. I am especially grateful to Peter Parker, Historical Society of Pennsylvania; William Joyce and Georgia Baumgardner, American Antiquarian Society; Eunice Gillman DiBella, Connecticut State Library; Tom Dunnings, New-York Historical Society; Carolyn Sung, Manuscript Division, Library of Congress; Kenneth Harris and George Chalou, National Archives; Winifred Collins,

Massachusetts Historical Society; George Stevenson and Ellen McGrew, North Carolina Division of Archives and History; Allan Stokes, South Caroliniana Library, University of South Carolina; Charles Lessor, South Carolina Department of Archives and History; George C. Rogers, The Papers of Henry Laurens, University of South Carolina; Kenneth Lohf and Ene Sirvet, Columbia University; Mrs. Granville T. Prior, South Carolina Historical Society; Suzanne Boorsch, Metropolitan Museum of Art; Roberta Wadell, Prints and Drawings, New York Public Library; Susan Burrows Swan and McSherry Fowble, Winterthur Museum. Keith Rageth has been an indefatigable director of the interlibrary loan division of the University of Iowa libraries. Mary-Jo Kline of The Papers of Aaron Burr, New-York Historical Society, generously shared her extensive knowledge of the period and pointed me to collections I would have missed.

The American Bar Foundation, the American Council of Learned Societies, and the National Endowment for the Humanities provided funds that supported both research and writing. I am deeply grateful, not least for the confidence that these foundations offered in the early stages of the project. I am indebted to the University of Iowa for an environment conducive to writing and for a research leave in 1976. My colleagues in the history department have encouraged this work from the beginning. Michel Dahlin of Stanford University and Robert Humphrey, Steven Krumpe, and Jill Harsin of the University of Iowa have been helpful research assistants. Eunice Prosser and Elaine Melcher of the University of Iowa typed the manuscript with precision and understanding.

I have been a beneficiary of the heightened interest in early American history that accompanied the Bicentennial. Audiences at the Columbia University Early American History Seminar, the University of Pennsylvania, the University of California–Irvine, Indiana University, Temple University, Brigham Young University, Baruch College–City University of New York, Marquette University, and at annual meetings of the American Historical Association, the Minnesota Historical Society, the Southern Historical Association, and the Organization of American Historians have asked questions that helped me refine my ideas. Portions of this work have been published in Stanley Elkins and Eric McKitrick, eds., *The Hofstadter Aegis: A Memorial* (New York, 1974); *American Quarterly*, XXVIII (1976), 187–205; and Jaroslaw Pelenski, ed., *The American and European Revolutions, 1776–1848: Sociopolitical and Ideological Ramifications* (Iowa City, Iowa, 1980).

Friends and colleagues have shown that a community of scholars really exists. Sydney V. James of the University of Iowa read the entire manuscript in a rough and early stage and his thoughtful reactions helped me to reshape and reform it. Donald Sutherland, another colleague, shared his immense knowledge of legal history. John S. Rosenberg of Arlington, Virginia, took time from his own work to read the entire draft with a fine editorial eye; he refined the prose and asked incisive questions. Anne Firor Scott of Duke University read the entire manuscript and helped me place it in perspective. Eric McKitrick, Stanley Elkins, John Diggins, and Joseph Ellis offered good counsel on early versions of chapters 1 and 7; Gerda Lerner, Blanche Wiesen Cook, and Dorothy Ross read the completed manuscript. Norman Fiering of the Institute of Early American History and Culture decided early that this book ought to be published; I appreciate the combination of patience and criticism that he, Clare Novak, and Cynthia Carter have displayed as they edited the manuscript.

My parents, Dorothy Haber Kaufman and Harry Hagman Kaufman, have made their belief in this book clear, and I appreciate their love and support. My greatest debt is to my husband, Richard Kerber, whose confidence has sustained me from the beginning. He has made many sacrifices in his own work so that mine could proceed unhindered, and his wise advice has sharpened my argument and clarified every page of my prose. This book is offered to our sons Ross and Justin, with gratitude for their patience, thanks for their love, and the resolve that my next book will have some boys in it.

Women of the Republic

Introduction

THE WOMEN'S WORLD OF

THE EARLY REPUBLIC

The word "idiot" comes from a Greek root meaning private person. Idiocy is the female defect; intent on their private lives, women follow their fate through a darkness deep as that cast by malformed cells in the brain. It is not worse than the male defect, which is lunacy: they are so obsessed by public affairs that they see the world as by moonlight, which shows the outlines of every object but not the details indicative of their nature.

—Rebecca West, *Black Lamb and Grey Falcon*

Benjamin Tanner after John J. Barralet, *America Guided by Wisdom* (1820). In Barralet's allegorical vision of the Republic, the major characters are female. The goddess of liberty, accompanied by Minerva, presides over a rich land. Nearby, Ceres sits with implements of agriculture and another woman spins. Washington, on a charger, is relegated to a niche in the background.
Courtesy The Henry Francis du Pont Winterthur Museum.

THE PRE-REVOLUTIONARY colonial world antedated both the political and industrial revolutions. Circumscribed by the lack of roads, bounded by the strength of local traditions, limited by the constraints of the preindustrial family economy, most people in pre-Revolutionary America lived out their lives in a rural culture and an agricultural economy. Like most women in preindustrial societies, eighteenth-century American women lived in what might be called a woman's domain. Their daily activities took place within a feminine, domestic circle: infants were delivered by midwives, the sick were cared for by nurses, women who traveled stayed overnight at boardinghouses owned or run by females. We may think of women as forming a tradition-bound, underdeveloped nation within a larger, more politically sophisticated one; the early Revolutionary crisis found most women and a substantial minority of men living lives shaped by local isolation, political apathy, and rudimentary literacy.

In the late eighteenth century, this traditional world was battered by the storms of political and technological change. Industrial technology reshaped the contours of domestic labor and thus began to erode the stability of households. The war of the Revolution and the constitutional experiments that followed composed one of the great ages of political innovation in Western history; in these years the terms were set by which future Americans would understand their relationship to the social order. A restrained, deferential democracy characteristic of American colonial localities gradually gave way to an aggressive, egalitarian, modern participatory democracy. A republican ideology redefined the political order and challenged fundamental assumptions: What does it mean to be a citizen? Who has a right to rule? Who ought to be content with being ruled?

But republican ideology primarily concerned a single sex rather than an American community of both sexes. Americans had inherited their political vocabulary from Aristotle, who believed that the good life could be realized only in the context of the public sector, a strictly male arena. Women were thought to make their moral choices in the context of the household, a woman's domain that Aristotle understood to be a nonpublic, lesser institution that served the polis. Having learned from Aristotle that politics was the affair of men, Americans continued to discuss political affairs in terms that largely excluded women, and that reflected the assumption that women were, as the political scientist Jean Elshtain writes, "*idiots* in the Greek sense of the word, that is, persons who do not participate in the polis."[1]

The assumption that women were not a central part of the political community continued to be made by the political theorists of the Enlightenment and of the British Whig Opposition. For at least a generation before 1776, American activists and pamphleteers had used the occasion of each imperial crisis to challenge American men to change their habitual obedience to elites and to England, to emerge from a world of custom and tradition, to behave as a serious political opposition. These pre-Revolutionary agitators addressed themselves to men. It was men who passed resolutions in town meetings, men who refused to try legal cases with stamped writs. The pre-Revolutionary crises were their political education.

Since the days of Anne Hutchinson, however, no secular group or institution had consistently sought to articulate the impact of imperial policy on women. There were many isolated exceptions: the crowds of women who fought the establishment of smallpox inoculation centers too close to their homes, the women who accompanied Maj. Gen. Edward Braddock's troops as cooks and nurses during the French and Indian War, the women merchants and traders who signed the famous "petition" of New York's "she-Merchants." Not until economic boycott became a major mode of resistance to England did it become obvious that women would also have to be pulled out of the privacy of their traditional domain and propelled into the public world of political decisions. A set of political arguments, explored in some detail in chapter 2, emerged to persuade—and to pressure—women to adhere to consumption codes. These arguments may be read as an effort to define the obligations women owed to the state, of which they were at last conceded to comprise a part.

How did the Revolution affect women? This is a difficult question to answer. The men who made the Revolution assumed that the war was theirs to make. There was no formal political context in which women might be consulted or might develop their collective judgment. But the war itself did speed the integration of women into the civil polity. Whether a woman was whig or tory, her services in a largely guerrilla war were much sought after—as a provider of essential services for troops, as a civilian source of food and shelter, as a contributor of funds

---

1. Jean Bethke Elshtain, "Moral Woman and Immoral Man: A Consideration of the Public-Private Split and Its Political Ramifications," *Politics and Society*, IV (1974), 455.

and supplies, as a spy. Women were challenged to commit themselves politically and then to justify their allegiance. The war raised once again the old question of whether a woman could be a patriot—that is, an essentially political person—and it also raised the question of what form female patriotism might take.

These questions were not resolved by the war's end. For example, one well-known element in British common law, which few Americans questioned, was coverture, the absorption of a married woman's property into her husband's control during the life of their marriage. Since only the citizen with independent control of property was thought to be able to exercise free will, it seemed to follow that the married woman had no independent political capacity. State legislatures in the new republic took care to show they understood that male and female political behavior required judgment by different standards. On the one hand women—married or unmarried—were responsible for acts of espionage or treason and were subject to the full penalties of the law. But except for overt acts of treason, the assumption still prevailed that married women could make no political choices of their own; for example, the wife of a tory was judged to be under such clear control of her husband that she perforce became a tory herself.

During wartime this assumption caught women in a double bind: women left at home while their husbands fought for the loyalists were often ostracized by their communities and forced into exile without being asked their own political opinions. But women with property may have been somewhat less vulnerable to patriot pressure. Confiscation acts normally excluded dower portions from seizure. Once the war was over, Americans permitted themselves to be even more sympathetic to the awkward position of the married woman and assumed she had been apolitical unless proven otherwise. Courts did not try to catch the loyalist's wife between the reality of dependence on her husband for support and the radical claim that she should have established her own individual commitment to the Republic; the woman who had gone into exile with her husband was generally able to reclaim her own property.

This sympathetic treatment was commendable and fair—judges did not change rules midstream—but it also suggests the conservatism of the legal revolution. Even the most radical American men had not intended to make a revolution in the status of their wives and sisters. Coverture continued into the early Republic and continued to shape the relations of women to the state. Separate equity jurisdiction, which had always been somewhat more accessible to women, declined as postwar court systems were rationalized, but such safeguards of women's control of property as married women's property acts, which were designed to replace equity jurisdiction, were more than a generation away. (The first was not passed until 1839.) Less and less care was taken in the postwar years to preserve dower thirds as commerce and speculation made land an even more liquid commodity than it had ever been—how was a man whose holdings changed annually and fluctuated wildly in value to tell what portion his wife ultimately ought to claim as one-third of all real property he had *ever* held?

Although the Revolution diluted the laws of coverture only slightly, it did have a clear impact on the law of divorce. The principles of the Revolution, after all, had laid great stress on the right to be free of burdensome masters, and the rhetoric of the Revolution had drawn heavily on the imagery of the happy and the unhappy family. After the war, a number of states passed laws that the British had disallowed in the colonial era, making divorce more accessible. In states such as Massachusetts and Connecticut more people seem to have taken advantage of existing laws, and the divorce history of these states suggests that some women became increasingly assertive and autonomous in their private behavior.

The new republic leaned on the law for structure. In turn, an educated citizenry was expected to maintain the spirit of the law; righteous mothers were asked to raise the virtuous male citizens on whom the health of the Republic depended. This assumption added political and ideological overtones even to technical discussions of education. A revolution in women's education had been underway in England and America when the Revolution began; in postwar America the ideology of female education came to be tied to ideas about the sort of woman who would be of greatest service to the Republic. Discussions of female education were apt to be highly ambivalent. On one hand, republican political theory called for a sensibly educated female citizenry to educate future generations of sensible republicans; on the other, domestic tradition condemned highly educated women as perverse threats to family stability. Consequently, when American educators discussed the uses of the female intellect, much of their discussion was explicitly anti-intellectual.

Caught between the rationalists of the Enlightenment and the romantics, ignoring ideologues who tried to tell them what to read, middle-class women of the early Republic persisted in choosing to write and to read fiction that with few exceptions acknowledged, even celebrated, female weakness and emotionalism. Excluded from the world of politics, women were understandably cool to Montesquieu, Gibbon, Rousseau. Female readers sought accounts of women grappling with reality; in epistolary fiction and in religious memoirs they found detailed accounts of women who overcame evil by purity, who overcame force by apparent concession. They learned that the seduced were likely to be abandoned; they were taught not to trust their own passions. Ambition, energy, originality —laudable in men—were to be distrusted in women.

The new nation also witnessed the development of an ambivalent ideology concerning the political role of women. Charles Brockden Brown, Benjamin Rush, and a few other men thought seriously about the implications of the new republic for women's lives. But the central architects of the new female ideology were women: not only Judith Sargent Murray and Susannah Rowson, but also the anonymous "Female Advocate" of Hartford, Connecticut, novelists like Hannah Webster Foster and her daughters, and playwrights like Mercy Otis Warren. Equally important were the throngs of anonymous women who read these female writers, wrote letters to each other, kept personal diaries, tested the responsiveness of the government to their needs by petitions to legislatures and lawsuits in courts, and began to organize themselves in benevolent and charitable societies.

For many women the Revolution had been a strongly politicizing experience, but the newly created republic made little room for them as political beings. The female experience of both the Revolution and the Republic was different from that of men, and not only because women did not fight in the army. Long before the famous New York Women's Rights Convention in 1848, American women had begun to explore the implications of the republican revolution for their lives. Searching for a political context in which private female virtues might comfortably coexist with the civic virtue that was widely regarded as the cement of the Republic, they found what they were seeking in the notion of what might be called "Republican Motherhood." The Republican Mother integrated political values into her domestic life. Dedicated as she was to the nurture of public-spirited male citizens, she guaranteed the steady infusion of virtue into the Republic. Political "virtue," a revolutionary concept that has troubled writers from Edmund Burke to Hannah Arendt, could be safely domesticated in eighteenth-century America; the mother, and not the masses, came to be seen as the custodian of civic morality.[2]

The language of Republican Motherhood provided the justification of

2. For a discussion of the dangers of absolute concepts of political virtue, see Hannah Arendt, *On Revolution* (New York, 1965), 74–83.

women's political behavior; it bridged the gap between idiocy and the polis. The woman now claimed a significant political role, though she played it in the home. This new identity had the advantage of appearing to reconcile politics and domesticity; it justified continued political education and political sensibility. But the role remained a severely limited one; it had no collective definition, provided no outlet for women to affect a real political decision. If women were no longer prepolitical, they certainly were not fully political. The image of the Republican Mother could be used to mask women's true place in the polis: they were still on its edges.

It is a measure of the conservatism of the Revolution that women remained on the periphery of the political community; it is possible to read the subsequent political history of women in America as the story of women's efforts to accomplish for themselves what the Revolution had failed to do. From the time of the Revolution until our own day, the language of Republican Motherhood remains the most readily accepted—though certainly not the most radical—justification for women's political behavior. This book is an account of its origins.

Chapter 1

"EMPIRE OF COMPLACENCY": THE INHERITANCE OF THE ENLIGHTENMENT

Are not women born as free as men?

—James Otis

Keep Within Compass (*ca.* 1785–1805). The message to the young woman, tatting even as she walks, is one of caution and restraint.
Courtesy The Henry Francis du Pont Winterthur Museum.

THE GREAT QUESTIONS of political liberty and civic freedom, of the relationship between law and liberty, the subjects of so many ideological struggles in the eighteenth century, are questions that ignore gender. Philosophes habitually indulged in vast generalizations about humanity: Montesquieu contemplated the nature of society; Rousseau formulated a scheme for the revitalized education of children; Lord Kames wrote four volumes on the history of mankind. The broad sweep of their generalizations indicates that Enlightenment writers indeed meant to include all people in their observations. Even their regular use of the generic *he*, which may disturb twentieth-century readers, is usually thought to be a matter of syntax and usage and without historical significance.

However, we should be skeptical of the generous assumption that the Enlightenment *man* was intended to be generic. *Philosophe* is a male noun: it describes Immanuel Kant, Adam Smith, Denis Diderot, G. E. Lessing, Benjamin Franklin, John Locke, Jean Jacques Rousseau. With the conspicuous exceptions of Catharine Macaulay and Mary Wollstonecraft, women are absent even from the second and third ranks of philosophes. They hover on the fringes, creating a milieu for discussions in their salons, offering personal and moral support to male friends and lovers, but making only minor intellectual contributions. Mme Helvétius and Mme Brillon, Mme Condorcet, even Catherine the Great of Russia, are consumers, not creators, of Enlightenment ideas. It is, then, not surprising that the Polly Stevensons, the Sophie Vollands, the Maria Cosways figure primarily as the addressees of letters by Franklin, Diderot, Jefferson.

A careful reading of the main texts of the Enlightenment in France, England, and the colonies reveals that the nature of the relationship between women and the state remained largely unexamined; the authors' use of *man* was in fact literal, not generic. Only by implication did the most prominent male writers say anything of substance about the function and responsibilities of women in the monarchies they knew and in the ideal communities they invented. Just as their inadvertent comments on the mob reveal the limits of their democratic theory, their comments on women reveal the limits of their conception of civic virtue.

Perhaps the most striking feature of Enlightenment literature is that the more abstract and theoretical a writer's intention, the more likely that his analysis of the social order would include women. A standard way of reinventing natural law was to imagine the first family in a state of nature and then to deduce political relationships from its situation. This approach virtually forced many philosophes to contemplate women's political role—even if, like Rousseau, they disapproved of women who intruded into politics. By contrast, writers (like those of the English Whig Opposition) whose primary intention was to criticize specific contemporary affairs were less likely to be driven to serious consideration of women as political beings.

The Enlightenment represented, Peter Gay has remarked, "man's claim to be recognized as an adult, responsible being" who would "take the risk of discovery, exercise the right of unfettered criticism, accept the loneliness of autonomy."[1] It is worth asking whether women were also expected to claim recognition as responsible beings. Could women also be enlightened? To what extent was there room for women in the philosophes' vision of the political order?

Let us begin with Thomas Hobbes, who normally spoke of the state as a male enterprise founded to prevent excesses of force. Hobbes understood the male-dominated state to be an artificial construction. "Dominion is acquired two ways," he wrote in *Leviathan*, "by generation, and by conquest. The right of dominion by generation, is that which the parent hath over his children." Immediately a logical problem presented itself: although power over the child seemed by definition to be appropriately shared by the child's two progenitors, only one parent could dominate, "for no man can obey two masters." In a "state of mere nature," before civil society had been organized and laws established, it seemed logical to Hobbes that natural "dominion is in the mother," if only because "it cannot be known who is the father, unless it be declared by the mother; and therefore the right of dominion over the child dependeth on her will, and is consequently hers." It also seemed clear to him that mothers made the crucial decision whether to nourish the child or to expose it to death; "if she nourish it, it oweth its life to the mother; and is therefore obliged to obey her, rather than any other."

Hobbes acknowledged that his reasoning might seem novel to his readers because they were accustomed to life in a polity in which "this controversy is decided by the civil law; and for the most part, but not always, the sentence is in favour of the father; because for the most part commonwealths have been erected by the fathers, not by the mothers of families."[2] Hobbes the skeptic believed that civilization is the result of conventions, not nature—this point accounts for his notoriety in his own time as well

1. Peter Gay, *The Enlightenment: An Interpretation. The Rise of Modern Paganism* (New York, 1966), 3.
2. Thomas Hobbes, *Leviathan* (New York, 1946), 130–131.

as his acceptance among moderns. What is not often noticed is that one element in the artificiality of the civic culture is the subjection of mothers to fathers. Hobbes did not question that subjection; indeed in discussing royal succession he comfortably made the point that male heirs were to be preferred to females "because men, are naturally fitter than women, for actions of labour and danger." But that female subjection is of human creation, Hobbes left no doubt; for proof, he offered Amazons (whom he thought historical) and sovereign queens as exceptions to the rule that dominion over the child belongs to the husband.[3]

In his *First Treatise of Government*, John Locke more fully integrated women into the political order. Locke's *Two Treatises of Government* are a direct attack on Robert Filmer's *Patriarcha*, which spins a justification for absolute monarchy by divine right out of the biblical injunction to "honor thy father." But the commandment, after all, is to "honor thy father and thy mother." Filmer's defense of absolutism in government conveniently forgot mothers. He described a power structure that was masculine, that was absolute, and that relied on primogeniture. To create and defend this structure as he did, Filmer had to ignore a large network of other relationships and impose a hierarchical order on all those he did acknowledge. Locke needed for his purposes only a reader who would concede that the biblical commandment was to "honor thy father and thy mother"; given this admission, Locke could proceed to race through Filmer, restoring mothers as he went, and by that device undercut Filmer's analogy between parental power and royal authority. If familial power is shared with women and limited by mutual responsibilities, the nature of royal authority must also be shared and limited. What Locke accomplished in the *First Treatise* was the integration of women into social theory.[4]

"The *first Society* was between Man and Wife," Locke wrote in the *Second Treatise*, "which gave beginning to that between Parents and Children; to which, in time, that between Master and Servant came to be added." But all relationships are not hierarchical: "*Conjugal Society* is made by a voluntary Compact between Man and Woman."[5] The grant of dominion made to Adam in Genesis did not, as Filmer contended, give

---

3. *Ibid.*, 128, 131.

4. John Locke, *Two Treatises of Government*, ed. Peter Laslett, 2d ed. (Cambridge, 1967); see especially I, secs. 62–65. See also Robert Filmer, *Patriarcha: or the Natural Power of Kings*, in Thomas I. Cook, ed., *Two Treatises of Government, with a Supplement, Patriarcha, by Robert Filmer* (New York, 1947).

5. Locke, *Two Treatises*, ed. Laslett, II, secs. 77, 78.

Adam monarchical power over all people and over Eve in particular, it gave all human beings authority over animals. If Adam was named lord of the world, Eve was lady. The curse of Eve, Locke thought, could not justify women's permanent and universal submission to men. The curse was part of her punishment for sin, but it was a sin that Adam had shared and for which he too was punished, not rewarded. Husbands reigned over wives, wives suffered the pains of childbirth; but these conditions could be changed by human intention. Labor might be medically eased, and a woman who was queen in her own right was not necessarily bound to become, when she married, her husband's subject.[6]

Locke came closer than most of his contemporaries and successors to specifying a political role for women. He underlined the rights and powers women ought to have in their domestic capacity. Mothers have, Locke thought, a right to filial respect that is not dependent on the husband's will; mothers have their own responsibilities to their children; women ought to control their own property. Locke coolly argued that the primary justification for marriage is the lengthy dependence and vulnerability of children. Indeed, he even came close to suggesting that divorce ought to be considered a reasonable resolution for an unhappy marriage by questioning "why this *Compact*, where Procreation and Education are secured, and Inheritance taken care for, may not be made determinable, either by consent, or at a certain time, or upon certain Conditions, as well as any other voluntary Compacts, there being no necessity in the nature of the thing . . . that it should always be for Life." There is not even a hint in his work that women unsex themselves when they step into the political domain.[7]

But once Filmer's argument had been disposed of, and Locke could generalize more broadly about civic powers and responsibilities, his interest in the role of women in the social order diminished. He did, however, phrase his most significant generalizations in the *Second Treatise* in terms of *persons*. His proposed legislative body was composed of persons; the supreme power was placed in them by the people; and war was defined as "using Force upon the People without Authority."[8] Women were included, presumably, among "the People," but an individual woman had no political mechanism for expressing her own will.[9] Locke obviously

6. *Ibid.*, I, secs. 30, 47.
7. *Ibid.*, secs. 61, 63, II, secs. 52, 65, 183, 80–83.
8. *Ibid.*, II, secs. 124, 153, 154, 155.
9. For women as a special case of relatively minor significance, see *ibid.*, secs. 180–183, 233.

assumed that women contributed in some way to the civic culture, but he provided no procedures by which they might act politically. Unfortunately, he did not write a *Third Treatise*.

Montesquieu also returned to first principles: "I have first of all considered mankind."[10] The principles that regulate governments—virtue in a republic, honor in a monarchy, fear in a despotism—are, for Montesquieu, abstractions apparently devoid of gender. The civic virtue that buttresses a republic is transmitted by parents (not only fathers) who are responsible for raising virtuous children (not only sons).

Sensitive to the implications of private manners for public style, Montesquieu found in the status of women an important index to the politics of a society. It was no accident, Montesquieu thought, that despotic societies, which delight "in treating all with severity," normally reduced women to a state of servitude. "In a government which requires, above all things, that a particular regard be paid to its tranquillity, . . . it is absolutely necessary to shut up the women." Montesquieu did not coin the modern term *sex object*, but he closely suggested it in his comment that women in despotisms "are themselves an object of luxury."

Montesquieu was very critical of "luxury," by which he meant not only wealth and expensive consumption but sexual self-indulgence as well. To banish luxury was to banish vice. Other forms of government came closer to this aim than did monarchies, and thereby gave women greater freedom. Monarchies offered women a higher social standing, but nevertheless left them vulnerable to manipulation: "Each courtier avails himself of their charms and passions, in order to advance his fortunes." On the other hand, "in republics women are free by the laws and constrained by manners." Yet even republics "constrain" women, if only by the force of manners and the threat of social ostracism. To the extent that women attract men's attentions, they always, in some measure, counteract the state's claim on men's emotions and loyalty. The traditional claim that women express their patriotism by sending their husbands off to war is not silly, for these women voluntarily relinquish a private claim on men in order that the public claim can have more force.[11]

Montesquieu explored some of these themes with great subtlety in the *Persian Letters*, which Marshall Berman calls "the first distinctively *political* novel written in the west." In Montesquieu's Persia, public despotism is mirrored in the private harem. Both are systems of dominance and

10. Charles Louis de Secondat, baron de Montesquieu, *The Spirit of the Laws*, trans. Thomas Nugent, I (New York, 1949), lxvii.

11. *Ibid.*, 101–104, 256.

submission, and one needs the other in order to exist. Sexual style is thus an adjunct of political style; when one is revised, so is the other. Indeed, as Berman eloquently argues, the core of Montesquieu's originality lies "in exposing and exploring the intimate relation between personal passion and political action. . . . Thus the freedom or repression, equality or inequality in a state is a function, not of its merely political organization, but of the structure of its personal and social life as a whole."[12] In the course of the novel, the Persian Uzbek is gradually sensitized to the evidence of individuality in his wives; the narrative culminates in a rebellion by the women of the seraglio, whose revolt takes the form of the assertion of their own sexual independence. The revolt is prefaced by an extraordinary myth in which a woman's heaven is defined as a place of complete sexual gratification, and in which real women will submit to a constraining political order only if they are free to express themselves sexually.[13] Montesquieu openly asks "whether women are subject to men by the law of nature"; the answer is negative. "Our authority over women is absolutely tyrannical; they have allowed us to impose it only because they are more gentle than we are, and consequently more humane and reasonable."[14]

Locke had implied that the availability of divorce is the ultimate test of marital freedom; Montesquieu came close to doing the same. He believed that affection and mutual benefit are the basic motives for continuing human relationships—between husband and wife, and between king and subject. The absence of divorce meant that roles, once chosen or assigned, must be played in perpetuity. Freedom within marriage, like freedom within the state, implied the ability to choose to leave.[15]

Montesquieu did not think that women played a central role in shaping the civic character of the government under which they lived. But he did think that the form of government had crucial implications for women's private lives. "In a republic the condition of citizens is moderate, equal, mild and agreeable. . . . an empire over women cannot . . . be so well exerted."[16] By his description of the "connection between domestic and

12. Marshall Berman, *The Politics of Authenticity: Radical Individualism and the Emergence of Modern Society* (New York, 1970), 7.

13. Charles Louis de Secondat, baron de Montesquieu, *Persian Letters*, trans. and ed. C. J. Betts (London, 1973), No. 141, 247–254.

14. *Ibid.*, No. 38, 93.

15. *Ibid.*, No. 104, 190–191, No. 116, 209–211.

16. Montesquieu, *Spirit of the Laws*, trans. Nugent, 255–256. Book 7 includes a curious pair of paragraphs headed "Of Female Administration" that offer the paradox that "it is contrary to reason and nature that women should reign in families . . . but not that they

political government," Montesquieu provided strong support for the conclusion that it is in women's self-interest to live in a republic. He offered no mechanism by which a woman unfortunate enough not to be born into a republic might change her condition, but he stated strongly that it was of crucial importance for women to live under certain forms of government and not under others.

Condorcet came closest to inventing procedures as well as justifications for including women in politics. His feminist comments emerge naturally from his general vision of the social order. They appear most extensively in his essay "Sur l'admission des Femmes au Droit de Cité" and in his "Lettres d'un Bourgeois de New-Heaven" (an appealing typographical error).[17]

Condorcet pointed out that although women had not exercised the right of citizenship in any "constitution called free," the right to political voice in a republic was generally claimed by men on grounds that might equally well be claimed by women—that they were "sensible beings, capable of reason, having moral ideas." "Men have . . . interests strongly different from those of women," Condorcet said in an unconventional and forceful statement (although he did not specify what those differences were), and have used their power to make laws that establish a "great inequality between the sexes." Once it was admitted that people cannot legitimately be taxed without representation, "it followed from this principle that all women are in their rights to refuse to pay parliamentary taxes." Condorcet then argued that except in matters requiring brute strength, women are obviously men's equals; the brightest women were already superior to men of limited talents, and improvements in education would readily narrow what gaps there were. He concluded what is perhaps his generation's most detailed statement of the political rights and responsibilities of women with the comment: "Perhaps you will find this discussion too long; but think that it is about the rights of

should govern an empire." In families women's natural weakness "does not permit them to have the pre-eminence"; however, in governments that same weakness means that women administer their governments with "more leniency and moderation" (ibid., 108). It is the classic double bind, and applies, in any event, only to women who inherit their thrones. Despite Montesquieu's defense of women's political abilities, he suggested no devices that would increase the use of these abilities.

17. Condorcet's essay "Sur l'admission des Femmes au Droit de Cité" originally appeared July 3, 1790, in the *Journal de la Société de 1789*; it is reprinted in *Oeuvres de Condorcet*, X (Paris, 1847), 119–130. The letters were published in Filippo Mazzei, *Recherches historiques et politiques sur les États-Unis . . . avec quatre lettres d'un bourgeois de New-Heaven sur l'unité de la législation*, I (Paris, 1788), 267–371.

half of human beings, rights forgotten by all the legislators; that it is not useless even for the liberty of men to indicate the means of destroying the single objection which could be made to republics, and to make between them and states which are not free a real difference."[18]

Condorcet's major political statement was his *Esquisse d'un tableau historique des progrès de l'esprit humain*. This book is a brave testament to the human spirit, written when that same spirit was hounding the author to a premature death in prison. In the *Esquisse*, Condorcet imagined that women had been an integral part of prehistoric society and important contributors to the social order. The original society consisted of a family, "formed at first by the want which children have of their parents, and by the affection of the mother as well as that of the father." Children gradually extended their natural affection for their parents to other family members and then to their clan. But before this first stage of primitive society was outgrown, women had lost their central position.

Condorcet suggested that the origins of governmental institutions resided in the meetings of men who planned hunting trips and wars. It seemed obvious to him that "the weakness of the females, which exempted them from the distant chase, and from war, the usual subjects of debate, excluded them alike from these consultations"; women were thus barred at the outset from "the first political institutions" and consigned to "a sort of slavery." Their slavery was modified in the second, or pastoral, epoch, and manners were "softened" and modified still more in the third epoch, which also marked the invention of alphabetical writing. "A more sedentary mode of life had introduced a greater equality between the sexes. . . . Man looked upon them [women] as companions, . . . [but] even in countries where they were treated with most respect . . . neither reason nor justice extended so far as to an entire reciprocity as to the right of divorce. . . . The history of this class of prejudices, and of their influence on the lot of the human species . . . [evinces] how closely man's happiness is connected with the progress of reason."[19]

The more rational the government, the more improved the status of women. This formulation was an important one, but Condorcet, oddly

18. My translation. Condorcet, "Lettres d'un Bourgeois," in Mazzei, *Recherches historiques*, I, 281–287.

19. Marie Jean Antoine Nicolas Caritat, marquis de Condorcet, *Outline of an Historical View of the Progress of the Human Mind* (Philadelphia, 1796), 24, 26, 28, 32, 43. In his list of tasks that remained unaccomplished, Condorcet specifically listed the improvement of the status of women; his words on this point have frequently been reprinted (*ibid.*, 280). A similar argument appears in [John Adams], *Sketches of the History, Genius, Disposition, Accomplishments, Employments, Customs, Virtues, and Vices of the Fair Sex, in All Parts*

enough, did not develop it further. Although he began the *Esquisse* as a history of mankind in the generic sense, by the "fourth epoch" the author fell into traditionalism: the pronoun *he* is used literally, and men represent the general case, women the rare and insignificant exception. Those who wish to find in Condorcet reiteration of the rule that the world is a man's world will find it in the *Esquisse*.[20]

Rousseau is well known for his sharp criticism of contemporary society and his vision of radical social change. His statements about women, however, usually reinforced the existing order; indeed Condorcet's comments on women and politics were offered as a direct challenge to those of Rousseau. Rousseau's conservatism about women may well have served to make his radical comments about men's behavior more palatable. If the world were to be changed into a new one, characterized by a new style of male behavior, governed by a General Will in accordance with a new social contract, it was surely reassuring to know that the women of that world would not change—that they would remain deferential to their men, clean in their household habits, complaisant in their conversation.

The key to Rousseau's understanding of women's political function is in his discussion of the origins of government in *The Social Contract*. The General Will, after all, is a concept without gender; the freedom of the social contract comes from the paradoxical identification of the ruler

---

of the World (Boston, 1807), 37: "The rank . . . and condition in which we find women in any country, mark out to us with the greatest precision the exact point in the scale of civil society, to which people of such country have arrived." Even critics of Condorcet's politics made use of this formulation. Jane West's conservative tract *Letters to a Young Lady in Which the Duties and Character of Women Are Considered* was published in England and Troy, N.Y., in 1806. "The nearer the country is to what is called the state of nature (but which, in correct language, should be termed savage degeneracy,) the more we find women depressed, servile, and miserable. . . . The progress of any people toward civilization is uniformly marked by allotting an increased degree of importance to the fair sex" (West, *Letters to a Young Lady*, 20–22).

20. See Keith Michael Baker's magisterial *Condorcet: From Natural Philosophy to Social Mathematics* (Chicago, 1975). Baker does not, however, comment on Condorcet's treatment of women's role in political society, the essay "Sur l'admission des Femmes au Droit de Cité," or the "Lettres d'un Bourgeois." In 1785 Condorcet's careful analysis of "the calculus of consent" was published as "Essai sur l'application de l'analyse à la probabilité des decisions rendues à la pluralité des voix." Condorcet viewed "the process of political decision-making . . . not as a means of ascertaining the strongest among a number of opposing parties—not, that is, as a mere expression of will—but as a method for the collective discovery of truth" (Baker, *Condorcet*, 228–229). His reasoning has something in common with Rousseau's General Will, in which all individuals choose to submit to the community. But even in Condorcet's more practical formulation, women are not explicitly part of the political community.

with the ruled. If it is obvious that women are among the ruled, ought they not also be among the legislators?

There is a hidden paradox in this generally paradoxical essay: the women who are ruled are, at the same time, not ruled; because they are not ruled, they need not participate in the General Will. They are invisible. As Rousseau explained in *Emile*, females live in another world. A woman's empire is "of softness, of address, of complacency; her commands are caresses; her menaces are tears."[21] This is not hyperbole: in Rousseau's social order, women have moral and physical relationships to men, but not political ones, nor do women have substantial relationships to any women other than their mothers. Rousseau was explicit. The shift from the generic to the literal *he* occurs before *The Social Contract* has scarcely begun. The most ancient and the only natural society is the family, Rousseau remarked, but children soon outgrow their dependence on their *fathers*.[22] After that obvious slight to mothers, Rousseau explained the General Will in specific, masculine terms; men alone were expected to display disinterested civic spirit. In *Emile* Rousseau took as self-evident that it is "the good son, the good father, the good husband, that constitute the good citizen."[23]

Emile is about the task of forming a citizen for an idealized society. Emile is a man whose body is at ease with his mind, a sophisticated innocent, a person as paradoxical as the society for which he is educated. Because men's education had strayed from the natural world into bookish abstraction, Rousseau needed a revolution to cause Emile to grow up among things rather than books, to postpone learning to read, to postpone studying foreign languages until he traveled to countries where they were used. But in creating Emile's wife, Sophie, Rousseau did not rethink the terms on which women ought to be educated for his new social order. Girls were already barred from books, rarely taught foreign languages, already limited to tasks relating to household chores. He did not posit for Sophie, as he did for Emile, a *tabula rasa* on which a rational mentor writes only what is necessary and natural; he did not provide for Sophie, as he did for Emile, a personality radically different from the one that standard systems of education were geared to create. Sophie is as tradi-

21. Jean Jacques Rousseau, *Emilius; or a Treatise of Education. Translated from the French*, III (Edinburgh, 1763), 10.

22. Jean Jacques Rousseau, *The Social Contract, and Discourses*, trans. G. D. H. Cole (London, 1913), Bk. I, chap. 2, 6.

23. Rousseau, *Emilius*, III, 14.

tional a woman as it is possible to imagine, reformed only in the sense that she does not dote on fashion or read novels.

Emile thanks his tutor for restoring him to "liberty, by teaching . . . [him] to yield to necessity." But Sophie's life is at all times largely directed by necessity. The more that a woman's life was governed by repeated cycles of pregnancy, lying-in, nursing, and child rearing, the closer she was to nature and the less the need to reform her education.[24]

In Book 5 of *The Wealth of Nations*, Adam Smith expressed similar admiration for the practical aspects of women's education.

> There are no public institutions for the education of women, and there is accordingly nothing useless, absurd, or fantastical in the common course of their education. They are taught what their parents or guardians judge it necessary or useful for them to learn; and they are taught nothing else. Every part of their education tends evidently to some useful purpose; either to improve the natural attractions of their person, or to form their mind to reserve, to modesty, to chastity, and to economy; to render them both likely to become the mistresses of a family, and to behave properly when they have become such. In every part of her life a woman feels some conveniency or advantage from every part of her education. It seldom happens that a man, in any part of his life, derives any conveniency or advantage from some of the most laborious and troublesome parts of his education.[25]

Smith's plan for reforming the educational system continued to exclude women. Men are to envy women's practical education and its direct relationship to female adult roles; it is harder to predict what skills boys will ultimately find most useful. That the practicality of women's education can be directly attributed to the limited and predictable nature of women's adult roles did not seem to bother Smith.

Rousseau's refusal to rethink the terms of Sophie's education was intentional. His own sadomasochistic sexual tastes gave him a substantial personal stake in the submissiveness of women. He was not loath to make the broadest generalizations: "To oblige us, to do us service, to gain our love and esteem . . . these are the duties of the sex at all times,

---

24. *Ibid.*, 229.

25. Adam Smith, *An Inquiry into the Nature and Causes of the Wealth of Nations*, ed. Edwin Canaan (New York, 1937), Bk. V, chap. 1, Pt. iii, art. 2, 734.

and what they ought to learn from their infancy." Relationships between men and women are always sexual and always verge on the uncontrollable: "Woman is framed particularly for the delight and pleasure of man. . . . Her violence consists in her charms. . . . [Her modesty masks her] unbounded desires."[26]

Rousseau's most substantial target was Plato. In Book 5 of *The Republic*, Plato had included women in the political community and had assigned the same employments to men and women. Rousseau was horrified by this "civil promiscuousness"; it represented, he sneered, the conversion of women into men.[27]

Repeatedly Rousseau insisted that the woman who seeks to be a politician or philosopher does violence to her own character and sexual identity. "A witty [i.e., articulate] woman is a scourge to her husband, to her children, to her friends, her servants, and to all the world. Elated by the sublimity of her genius, she scorns to stoop to the duties of a woman, and is sure to commence a man." Rousseau was sure his readers would share his scorn of "a female genius, scribbling verses in her toilette, and surrounded by pamphlets" (although if she were scribbling emotional effusions, as Julie does throughout all six books of *La Nouvelle Héloïse*, he apparently had no objection). "The art of thinking is not foreign to women," Rousseau contended, "but they ought only to skim the surface of abstruse sciences."[28]

Attacks on masculine, articulate women are one of the more common themes of English literature (both British and American) in the late eighteenth and early nineteenth centuries. The negative image of the bluestocking would prove to be a formidable obstacle to feminists throughout the nineteenth and twentieth centuries. Although Rousseau did not create this image, surely he did much to strengthen it in precisely those liberal and reformist circles where it would be logically predicted to die out.

Rousseau's impact on American thought is difficult to measure. *Emile* was available in an English translation. People who did not read Rousseau directly may have encountered ideas similar to his in Lord Kames's *Sketches of the History of Man*, which did circulate widely and which included comments on women's place in society that are in rough congruence with Rousseau's. For Lord Kames, women's history was "a capital branch of the history of man." It demonstrated a crude progress from

26. Rousseau, *Emilius*, III, 74–75, 5–6.
27. Plato, *The Republic*, trans. H. D. P. Lee (London, 1955), 209–210. Rousseau's comments appear in *Emilius*, III, 14.
28. Rousseau, *Emilius*, III, 104–105, 139.

women's debased condition among savages to "their elevated state in civilized nations." He explicitly denied that women have a direct responsibility to their nation; because their relationship to their country is determined by the secondhand experience of husbands and sons, they therefore have "less patriotism than men." Like Rousseau, Kames feared masculinization: "Remove a female out of her proper sphere, and it is easy to convert her into a male." He agreed that women's education ought to produce sensible companions and mothers; the great dangers to be guarded against were frivolity and disorderly manners. Having disposed of women in 97 pages, he was free to ignore them in the remaining 1,770 pages of his four-volume treatise. His final conclusion is merciless: "Cultivation of the female mind, is not of great importance in a republic, where men pass little of their time with women."[29]

We are left with an intellectual gap. The great treatises of the Enlightenment, which criticized and helped to change attitudes toward the state, offered no guidance to women analyzing their relationship to liberty or civic virtue. Even Rousseau, one of the most radical political theorists of an age famous for its ability to examine inherited assumptions, failed to examine his own assumptions about women. Ought a woman dare to think? Might a woman accept "the loneliness of autonomy"? To be alone, in fact, was to be male; women were invariably described, even by Locke, in relationship to others. Condorcet occasionally imagined an autonomous woman, but for Locke, Montesquieu, Rousseau, and Kames, women existed only as mothers and wives. If Fred Weinstein and Gerald M. Platt correctly define the Enlightenment as the expression of "a desire to end the commitments to passivity and dependence in the area of politics," women were not a part of this reform.[30]

Americans were more directly attracted to the literature of the Commonwealth and Radical Whig Opposition than to other branches of

29. Henry Home, Lord Kames, *Sketches of the History of Man*, II (Edinburgh, 1778), 1–2, 5, 85, 97. This theme also appears in [Adams], *Sketches of the History of the Fair Sex*, 106, where the author insists that women are less susceptible to patriotism than men because patriotism is produced "by the ideas of interest and property." He concedes that women are capable of patriotism if sufficiently aroused and excited, as Roman and Spartan women had been. Kames, like his cousin David Hume, Adam Ferguson, and others of the Scottish common sense school, was skeptical of the usefulness of a "state of nature" fiction. None of them dealt extensively with the role of women in a polity. See David Hume, "Of the Passions," in *The Philosophical Works of David Hume* (Edinburgh, 1826), II, Pt. i, sec. 9, 43.

30. Fred Weinstein and Gerald M. Platt, *The Wish To Be Free: Society, Psyche and Value Change* (Berkeley, Calif., 1969), 49.

Enlightenment thought. Many eighteenth-century Americans were familiar with the works of John Trenchard and Thomas Gordon, Algernon Sidney, James Harrington, James Burgh, and Catharine Macaulay. Political theorists made much use of this literature. But these writers were largely concerned with specific issues of opposition to crown policy; they rarely needed a presocial family to make an argument. One result of the overwhelming influence of the English Whig tradition in America was that American political theory was rooted in assumptions that never gave explicit attention to basic questions about women. Male Whigs were fortunate; they did not need to begin at the beginning to develop their cases, but that same good fortune inhibited the likelihood that they would include women in their contemplations of the good society.

As Edwin Burrows and Michael Wallace have brilliantly shown, Whigs had a major ideological concern for parent-child relationships, but their discussions were restricted to the specific case of sons and fathers or to the limits of the obligations of sons to mothers.[31] Other variants of familial relationships were less thoroughly explored. John Trenchard, for example, addressed himself only to the evils of marrying women for money. In all four volumes of vigorously egalitarian rhetoric in *Cato's Letters* that rang the changes on the theme of the relationship between the state and the individual, Trenchard always contemplated political man, narrowly defined.[32] Not even so articulate a feminist as Catharine Macaulay felt the need to discuss women's education extensively. She attacked Rousseau and wrote in the seven small pages of her twenty-second "Letter on Education" most of what it took Wollstonecraft hundreds of pages to argue in her *Vindication of the Rights of Woman*. But

31. Edwin G. Burrows and Michael Wallace, "The American Revolution: The Ideology and Psychology of National Liberation," *Perspectives in American History*, VI (1972), 167–306; see especially Pts. ii and iii. The extent to which the imagery of mother/daughter relationships was used varied widely. The Resolves of the Inhabitants of the Town of Gorham [Massachusetts] on the Port Bill, written in June 1774, made more extensive use of this imagery than most: "In this golden Age mutual Love subsisted between the Mother State and her Colonies, the Mother extended her Powerfull Arm to skreen and to Protect her Children.... In return the Children have ever been Obedient to the requisitions of the Mother" (in L. Kinvin Wroth *et al.*, eds., *Province in Rebellion: A Documentary History of the Founding of the Commonwealth of Massachusetts, 1774–1775* [Cambridge, Mass., 1975], doc. 224). It was signed by 220 men and 6 women (5 of whom identified themselves as "widow").

32. John Trenchard and Thomas Gordon, *Cato's Letters; or, Essays on Liberty, Civil and Religious, And other important Subjects*, 3d ed., II (London, 1733), 201–212. There are no comments on women in John Trenchard and Thomas Gordon, *The Independent Whig* (London, 1721).

Jonathan Spilsbury after Catharine Read, *Catharine Macaulay* (1764).
Courtesy National Portrait Gallery, London.

Macaulay, who was confident enough to plunge directly into public political debate and to criticize Hobbes and Burke without even a passing apology for the frailties of her sex, apparently felt no need to address the responsibilities of women to political society. Perhaps she believed she had made her position clear by implication and in practice. But her direct comments speak of the private responsibilities of women—even reformed, chaste, nonfrivolous women—to individual men. In this she was more in agreement with Rousseau than she thought.[33]

American whigs were as unlikely as their British counterparts to integrate into political theory a concept of the proper relationship between women and the body politic. It may even be that Americans ignored the problem because the British did. Any body of theory that addresses basic issues of sex roles must reach back to presocial or psychological sources of human behavior. The issues are so basic that they demand probing the deepest and most archetypal layers of human experience. Americans felt little need to do this. James Otis was one of the few to try, in the opening pages of the 1764 pamphlet *The Rights of the British Colonies Asserted and Proved.*

> The origin of *government* has in all ages no less perplexed the heads of lawyers and politicians than the origin of *evil* has embarrassed divines. . . . the gentlemen in favor of [the theory that government is based on] the *original compact* have often been told that *their* system is chimerical and unsupported by reason or experience. Questions like the following have been frequently asked them. . . . "Who were present and parties to such compact? Who acted for infants and women, or who appointed guardians for them? Had these guardians power to bind both infants and women during life and their posterity after them? . . . What will there be to distinguish the next generation of men from their forefathers, that they should not have the same right to make original compacts as their ancestors had? If every man has such right, may there not be as many original compacts as there are men and women born or to be born? Are not women born as free as men? Would it not be infamous to assert that

33. Catharine Macaulay, *Letters on Education; with Observations on Religious and Metaphysical Subjects* (London, 1790); Catharine Macaulay, *An Address to the People of England, Ireland and Scotland, on the Present Crisis of Affairs,* 3d ed. (New York, 1775); Catharine Macaulay, *Observations on the Reflections of . . . Edmund Burke* (Boston, 1791); Catharine Macaulay, *Loose Remarks on Certain Positions to be Found in Mr. Hobbes . . .* (London, 1767).

the ladies are all slaves by nature? If every man and woman born or to be born has and will have a right to be consulted and must accede to the original compact before they can with any kind of justice be said to be bound by it, will not the compact be ever forming and never finished?"

Otis raised embarrassing questions about women's political role. "If upon the abdication all were reduced to a state of nature, had not apple women and orange girls as good a right to give their respectable suffrages for a new King as the philosopher, courtier, *petit-maître* and politician? Were these and ten millions of other such . . . consulted?"[34] Although Otis could ask embarrassing questions and imply their answers, on this as on so many points of theory, his developing mental illness prevented him from suggesting constitutional devices for implementing them.

As American men entered the Revolution, then, they had not dealt with the matter of whether the new social order they envisioned would be new for women. They made this plain in a myriad of direct and indirect ways. Nowhere is it clearer than in a splendid patriotic discourse prepared by Henry Laurens in which he addressed "the inhabitants of America," who were fighting to protect their "wives from insult or violation." It did not seem to him that women too were inhabitants.[35]

Indeed, female qualities were commonly made the measure of what a good republican ought to avoid. "Luxury, effeminacy, and corruption" was a recurrent cautionary triad; so was "ignorance, effeminacy, and vice." Samuel Adams warned against the undermining of public virtue by the "effeminate" refinements of the theater. Effeminacy was associated with timidity, dependence, and foppishness—even homosexuality. It was associated with luxury and self-indulgence, suggesting perhaps that those who denounced it may have found it tempting. If Americans lived in a world of the political imagination in which virtue was ever threatened by corruption, it must be added that the overtones of virtue were male, and those of corruption, female.[36]

34. James Otis, *The Rights of the British Colonies Asserted and Proved* (Boston, 1764), in Bernard Bailyn, ed., *Pamphlets of the American Revolution, 1750–1776*, I (Cambridge, Mass., 1965), 419–422.

35. Laurens's speech was reprinted in the *New-Jersey Gazette* (Trenton), May 27, 1778.

36. George Washington to James Warren, Oct. 7, 1785, John C. Fitzpatrick, ed., *The Writings of George Washington from the Original Manuscript Sources, 1745–1799* (Washington, D.C., 1931–1944), XXVIII, 290; William Hillhouse, *A Dissertation, in Answer to a late Lecture* (New Haven, Conn., 1789), 4–5; Samuel Adams, "The Observer," No. VII, *Massachusetts Centinel* (Boston), Jan. 15, 1785, in Gordon S. Wood, ed.,

As American women entered the Revolution, they had few theoretical analyses of their place in society on which they might draw for sustenance. There was no dearth of argument telling them that they were peripheral to the world of politics and decision making. If they compiled lists of illustrious women, they had to range far back in the past: to Catherine of Siena, to Elizabeth I. The Enlightenment provided little guidance; prewar republican ideology provided less. Mary Wollstonecraft was only seventeen years old when the first shots were fired at Lexington. If American women were to count themselves as the daughters of Liberty, they would have to invent their own ideology.[37]

The Rising Glory of America, 1760–1820 (New York, 1971), 137–138. For thoughtful reflections on this theme, see J. G. A. Pocock, *The Machiavellian Moment: Florentine Political Thought and the Atlantic Republican Tradition* (Princeton, N.J., 1975), chaps. 14 and 15, 405, 462–552.

37. See also Mary Sumner Benson, *Women in Eighteenth-Century America: A Study of Opinion and Social Usage* (New York, 1935).

Chapter 2

"WOMEN INVITED TO WAR":

SACRIFICE AND SURVIVAL

I have Don as much to Carrey on the warr
as maney that Sett Now at the healm of
goverment.

—Rachel Wells

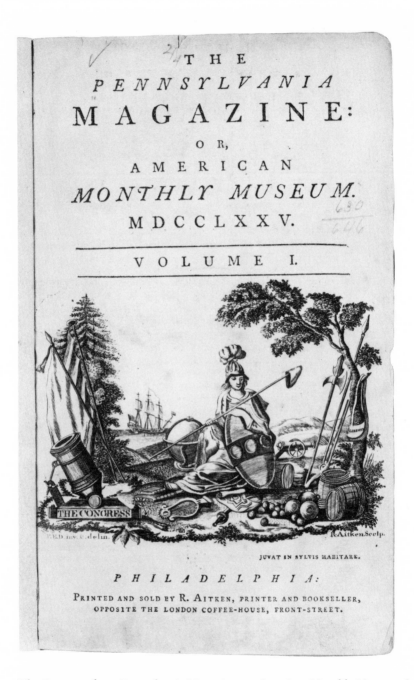

THE
PENNSYLVANIA
MAGAZINE:
OR,
AMERICAN
MONTHLY MUSEUM.
MDCCLXXV.

VOLUME I.

THE CONGRESS

P.E.D inv. C. delin.   R. Aitken Sculp.

JUVAT IN SYLVIS HABITARE.

PHILADELPHIA:

PRINTED AND SOLD BY R. AITKEN, PRINTER AND BOOKSELLER,
OPPOSITE THE LONDON COFFEE-HOUSE, FRONT-STREET.

The Congress, from Pennsylvania Magazine: or, American Monthly Museum, I
(1775).
Courtesy The Library of Congress, Washington, D.C.

"PATRIOTISM IN THE FEMALE SEX," wrote Abigail Adams as the American Revolution drew to a close, "is the most disinterested of all virtues. Excluded from honours and from offices, we cannot attach ourselves to the State of Government from having held a place of Eminence. Even in freest countrys our property is subject to the controul and disposal of our partners, to whom the Laws have given a sovereign Authority. Deprived of a voice in Legislation, obliged to submit to those Laws which are imposed upon us, is it not sufficient to make us indifferent to the publick Welfare? Yet all History and every age exhibit Instances of patriotic virtue in the female Sex; which considering our situation equals the most Heroick."[1]

We cannot know how widely shared were these opinions, expressed in a private letter from wife to husband. They certainly challenged much of the accepted wisdom of the Revolutionary generation. It had been the common sense of eighteenth-century political theory that women had "less patriotism than men." Because women were excluded from honors and offices, the usual methods of attaching subjects' self-interest to the outcome of national policy, women's relationship to their nation seemed to be secondhand. They were thought to experience politics through husbands, fathers, sons.[2]

This distrust of the female capacity to take politics seriously was present in the American colonies when the Revolution began and persisted long after the war's close. That many women shared this distrust is clear. "I can't help exclaiming now and then, dreadful fruits of Liberty. I confess I have not such romantic notions of the Goddess," Margaret Livingston wrote shortly after the war began. "You know that our Sex are *doomed* to be obedient in every stage of life so that *we* shant be great gainers by this contest."[3] The social correspondence of women from even the most political families—Jays, Livingstons, Pinckneys—often expressed the complaint that however the war turned out it would mean only inconvenience and trouble for them.

Despite anecdotal evidence of the economic and physical sacrifice of individual women, a folklore persisted that discounted women's political behavior, assumed that women were incapable of making reasoned and

1. Abigail Adams to John Adams, June 17, 1782, L. H. Butterfield *et al.*, eds., *Adams Family Correspondence* (Cambridge, Mass., 1963–), IV, 328, hereafter cited as *Adams Family Correspondence*.

2. Kames, *Sketches of the History of Man*, II, 4–5, 85, 97.

3. Margaret Livingston to [Catharine Livingston], Oct. 20, 1776, Ridley Papers, Massachusetts Historical Society, Boston.

unbiased political judgments, and emphasized the hesitancy of women to sacrifice their creature comforts for higher national purposes. The popular press shrilly insisted both before and after the war that American women were excessive in their consumption of British goods and books; the critics held that by indulging in British products, American women were undercutting the efforts of American men to develop a fully independent national culture.

Could a woman be a patriot? If any experience could have provided unambivalent answers to that question, the Revolution ought to have done so. But the answers seemed little clearer at the end of the war—in part because memories of women who supported the Revolution were counterbalanced by memories of women who were loyalists. Evidence of unprecedented female political behavior in both camps was outweighed by the winners' scorn for the losers and by the belief that women's political choices had been controlled by male relatives. Women were expelled from patriot-held territory, for example, not because of their own political identities, but because of their husbands'; the burden rested heavily on the wife of the tory to prove that she indeed did not share her husband's political opinions. Few were prepared to agree that a wife and mother could also be an independent political being. Those who, like Abigail Adams, thought women could be both, faced a difficult task if they were to carry this idea past private conceptions. They would need to persuade a hostile public that expressive political behavior did not threaten the traditional domestic domain; by adopting the ideals of what may be called "Republican Motherhood," a patriotic woman could unite her seemingly contradictory loyalties to the home and to the state. Their task was made more difficult by the liberal hesitancy to believe that propertyless people could make reasoned political decisions; yet even unmarried women who were independent property holders found resistance to their political claims. That women of the Revolutionary generation were not fully successful in their attempt ought not to blind us to their effort to articulate a political ideology that blended the domestic and public spheres. The creators and advocates of Republican Motherhood produced the terms and rhetoric in which much of the nineteenth- and twentieth-century debate on the proper dimensions of female patriotism would be expressed.

In 1769, mulling over what needed to be done to make the resistance to England effective, Christopher Gadsden formulated an explicit rationale for a direct ideological appeal to women that included domestic loyalties as well as a political consideration:

> I come now to the last, and what many say and think is the *greatest difficulty* of all we have to encounter, that is, to persuade our wives to give us their assistance, without which 'tis impossible to succeed. I allow of the impossibility of succeeding without their concurrence. But, for my part, so far from doubting that we shall have it, I could wish, as our political salvation, at this crisis, depends altogether upon the strictest oeconomy, that the women could, with propriety, have the principal management thereof; for 'tis well known, that none in the world are better oeconomists, make better wives or more tender mothers, than ours. Only let their husbands point out the necessity of such a conduct; convince them, that it is the only thing that can save them and their children, from distresses, slavery, and disgrace; their affections will soon be awakened, and cooperate with their reason. When that is done, all that is necessary will be done; for I am persuaded, that they will be then as anxious and persevering in this matter, as any the most zealous of us can possibly wish.[4]

Gadsden's formulation is traditional in its easy telescoping of "women" into wives. His appeal is not to women, but to the men who are their husbands; he does not seek to sway the independent single woman. But he did perceive that because women manage household economies, it would be easy for them to undermine political boycotts. Women would make political decisions whether they meant to or not. He also understood that they would make their decisions on the basis of their perception of their domestic duties and responsibilities. The men who sought to persuade them would have to do their persuading in women's terms: in terms of the ultimate security of children and homes. Republican rhetoric would have to be adapted to the protection of the woman's domain if it were to be effective.

Perhaps men habitually overstated the need to appeal to women on the basis of their desire to protect domesticity. We have direct written expressions by women that justify boycotts squarely on the grounds of public

---

4. Christopher Gadsden, "To the Planters, Mechanics, and Freeholders of the Province of South Carolina, No Ways Concerned in the Importation of British Manufacturers" (June 22, 1769), in Richard Walsh, ed., *The Writings of Christopher Gadsden* (Columbia, S.C., 1966), 83–84.

political commitments. Indeed, they assert that women can be firmer than men in their patriotism. Milcah Martha Moore of Philadelphia copied a long verse into her commonplace book in 1768; it is based on the assumption that women can make up for men's political weaknesses.

Since the Men from a Party, on fear of a Frown,
Are kept by a Sugar-Plumb, quietly down,
Supinely asleep, and depriv'd of their Sight
Are strip'd of their Freedom, and rob'd of their Right.
If the Sons (so degenerate) the Blessing despise,
Let the Daughters of Liberty, nobly arise,
And tho' we've no Voice, but a negative here,
The use of the Taxables, let us forbear,
(Then Merchants import till yr. Stores are all full
May the Buyers be few and yr. Traffick be dull.)
Stand firmly resolved and bid Grenville to see
That rather than Freedom, we'll part with our Tea
And well as we love the dear Draught when adry,
As American Patriots,—our Taste we deny.
  .   .   .   .
And Paper sufficient (at home) still we have,
To assure the Wise-acre, we will not sign Slave.[5]

The first stage in raised political consciousness was to wear homespun or else old clothes of British cloth. Gadsden even urged women to put off wearing old British clothes lest they set a bad example. Women were in effect being asked to police themselves.

If purchasing was politicized, so was manufacture. In Newport, Rhode Island, Congregational minister Ezra Stiles played host to "ninety-two daughters of Liberty" who brought seventy spinning wheels at the break of day to his house and "spun and reeled, respiting and assisting one another" until 170 skeins were done.[6] Because ordinary behaviors suddenly became charged with political significance, political decisions might be ascribed where none were intended, and even those who wished to remain neutral might find themselves accused of aligning themselves one

5. "Patriotic Poesy" [1768], William and Mary Quarterly, 3d Ser., XXXIV (1977), 307–308.

6. Franklin Bowditch Dexter, ed., The Literary Diary of Ezra Stiles (New York, 1901), I, 8, 53. For other spinning contests, see the New-York Journal; or, the General Advertiser (New York City), Mar. 23, 1769.

way or another. If patriots wore homespun, could one wear an old silk dress? If "daughters of Liberty" brought their wheels to a communal spinning bee, could one stay home? Perhaps the headache caused by seventy wheels whirring at once discouraged some from attending. But attendance was also a way of identifying those with loyalist leanings.

The sharpest of these challenges to consumption behaviors came in the form of the tea boycott. Like the grape or lettuce boycotts of recent years, the tea boycott provided a relatively mild way of identifying oneself with the patriotic effort, for it was easy to refrain from drinking tea. If one wished, one could be emphatic, like the landlady with whom John Adams lodged briefly and who lectured him on the need to drink coffee, or like nine-year-old Susan Boudinot, daughter of a New Jersey patriot, who was taken to visit the tory governor William Franklin. When she was offered a cup of tea, she curtsied, raised it to her lips, and tossed the contents out the window. Doggerel verse on patriotic boycotts appeared in newspapers and in women's private papers, passed around from hand to hand.[7] In Philadelphia, Hannah Griffitts referred to the tea act as North's "Ministerial blunder" and drafted a poem:

> . . . for the sake of Freedom's name,
>   (Since British Wisdom scorns repealing,)
> Come, sacrifice to Patriot fame,
>   And give up Tea, by way of healing,
> This done, within ourselves retreat,
>   The Industrious arts of life to follow,
> Let the Proud Nabobs storm & fret,
>   They Cannot force our lips to swallow.[8]

7. Milton Halsey Thomas, ed., *Elias Boudinot's Journey to Boston* (Princeton, N.J., 1955), preface.

8. "Beware the Ides of March," Feb. 28, 1775, Hannah Griffitts Papers, Library Company of Philadelphia. Mercy Otis Warren invented a versified conversation among women who were deciding whether to participate in the 1774 boycott; she admitted that there were some who insisted on their rights to British imports, but she held up "Prudentia" as a model: "Let us resolve on a small sacrifice/And in the pride of Roman matrons rise;/Good as Cornelia, or a Pompey's wife/We'll quit the useless vanities of life" ("To the Hon. J. Winthrop, Esq., Who, on the American Determination, in 1774, to suspend all Commerce with Britain . . . requested a poetical List of the Articles the Ladies might comprise under that Head," *Poems, Dramatic and Miscellaneous* [Boston, 1790], 208–212). See also the poem "To the Ladies" (1769), in Frank Moore, ed., *Songs and Ballads of the American Revolution* (New York, 1855), 48–50, and the verses in the *Pennsylvania Gazette* (Philadelphia), Oct. 16, 1775.

The able Doctor, or America Swallowing the Bitter Draught.

Paul Revere, *The able Doctor, or America Swallowing the Bitter Draught.* A well-established iconographical tradition represented each of the four continents by a female figure dressed to symbolize her land. America had long been represented as an Indian. The tradition continues in this engraving. America is a vulnerable, naked woman. Down her unwilling throat the British author of the Boston Port Bill forcibly pours tea, while leering politicians gather round, enjoying her distress. One takes advantage of the moment to peer up her skirts. Britannia cannot bear to watch, but she can do nothing to help.
Courtesy The Colonial Williamsburg Foundation, Williamsburg, Virginia.

Occasionally political awareness became sharp enough to prompt a petition circulated and signed by women. In the 1830s women's petitions would be a familiar device, widely circulated by female antislavery societies. But they were virtually unknown before the 1770s. For many women, signing such a petition was surely their first political act. Fifty-one women of Edenton, North Carolina, endorsed the nonimportation Association resolves of 1774:

> As we cannot be indifferent on any occasion that appears nearly to affect the peace and happiness of our country, and as it has been thought necessary for the public good, to enter into several particular resolves by a meeting of members deputed from the whole Province, it is a duty which we owe, not only to our near and dear relations and connections . . . but to ourselves, who are essentially interested in their welfare, to do everything as far as lies in our power, to testify our sincere adherence to the same; and we do therefore accordingly subscribe this paper, as a witness of our fixed intention and solemn determination to do so.

The dismay with which this sober and straightforward petition was received suggests its novelty. Arthur Iredell, who was living in England, wrote to his North Carolina relatives: "Is there a Female Congress at Edenton too? I hope not, for we Englishmen are afraid of the Male Congress, but if the Ladies, who have ever, since the Amazonian Era, been esteemd the most formidable Enemies, if they, I say, should attack us, the most fatal consequences is to be dreaded."[9]

The prewar boycotts initiated the politicization of the household economy and marked the beginning of the use of a political language that explicitly included women. This politicization of the household economy intensified during the war. "Was not every fireside, indeed," John Adams would recall, "a theatre of politics?" Disruption of trade with Britain meant that consumption codes became self-enforcing. Nonconsumption depended on national policy rather than on individual choice, but other

---

9. Arthur Iredell to James Iredell, Jan. 31, 1775, Don Higginbotham, ed., *The Papers of James Iredell*, I (Raleigh, N.C., 1976), 282–286. Portions of the petition are reprinted *ibid.*, 285–286. The petition and the names of the signers are reprinted in Richard T. H. Halsey, *The Boston Port Bill as Pictured by a Contemporary London Cartoonist* (New York, 1904), 314–315. See also Samuel Ashe, *History of North Carolina* (Greensboro, N.C., 1925), 427–429.

demands were addressed to women and to housekeepers. They were asked to spin thread for cloth manufacturers. A good spinner could consistently produce perhaps two and one-half pounds a day. Sometimes the appeal made to women was patriotic, sometimes commercial, sometimes quasi-religious, sometimes all three—as in a Philadelphia advertisement that encouraged women to spin by emphasizing that the distinguishing characteristic of an excellent woman was that she "seeketh wool and flax and worketh willingly with her hands. She layeth her hands to the spindle, and her hand holdeth the distaff." Each spinner was to feel strengthened by the sense that she was part of a long line of women stretching back to antiquity: "In this time of public distress, you have now, each of you, an opportunity not only to help to sustain your families, but likewise to cast your mite into the treasury of the public good." Women saved rags for papermaking and for bandages; they turned in lead weights from windows to be melted down for bullets; they saved the family urine for saltpeter.[10]

State statutes usually relied on the generic *he*, but those dealing with commodity production for the war made it very clear that women were specifically regarded as sources of the clothing and blankets the army needed. A New Jersey procurement act for November 1777, for example, made a point of prescribing penalties "if any person having any blankets to sell, or such sufficiency as to enable him or her to spare a part without distressing his or her family, and shall rate them at an exorbitant price, ... or if any commissioner shall have reason to believe that any person hath secreted his or her blankets." The amount expected from each county was large, and it is hard to imagine that the commissioners could have approached their quotas if women in large numbers had not taken to their looms. Male suppliers of clothing—tailors, weavers, shoemakers —were exempted from military service, but no sweeteners were offered

10. John Adams to Mercy Otis Warren, July 27, 1807, "Correspondence between John Adams and Mercy Otis Warren," Massachusetts Historical Society, *Collections*, 5th Ser., IV (Boston, 1878), 355; "To the Spinners in this City and County" (Aug. 1775), in William Duane, Jr., ed., *Passages from the Remembrancer of Christopher Marshall* (Philadelphia, 1839), 40. For other evidence of women's supply services, see William S. Stryker *et al.*, eds., *Documents Relating to the Revolutionary History of New Jersey (Archives of the State of N.J.*, 2d Ser., I-V [Trenton, N.J., 1901–1917]), III, 34, hereafter cited as *N.J. Archives*, 2d Ser.; Duane, ed., *Remembrancer of Marshall*, 35n; William Hand Browne *et al.*, eds., *Archives of Maryland* (Baltimore, 1883–), XII, 427–428; and Samuel Hazard, ed., *Minutes of the Provincial Council of Pennsylvania* ... [Colonial Records of Pennsylvania], X (Philadelphia and Harrisburg, Pa., 1852–1853), 633.

for the services provided by women, only the threat that the items they made could be seized by the commissioners.[11]

Old clothing collected for the army could rarely be used in the condition in which it was contributed. During the dreadful Valley Forge winter of 1777–1778, Mary Frazier of Chester County, Pennsylvania, rode

> day after day collecting from neighbors and friends far and near, whatever they could spare for the comfort of the destitute soldiers, the blankets, and yarn, and half worn clothing thus obtained she brought to her own house, where they would be patched, and darned, and made wearable and comfortable, the stockings newly footed, or new ones knit, adding what clothing she could give of her own. She often sat up half the night, sometimes all, to get clothing ready. Then with it, and whatever could be obtained for food, she would have packed on her horse and set out on her cold lonely journey to the camp—which she went to repeatedly during the winter.[12]

Women undertook to police local merchants who hoarded scarce commodities. In May 1777, for example, a series of attacks were made on the Poughkeepsie, New York, home of Peter Mesier, a reputed loyalist who was rumored to be hoarding tea. Mesier's wife offered to sell the cache at four dollars a pound, but twenty-two women, accompanied by two Continental soldiers, demanded entry to her home, saying that they "would . . . have it at their own Price, and brought a Hammer and Scales, and proceeded to weigh as much as they chose to take, untill they had taken near One hundred weight . . . for which they left about Seventeen Pounds in Money." The next day some men "and a number of Women to the amount of about 20" returned to the Mesier home and broke in without a warrant. The mob searched the house, "drew his Liquors and Drank of

11. "I know it to be the Duty of all to contribute as far in their Power to the public assistance," wrote Elizabeth Sinkler to Gen. Nathanael Greene in June 1782. She reported that "upwards of six thousand Bushels of Provisions have been delivered for the Use of the State since November last," and wondered if she might be thought to have done her share because her plantation was more accessible to the road than most. Her husband had died in the war, and she had the management of the estate, which included 200 residents (Elizabeth Sinkler to Nathanael Greene, June 22, 1782, South Caroliniana Library, University of South Carolina, Columbia). See also N.-J. Gaz., Dec. 17, 1777.

12. [Sarah Frazier], "A Reminiscence," *Pennsylvania Magazine of History and Biography*, XLVI (1922), 55.

them, broke open every Cask in the Cellar and the case of his Clock. . . . After they had searched the house, they went into the yard and beat his Dep[onen]t's Servants, threw Stones at and otherwise greatly abused him."[13] In July 1778 Abigail Adams reported that "a Number of Females, some say a hundred, some say more assembled with a cart and trucks, marched down to the Ware House" of an "eminent, wealthy, stingy Merchant" who was rumored to be hoarding coffee. When he refused to deliver the keys, "one of them seazd him by his Neck and tossed him into the cart. . . . he delivered the keys. . . . they . . . opened the Warehouse. Hoisted out the Coffee themselves, put it into trucks and drove off. . . . A large concourse of Men stood amazed silent Spectators." Throughout the war, open hostility to British fashion continued to be a way of mobilizing civilian enthusiasms and of offering a target for civilian anger. When the patriots recaptured Philadelphia in 1778, they celebrated the Fourth of July with understandable enthusiasm. Among their displays, Elizabeth Drinker reported, was "a very high Head dress . . . exhibited thro the Streets this afternoon on a very dirty Woman with a mob after her, with Drums &c by way of ridiculing that very foolish fashion." Of course women had been participants in crowds before the Revolution, but the war intruded into the family economy and gave more obvious and more frequent opportunity for the enforcement of consumption codes and for the display of aggressive political behavior by women.[14]

The belief that consumption behaviors had political implications would persist long after the Revolution. With every international crisis in the years of the early Republic, women would be asked to make contributions from the family economy to the public account. For example, at the beginning of a national drive to improve domestic manufactures in the fall of 1787, an anonymous author published an "Address to the ladies of America" in the *American Museum*: "Your country is inde-

13. *Minutes of the Committee and of the First Commission for Detecting and Defeating Conspiracies in the State of New-York*, I (New York, 1924), 301–303, hereafter cited as N.-Y. *Committee for Detecting Conspiracies*.

14. Abigail Adams to John Adams, July 31, 1777, *Adams Family Correspondence*, II, 295; Diary of Elizabeth Sandwith Drinker, July 4, 1778, Historical Society of Pennsylvania, Philadelphia. In the French Revolution, the comparable women's riots were more desperate, frequent, and violent; the issue was bread, not the luxury of coffee or tea. William Livingston satirized the sumptuary campaign in the guise of a letter to the *New-Jersey Gazette* in which he proposed that woolen petticoats be remade into clothes for the army. "And to clear this measure from every imputation of injustice, I have only to observe, that the generality of the *women* of that county, having for above a century, *worn the breeches*; it is highly reasonable that the *men* should now, . . . make booty of the *petticoats*" (Dec. 1777, *N.J. Archives*, 2d Ser., I, 532).

pendent of European power: and your modes of dress should be independent of a group of coquettes, milliners and manufacturers, who, from motives of vanity on one hand, and avarice on the other, endeavour to enslave the fancy of the whole world." Buying American wares became a patriotic gesture, intended to support "infant" manufacturers threatened by more fashionable products from abroad; it was up to American women to provide a protected market for domestic goods. A Virginia papermaker was frank to admit that when he had asked women to sell household rags to him as a matter of profit, few were forthcoming, but he proceeded to appeal "to the *Public Spirit* of the Ladies." Since support of home manufactures was patriotic, "the lady favouring them with the largest supply will be entitled to a distinguished place in the temple of PATRIOTISM."[15] On the eve of the next war with England, papermakers were still begging for rags with the same pleas:

> The scraps which you reject, unfit
>> To clothe the tenant of a hovel,
> May shine in sentiment and wit,
>> And help to make a charming novel.

Gradually American ideologues developed an imaginary sumptuary system that applied only to women. They appealed to women on the most frivolous terms. This voluntary effort was a far cry from the bitter sumptuary restraint of the Revolution.[16]

During the war women, like most men, were civilians. The role of the private citizen in a civil war can be vague and unclear; it is not surprising

15. *American Museum*, I (1787), 475; *Virginia Gazette and Alexandria Advertiser* (Alexandria), Dec. 2, 1790. See also the "Patriotic and Economic Association of the Ladies of Hartford," Nov. 6, 1786. "Saving of Rags may perhaps be thought too trifling, and below the Notice of the good Matrons of the State; but when they consider they are aiding and assisting in a necessary Manufacture, and when the young Ladies are assured, that by sending to the Paper Mill an old Handkerchief, no longer fit to cover their snowy Breasts, there is a Possibility of its returning to them again in the more pleasing form of a Billet Doux from their Lovers, the Proprietors flatter themselves with great Success" (*North-Carolina Gazette* [New Bern], Nov. 14, 1777, William L. Saunders and Walter Clark, eds., *The State Records of North Carolina* [Winston and Goldsboro, N.C., 1886–1907], XI, 804).

16. 1811, in Harriet Silvester Tapley, *Salem Imprints, 1768–1825: A History of the First Fifty Years of Printing in Salem, Massachusetts* . . . (Salem, Mass., 1927), 89. Earlier themes persisted, as is shown in this 1801 New Jersey toast: "The fair daughters of Columbia— May their modesty, industry, ingenuity and economy, supercede the necessity of such large importations; and these accomplishments be their only recommendation to procure the best of husbands" (*New-Jersey Journal* [Elizabeth Town], Mar. 17, 1801).

that whether whig or tory, women had something of a collective reputation for hesitant patriotism or outright neutrality. But women soon discovered that in this civil war any theater of conflict could create violence that would change their lives. They might not be soldiers, but they were not immune from attack.

Documented cases of rape are relatively rare, but those we have are vicious in the extreme. Rape by the British was a crime for which there could be little redress. Those who reoccupied areas held by enemy troops gave low priority to documenting crimes for the sake of the record. We do have, however, the pathetic testimony, signed only with a mark, of thirteen-year-old Abigail Palmer, who was at home with her grandfather when the British troops came through Hunterdon County, New Jersey, in the winter of 1777. "A great number of soldiers Belonging to the British Army came there, when one of them said to the Deponent, I want to speak with you in the next Room & she told him she woud not go with him when he seizd hold of her & dragd her into a back Room and she screamd & begd of him to let her alone. . . . her Grandfather also & Aunt Intreated . . . telling them how Cruel & what a shame it was to Use a Girl of that Age after that manner, but . . . finally three of Said Soldiers Ravished her."[17]

Mistreatment and indignity, the more frightening because the threat of rape was always present, were possible wherever armies roamed. Examples are easy to find, but difficult to quantify; they form a substantial segment of the memoir material compiled by both sides. The murder of Mrs. Caldwell in Connecticut Farms, New Jersey, by a British sharpshooter in 1780 took on the proportions of a patriotic myth; likewise, the loyalists made a legend of Flora MacDonald's daughters, whose rebel captors in the fall of 1777 put "their swords into their bosoms, split down their silk dresses and, taking them out into the yard, stripped them of all their outer clothing." The loyalist Ann Hulton reported that "at

17. Eventually the soldiers dragged her and another girl, Elizabeth Cain, off to their camp, "where they was both Treated by some others of the soldiers in the same cruel Manner . . . until an officer came" and returned the girls to their homes. Papers of the Continental Congress (M-247), Roll 66, Item 53: 31, National Archives. Other Hunterdon County cases were testified to: Mary Campbell, Sarah Cain, Mary Phillips, ibid., 29–39. The widow Rebekah Christopher fought off an attack on herself and then "found her Daughter about Ten year old among five or six of sd soldiers, & one of them had hold of her, & she this Deponent believed would have Ravished her if her coming into the Barn had not prevented him" (ibid., 39). All the Hunterdon County women's depositions were signed with marks. Orderly books of American regiments record soldiers whipped for rape, but details of the cases are rarely, if ever, given.

Roxbury Mr. Ed. Brinleys wife whilst lying in, had a guard of Rebels always in her room, who treated her with rudeness & indecency, exposing her to the view of their banditti, as a sight 'See a tory woman' and stripd her & her Children of all their Linnen & Cloths." The king's troops were even more cruel to Hannah Adams, the wife of Deacon Joseph Adams of Cambridge, Massachusetts; on their retreat from Concord, three soldiers broke into her room where she was lying in bed, "scarcely able to walk ... to the fire, not having been to [her] chamber door ... [since] being delivered in child-birth." They forced her outside with bayonets and set the house on fire while her five children were still inside.[18]

Women were made refugees by the war. The war was so disruptive to family life that one begins to wonder whether the cult of domesticity—the ideological celebration of women's domestic roles—was not in large measure a response to the wartime disruption and threat of separation of families. Peace would bring renewed appreciation of what had once been taken for granted.

When the patriots evacuated New York City in 1776, Margaret Livingston moved from the city to Fairfield, Connecticut, only to find the British nearby. "I cant help thinking," she wrote, "... it would have been better for us to have staid in N. Y. the expence of moving has been very great & the loss of a good deal property in the City, makes me envy those who have had courage to stay. I have [learnt] experience by it. I am determin'd should I ever be so unfortunate as to see another War, never to move from the place providence has placed me in come what Foe that will. nothing new from the British Army today, but expect soon to hear of a bloody battle, seventeen thousand Men have not landed to look at one another."[19] Many of the poor who had been cared for in the city almshouse had to leave also, and money was allocated to transport them to upstate counties. More than half of the approximately 550 who were sent out were women, and it is possible that more married women were subsumed under their husbands' names, as they were in other lists. When Ezra Stiles counted the refugees who had come to New Haven in 1782, eighteen were male and twenty-eight female. Most unfortunate were the

---

18. For stages in the mythologizing of Mrs. Caldwell, see *N.J. Archives*, 2d Ser., IV, 446, 453, and Princeton commencement dialogue, Oct. 2, 1780, *ibid.*, V, 31. Ann Hulton is quoted in Catherine S. Crary, ed., *The Price of Loyalty: Tory Writings from the Revolutionary Era* (New York, 1973), 57. The account of Hannah Adams is in Wroth *et al.*, eds., *Province in Rebellion*.

19. Margaret Livingston to [Catharine Livingston], Oct. 20, 1776, Ridley Papers.

170 Kentucky women and children taken captive by a force of British and Shawnee in June 1780; after a two-year internment in Canada, they were sent home in a condition that aroused public sympathy.[20]

It was taken for granted that women would maintain the household economy while their menfolk were at war. Sarah Frazier described her grandmother's war effort: "All the cloth and linen that my Grandfather wore during the war were spun at home, most of it by her own hands. All the clothing of the family, (and it was not a small one) during this time was made at home except weaving. All the business of every kind, she attended to Farm, Iron Works, and domestic matters. In Summer as soon as it was light she had her horse saddled, rode over the farm and directed the men about their work, often rode down to the creek, where Sharpless' Iron Works are now, and was back at breakfast time to give her attention and toil to the children, servants, & household affairs." Abigail Adams maintained the family farm, hired and fired the hands, bought and sold lands. "Mrs. Adams Native Genius will Excel us all in Husbandry," James Warren reported. "She was much Engaged when I came along, and the Farm at Braintree Appeared to be Under Excellent Management."[21]

Because the Revolution was a civil war, each adult had to assume a political identity and maintain it with sufficient clarity to satisfy the local authorities. Women had the advantage. Because they were not being recruited into the conflicting armies, their political choices were less carefully scrutinized than those of men; they could even shift back and forth between camps with some ease.

Patriots continually complained that women were moving into areas occupied by the British, bringing property and information behind enemy lines. "I have good reason to suspect," George Washington wrote, "that many persons (Women particularly) who obtain leave from the Executive Council of Pennsylvania to go and come to and from New York under

20. James A. Roberts, ed., *New York in the Revolution as Colony and State*, 2d ed., II (Albany, N.Y., 1898), 118–125; Dexter, ed., *Literary Diary of Ezra Stiles*, III, 60–61; Timothy Pickering to Virginia Delegates, Nov. 23, 1782, William T. Hutchinson, William M. E. Rachal *et al.*, eds., *The Papers of James Madison* (Chicago, 1962–), V, 314–315.

21. [Frazier], "A Reminiscence," *PMHB*, XLVI (1922), 56; James Warren to John Adams, Apr. 27, 1777, *Adams Family Correspondence*, II, 239n. The explicit instructions given to women by patriots imply the expectation that major farming enterprises will be pursued. "I see you have let the Island," Philip Livingston wrote to his married daughter Catherine Van Rensselaer. "You must agree with the Tenants to pay Taxes—not to plant more than 30 acres of Corn in one year, nor nearer together than common" (May 5, 1775, *Magazine of History*, III [1906], 391–392).

pretence of visiting their Friends, have, in fact, no other Business but that of bringing out Goods to trade with." Henry Livingston complained that the British "were informed of every thing that passed among us and that Women were the most proper persons for that purpose."[22]

Women who were intercepted in circulating British proclamations or passing information about American troops were numerically few, but dangerous enough to be taken seriously. In 1780, for example, some thirty-two women, along with over four hundred men, were brought to the attention of the Albany County Board of the New York State Commissioners for Detecting and Defeating Conspiracies, accused of being spies or sympathizers. Among the accused were women who had given sanctuary in their homes to loyalists and to British soldiers. Rachael Ferguson, confined in an Albany jail "for harbouring and entertaining a Number of Tories" en route from Canada, was released on the very high bail of eight hundred pounds. Lidia Currey was similarly jailed for "assisting in concealing and harbouring Persons from the Enemy." A Mrs. Henderson of Dutchess County, New York, smuggled a message from a husband who was fighting with the British to his wife at home, and publicly "expressed herself much in favor of the Superiority and Success of the British Arms and observed that She had no doubt that finally they would subdue this Country and therefore that it would be best for all Persons to come in and submit."[23]

Not only British sympathizers were suspected as conspirators. Pacifist Shakers were carefully watched. Founded by Mother Ann Lee, the Shaker sect had a strong appeal to women. The Albany committee interrogated Ann Standerren and two men with the carefully phrased question "whether they are principled against taking up Arms in defence of

22. George Washington to Joseph Reed, Feb. 12, 1779, Papers Cont. Cong. (M-247), Roll 33, Item 69: II, 129; Testimony of Henry Livingston, Feb. 5, 1777, N.-Y. *Committee for Detecting Conspiracies,* I, 120. For fears that spies were hiding in women's clothes, see Victor H. Paltsits, ed., *Minutes of the Commissioners for Detecting and Defeating Conspiracies in the State of New York: Albany County Sessions* (New York, 1909–1919), II, 563, hereafter cited as *N.Y. Commissioners for Detecting Conspiracies.* See also *N.J. Archives,* 2d Ser., I, 531.

23. *N.Y. Commissioners for Detecting Conspiracies,* II, 445–446; *N.-Y. Committee for Detecting Conspiracies,* I, 67–68. For interception of copies of Howe's *Proclamation* that had been sent to two women, see *N.-Y. Committee for Detecting Conspiracies,* I, 64–65. See also *N.Y. Commissioners for Detecting Conspiracies,* I, 199, II, 751, and *N.-Y. Committee for Detecting Conspiracies,* I, 106, 264–265. For a case in which a recruiter for the tories was jailed, see the testimony of Margarethe Beeckmann before the Tryon County Committee of Safety at Canajoharie, Feb. 9, 1778, Tryon County Committee of Safety Papers, New-York Historical Society, New York City.

the American cause and whether they have not endeavored to influence other persons against taking up arms." When the three "answered in the affirmative," the committee resolved that they be committed [to jail]." Not until December, when the board conceded that "many of the Persons of the said Persuasion [Shaking Quakers] have been reformed and that no further Evil is to be apprehended from her influence," was Standerren permitted to return home on the basis of a two hundred pound bond for good behavior.[24]

Wives of tories, as a class, were regarded with partisan hostility, especially if their husbands had actually joined the British. In patriot areas, their homes might be robbed and plundered with relative impunity. After the fall of Ticonderoga, insecurity ran especially high on the New York frontier; it was suspected that tories were hiding out in the woods, secretly provided with supplies by their wives, and readying themselves to assist in the expected attack on Fort Schuyler. "The Women of those Enemies is still living among us," growled the chairman of the Tryon County Committee of Safety to Governor George Clinton. "Some behave very rudely at present, and have proved very active to support and spirit up the opposite Cause." The tory women saw their position rather differently. In a rare joint petition, signed with their marks and sent to the committee, they complained that "being left by . . . [their] Husbands and . . . [their] Effects sold," they were "reduced to the greatest distress imaginable." They "humbly" asked that they be provided for or that they be permitted to join their husbands, and eventually they got their request. In the summer of 1777, the Tryon County Committee of Safety rounded up eleven women and placed them under house arrest, and in October they were given seven days notice to leave.[25]

Suspicion of tory wives was not confined to Tryon County. The New York State Commissioners for Detecting and Defeating Conspiracies wrote to Governor Clinton, "From the frequent complaints which are exhibited to this Board that the wives of such disaffected Persons who are gone over to the Enemy daily harbour Persons who through fear of being punished for their Crimes against the State conceal themselves and their holding Correspondance with their Husbands it is conceived necessary that some mode should be adopted to prevent this evil." The commis-

---

24. N.Y. *Commissioners for Detecting Conspiracies*, II, 469–471, 592.

25. Peter S. Deygart to George Clinton, Aug. 25, 1777, Tryon Co. Comm. of Safety Papers; "Petition of sundry women wives of tories for relief," n.d., *ibid*. See also *N.Y. Commissioners for Detecting Conspiracies*, II, 560.

sioners begged the governor to see to it that women whose husbands had joined the enemy were sent to the enemy themselves. By the summer of 1780 New York State had passed "An Act for the Removal of the Families of Persons who have joined the Enemy," justifying the removal on the basis of the "many and great Mischiefs" that arise "by permitting the Families of Persons who have joined the Enemy, to remain at their respective Habitations, inasmuch as such Persons frequently come out in a private Manner, to gain Intelligence and commit Robberies, Thefts and Murders . . . and are concealed and comforted by their respective Families." This measure empowered justices of the peace to give a twenty-day notice to the wives of persons who were with the enemy "that they depart this State . . . or repair to such Parts of it as are within the Power of the Enemy; and at their Discretion to take with them all or any of their Children, not above the Age of twelve Years."[26]

As early as the fall of 1777 the New Jersey legislature had authorized the New Jersey Council of Safety "to send into the Enemy's Lines such of the wives and Children of Persons lately residing within this State, who have gone over to the Enemy, as they shall think necessary." Even after Sally Medlis promised that she would "never hold any correspondence whatsoever with her Husband or in any Manner or Way injure the State," she was exiled along with other wives of Newark loyalists.[27] And when patriots reoccupied Philadelphia in 1779, they too assumed that wives' political loyalties were the same as their husbands', and that wives had remained behind either to protect their property or to function as a fifth column should opportunity arise. In Philadelphia, too, wives of tories were summarily expelled in 1780.[28]

There was little room in the patriot position for the admission that women might make political choices that were distinct from—and at odds with—those of their husbands. The Albany commission did permit one tory wife to remain after the passage of the expulsion law on the

26. *N.Y. Commissioners for Detecting Conspiracies*, I, 327, II, 794–796, 799; "An Act for the Removal of the Families of Persons who have joined the Enemy," July 1, 1780, in *Laws of the State of New York, Passed at the Sessions of the Legislature, Held in the Years 1777 . . . 1784*, I (Albany, N.Y., 1886), 282–283.

27. "Act for Constituting a Council of Safety," Sept. 1777, in *Acts of the General Assembly of the State of New Jersey* (Trenton, N.J., 1777), 87; Petition of Sally Medlis, Aug. 11, 1779, Manuscript Collection, Revolutionary War Records, Bureau of Archives and History, Trenton, N.J., in Dennis P. Ryan, "Six Towns: Continuity and Change in Revolutionary New Jersey, 1770–1792" (Ph.D. diss., New York University, 1974), 188.

28. See Raymond C. Werner, ed., "Diary of Grace Growden Galloway, Kept at Philadelphia . . . ," *PMHB*, LVIII (1934), 162, 186.

grounds that "notwithstanding the Political Sentiments of her husband ... Jane Moffit has always been esteemed a Friend to the American Cause." But in other cases a woman's harmlessness and her willingness to promise that she would not be a burden on the public treasury were the major considerations. Tories' wives who petitioned to be allowed to stay brought certificates signed by their patriot neighbors to the effect that they had "behaved themselves in an unexceptionable Manner" and that permitting them to remain would not be "detrimental to the Freedom and independence of this and the United States."[29]

One of the most explicit of these pleas is a petition of twenty-one patriot women who had themselves been temporarily expelled from their homes in Wilmington, North Carolina, when the British occupied the town. When Wilmington was retaken in 1782, the Americans responded by issuing an order that summarily expelled the wives and children of absent loyalists. Women who signed the petition protesting this action included the wives of some of the most prominent patriots of the Cape Fear region. Anne Hooper, whose husband had signed the Declaration of Independence, signed first. Initially the petitioners bowed to tradition: "It is not the province of our sex to reason deeply upon the policy of the order." Yet they insisted that they had an obligation to respond, partly because the policy "must affect the helpless and innocent," partly because they suspected it had been drafted in retaliation for their own expulsion. The loyalists' wives had neither inspired the British expulsion order nor aided its execution, said the patriot women. "On the contrary, they expressed the greatest indignation at it, and with all their power strove to mitigate our sufferings." Mrs. Hooper and her colleagues saw that there was a real difference between sending patriot wives to their friends on the outskirts of town, friends who had taken them in and made them comfortable, and expelling "Town women" whose husbands were far away in Charleston and who lacked means of traveling there. The patriot women claimed a patriot's privilege. "If we may be allowed to claim any merit with the public for our steady adherence to the Whig principles of America . . . we shall hold it as a very signal mark of your respect for us if you will condescend to suffer to remain amongst us our old friends and acquaintances whose husbands, though estranged from us in political opinions, have left wives and children much endeared to us. . . . The

29. Jane Moffit's petition is reported in *N.Y. Commissioners for Detecting Conspiracies*, II, 619–620. For other petitions see *ibid.*, 619–620, 523, 528, 541, 540. A successful certificate dated Jan. 5, 1781, signed by two justices of the peace on behalf of 15 tory wives, appears *ibid.*, 612–613, 620.

safety of this State, we trust in God, is now secured beyond the most powerful exertions of our Enemies, and it would be a system of abject weakness to fear the feeble efforts of women and children."[30]

A woman's plea to resist expulsion may not always have represented a clearly political choice. The desire to remain in one's own home and in control of one's own property was of course very strong, and few wished to wander in the crowds of women who followed the British troops. The woman who went behind the British lines could not be certain she would find the man she sought. But surely some women, like Jane Moffit, had political allegiances that differed from those of their husbands. If they did, they would find it difficult to persuade committees of safety to respect these distinctions. Robert Morris's wife, Mary, watched the expulsion of women from Philadelphia with misgivings:

> My feelings [are] . . . wounded for the sufferings of a Number of my Sex in this State, who are compeld to leave it, by that Cruell Edict of our Counsel: a resolve which Oblidges all the women whose Husbands are with the enemy, and Children whose parents are there, to repair to *them* Immediately; a determination like this which admits of no Exception, is unjust, and cruell, . . . there is many whose conduct has not Merited it, tho there is others that have, yet why not discriminate between the Innocent and guilty. . . . Mrs. Furgerson is determind not to go, she says they may take her life, but shall never banish her from Her Country.

Then she concluded wryly, "There are others [who are] . . . renderd happyer by the banishment of a worthless Husband and who by honest industry gains a Subsistence for themselves and Children."[31]

30. Petition of Anne Hooper, Sarah Nash, Mary Nash, and others, to Gov. Alexander Martin and the Members of the Honorable Council, Saunders and Clark, eds., *N.C. State Recs.*, XVI, 467–469. For a subtle exploration of the situation of loyalist women, see Mary Beth Norton, "Eighteenth-Century Women in Peace and War: The Case of the Loyalists," *WMQ*, 3d Ser., XXXIII (1976), 386–409.

31. Mary Morris to Catharine Livingston, June 10, [1780], Ridley Papers. The local level of hostility toward loyalist families may have depended on the political balance of the region. Adele Hast has demonstrated that absentees' wives who remained in the Northern Neck of Virginia suffered no more extensively than the other women in that area: "Relations with friends and relatives were more important determinants of the treatment of these women than was their alliance with opponents of the struggle for independence" (Adele Hast, "Loyalism in Eastern Virginia during the American Revolution: The Norfolk Area and the Eastern Shore" [Ph.D. diss., University of Iowa, 1979], chap. 6). Margaret Parker described her struggle to maintain a household along with her sister Rebecca Aitchison:

The emergencies of war pulled women into political relationships and forced unfamiliar political choices. Women appear in substantial numbers among those who appealed for tax abatements because their property had been destroyed. Even menial jobs were politicized. Mary Pratt was turned out of her job as housekeeper for the South Carolina State House after the capture of Charleston "to make room for another person who was more attached to the British Government."[32] Patriot forces, too, had employment to offer and new roles to suggest to sympathetic women who were willing to emerge, even if only to a modest extent, from their traditional domain. Women represent only a small proportion of those who came before committees of safety to testify against tories, but that these women would bring their traditionally private judgments of male political behavior into public tribunals is testimony to the intensity of wartime politics. Committees of safety had employment for "discreet Women, of known attachment to the American Cause" to search suspected women smugglers and tories for illegal papers.[33] Abigail Adams seems to have been pulled into this effort. On April 21, 1776, she reported that "a Number of Gentlemen who were together at Cambridge thought it highly proper that a Committee of Ladies should be

---

"We spin our own cloaths, milk, sew, raise poultry and everything we are capable of doing to maintain ourselves. . . . we buy nothing that we can do with out. Our girls are all dressed in their own spinning. . . . Jenny is as notable at the country work as if she had been brought up to it. . . . I am sorry our present circumstances prevents them from improving themselves by reading, writing, keeping polite company etc" (Jan. 3, 1779, "Letters from Virginia, 1774–1781," *Mag. of Hist.*, III [1906], 214–215).

32. For tax abatements, see Charles J. Hoadly *et al.*, eds., *The Public Records of the State of Connecticut* . . . (Hartford, Conn., 1894–), VII, 449–471, hereafter cited as *Conn. State Recs.*, and Papers Cont. Cong. (M-247), Roll 66, Item 53: 165–220. Mary Pratt's petition of Jan. 29, 1783, is published in Theodora J. Thompson, ed., *The State Records of South Carolina: Journals of the House of Representatives 1783–1784* (Columbia, S.C., 1977), 61. After the war she petitioned for the 16 months' salary owed her, but she received only "rations of Meat, Bread and Wood in order to relieve her present distress"; the amount of that payment was "deducted from her account against the Publick" (*ibid.*, 60).

33. Examples of women who testify against tories are numerous. See *N.-Y. Committee for Detecting Conspiracies*, I, 87, 98, 102–103, 106, 264–265; Tryon Co. Comm. of Safety Papers, Feb. and Mar. 1778; and *N.Y. Commissioners for Detecting Conspiracies*, I, 290–294, 354, II, 475, 508, 517, 519, 534, 548, 615, 717. For women who searched people leaving Philadelphia during the British occupation, see [Frazier], "A Reminiscence," *PMHB*, XLVI (1922), 53. Mary Frazier successfully smuggled out an appeal to Washington complaining of British treatment of American prisoners in Philadelphia. "Mrs. Gibbons and myself were taken into a room and two women came forward to undress us. Mrs. Gibbons declared they should not touch her, and made so much fuss, kicking, slapping and scolding, that they were sure she had something to struggle for, & they undressed her even taking off her shoes and stockings. I had slipped the quilting of my petticoat and put the paper in and sewed it up again" (*ibid.*).

chosen to examine the Torys Ladies, and proceeded to the choice of 3 Mrs. Winthrope, Mrs. Warren and your Humble Servant."[34]

There were women who went to great risks for the patriot cause. Elizabeth Burgin came under suspicion for "helping the American prisiners to make their [es]cap" from New York in 1779. "The British offered," she reported, "a bounty of two Houndred pounds for taking me." Her friends smuggled her out to Long Island and then on to Philadelphia in a "wale boat," which was "chased by two Boats half way [across] the Sound." It was more than a month before she was able to get back to New York under a flag of truce to retrieve her children.[35]

The American army offered political uses for traditional domestic skills. Conspicuous military heroines like Margaret Corbin were only a tiny proportion of the thousands of dependents who drifted after the troops. Wives and children who had no means of support when their husbands and fathers were pressed into service followed after and cared for their own men, earning their subsistence by cooking and washing for troops in an era when the offices of quartermaster and commissary were inadequately run.[36]

The richest fictional portrait of such a woman was provided by James Fenimore Cooper in *The Spy: A Tale of the Neutral Ground*, published in 1821. Elizabeth Flanagan is "a female sutler, washerwoman, and . . . petticoat doctor to the troops. She was the widow of a soldier who had been killed in the service. . . . She constantly migrated with the troops. . . . sometimes the cart itself was her shop; at others the soldiers made her a rude shelter of such materials as offered." Her motive is not simply financial; she is as proud a patriot as any of Cooper's characters, with a clear sense of the value of her services to the political cause. "What

34. Abigail Adams to John Adams, *Adams Family Correspondence*, I, 391. John Adams replied, "As you are a Politician, and now elected into an important Office, that of Judgess of the Tory Ladies, which will give you naturally an Influence with your sex, I hope you will be instant, in season and out of season, in exhorting them to use their Influence with the Gentlemen, to fortify upon Georges Island, Lovells, Petticks [Peddocks], Long, or wherever else it is proper. Send down Fire ships and Rafts and burn to Ashes those Pirates" (John Adams to Abigail Adams, May 12, 1776, *ibid.*, 406). His answer suggests his continuing assumption that women's political processes were not men's, though they might share goals. See also Abigail Adams to Mercy Otis Warren, Apr. 27, 1776, *ibid.*, 398.

35. Petition of Elizabeth Burgin, Nov. 19, 1779, Papers Cont. Cong. (M-247), Roll 170: 312.

36. The practice was an old one; it was common during the French and Indian War. The journal of Sgt. David Holden for 1760 records allowances for women, allocation of women to companies, and rivalry for women in the camp ([David] Holden, "A Journal of What was Transacted in the Expedition for the Total Reduction of Canada in the Year A. D. 1760," Massachusetts Historical Society, *Proceedings*, 2d Ser., IV [1888], 387–409).

would become of the States and liberty," she asks, "if the boys had never a clane shirt, or a drop to comfort them? Ask Captain Jack, there, if they'd fight . . . and they no clane linen to keep the victory in." When, at the end of the novel, the brave Capt. Jack Lawton is killed by the British in a hopeless engagement from which both sides ultimately retreat, it is Elizabeth Flanagan who is left to keen the grandeur of the hero and the wastefulness of war: "It's no more will he hear, and it's but little will he mind yee're probes and yee're medicines. Och! hone—och! hone—and where will be the liberty now? or who will there be to fight the battles, or gain the day? . . . Och! he's gone! he's gone! and the liberty is gone wid him!"[37]

The real women who followed the troops were usually regarded as a nuisance, and they appear in orderly books in terms of what they might not do. Sometimes they are not to ride the wagons when the army moves; sometimes they are required to ride "as the weomin going on horses Back will deminish the Number of Drivers taken from the Army." When provisions were scarce in 1780, officers at West Point were instructed to "without Delay make the Strictest inspection into the Carractor of the women who Draw [rations] in their Corps and Report on their honour the Names of Such as are Maryed to non Commsd officers, privates and Artificers." Married women were to be given certificates, unmarried women to be "sent off." Women who were permitted to stay might not draw provisions unless they washed clothes "at . . . a Reasonable Rate" fixed by "the Commanding officers of the Corps in which they Draw." The rates for washing were set low: "for washing and ironing a plain shirt, 4 shillings . . . sheat 2/6." In 1782 women were allowed "two shillings a dozen for all articles which they wash reckoning both large and small provided they find their own soape."[38]

At Fishkill, New York, the wives of several artisans were employed as cooks; however, cooking was not regarded as a skilled trade, and the women were paid substantially less than their husbands. John Parsell, who was superintendent of the wheelwrights for two weeks, was paid fourteen shillings a day; Thomas Parsell, the foreman, was paid twelve

37. James Fenimore Cooper, *The Spy: A Tale of the Neutral Ground* (London, 1882), II, 95–96, 307–308, 275–277.

38. Thomas Lynch Montgomery, ed., *Pennsylvania Archives*, 6th Ser., XIV (Harrisburg, Pa., 1907), 71, 127; Tallmadge Orderly Books, Fourth New York Regiment, June 25–27, [1780], June 29, 1780, Aug. 19, 1782, Almon W. Lauber, ed., *Orderly Books of the Fourth New York Regiment, 1778–1780, The Second New York Regiment, 1780–1783, by Samuel Tallmadge and Others, With Diaries of Samuel Tallmadge, 1780–1782* . . . (Albany, N.Y., 1932), 381–384, 386, 610.

shillings a day. Their relative Sarah Parsell was cook—at two shillings a day. The cook for the express riders was Mrs. Lloyd, wife of the hostler, and she was paid four dollars per month while her husband got ten dollars.[39]

Even when given specific orders and employment, many women resisted military discipline. The pattern is clearly revealed in Washington's General Orders: from the beginning to the end of the war, his notes are dotted with the complaint that women slowed down the progress of the army. They are an "incumbrance," "a clog upon every movement." Women were sent with the slowest section of the moving troops, the baggage wagons, for two reasons. First, burdened as they were with children or pregnancies, the female dependents maintained the slowest pace. Second, it was an embarrassment to let them be seen with men. When the army retreated through Philadelphia after the battle of Germantown, Washington was explicit: baggage wagons were "to avoid the City entirely. . . . Not a woman belonging to the army is to be seen with the troops on their march." Much as he would have liked, Washington could not deny that in some sense the women did "belong" to the army. He was reduced to insisting that they be put to work or sent off to serve as nurses. Washington issued order after order forbidding women to ride in any wagon without leave in writing from the brigadier in command. "And," he added, "the Brigadiers are requested to be cautious in giving leave to those who are able to walk." Further, "the women are expressly forbid any longer, under any licence at all, to ride in the waggons, and the officers earnestly called upon to permit no more than are absolutely necessary, and such as are actually useful, to follow the army." By 1778 he was complaining that women were still in the wagons. When officers questioned the female passengers, they always maintained they had been given permission to ride by someone else. By the summer of 1778 Washington was requiring permission in writing with the sole allowable basis of such permission being "inability to march." But a year later he had to admit that "the pernicious practice of suffering the women to incumber the Waggons still continues notwithstanding every former prohibition," and on the eve of Yorktown he was still fuming about the women encumbering the army.[40]

---

39. "Pay Roll of Sundry Persons employed in the publick Service by Hugh Hughes Deputy Quarter Master for the State of New York," Jan.–Dec. 1782, Papers of the Revolutionary War (M-246), Roll 135, Jacket 4, Natl. Archives.

40. General Orders, Fitzpatrick, ed., *Writings of Washington*, Aug. 4, 1777, IX, 17, Aug. 23, 1777, IX, 126, June 17, 1777, VIII, 257, July 4, 1777, VIII, 347, Aug. 27, 1777, IX,

The women not only had to be transported, they had to be fed. Washington was perplexed. "I cannot see," he wrote to Brig. Gen. John Stark at White Plains, "why the soldiers Wives in Albany should be supported at public expence. They may get most extravagant Wages of any kind of Work in the Country and to feed them, when that is the case, would be robbing the public and encouraging idleness." A year later, New York women whose husbands were away fighting in the west apparently demanded what we would now call dependents' allowances. Washington threw up his hands. "This is a thing which I have never known to be allowed, and which, if admitted in one instance, might be claimed by the whole Army." He was helpless to change things and conceded that "the New York troops will be at this post in a few days, when the Wives of as many Soldiers, as are generally allowed to follow the Army, may join and be subsisted as usual. If any remain, I cannot undertake to give an order for them to draw provisions." Washington's frustration affords an indirect glimpse of these hundreds of women who would not be separated from their husbands or from their ad hoc work in the camps, thus making it impossible to keep them off the wagons or from drawing their own subsistence rations. Like it or not, Washington was stuck with what even he had to refer to as the "Women of the Army."[41]

The most common official position that the American forces offered women was that of nurse, an obvious employment of domestic skills. Occasionally military nurses could earn premium pay, but it is important to recognize that, two generations before Florence Nightingale and Clara Barton upgraded the profession, the work of military nurses was largely custodial and therefore ill-paid. Women were recruited for this labor because, in Washington's words, if female nurses were not found, the army was "under the necessity of substituting in their place a number of men from the respective Regiments" who would then be "entirely lost in

---

139, June 19, 1778, XII, 94, June 7, 1779, XV, 240, June 19, 1781, XXII, 233.

41. George Washington to John Stark, Aug. 5, 1778, *ibid.*, XII, 283; George Washington to Goose Van Schaick, Oct. 19, 1779, *ibid.*, XVI, 489; General Orders, May 31, 1778, *ibid.*, XI, 497. At the end of the war, the garrison at West Point, which included 10,501 men, also had 405 women and 302 children. The largest numbers of dependents were associated with the New York and Massachusetts units, but there was no unit without its small contingent of women and children. See Papers Rev. War (M-246), Roll 136. I am grateful to George Chalou for providing this reference. Descriptions of "Those women which belonged to the Garrison" appear in William Colbraith, "A Diary of the Siege of Fort Schuyler, [April 17–August 23, 1777]," *Mag. of Hist.*, III (1906), 90–104. For women following the Hessians, see Sarah Logan Fisher, "A Diary of Trifling Occurrences," ed. Nicholas B. Wainwright, *PMHB*, LXXXII (1958), 419.

the proper line of their duty." Most of the skilled tasks of nursing were performed throughout the war by male surgeon's mates. The official duties left to the nurse were closer to those of the modern orderly, and only in the absence of the mates did nurses administer medicines. The formal job description below suggests the menial role of the army nurses and, in its direct warnings against drunkenness and theft, also reveals the nurses' low status in the hospital staff:

The N U R S E S, in the absence of the Mates, administer the medicine and diet prescribed for the sick according to order; they obey all orders they receive from the Matron; not only to be attentive to the cleanliness of the wards and patients, but to keep themselves clean they are never to be disguised with liquor [a stricture which is not placed on the males]; they are to see that the close-stools or pots are emptied as soon as possible after they are used, into a necessary house. . . . they are to see that every patient, upon his admission into the Hospital is immediately washed with warm water, and that his face and hands are washed and head combed every morning . . . that their wards are swept over every morning or oftener if necessary and sprinkled with vinegar three or four times a day; nor are they ever to be absent without leave from the Physicians, Surgeons or Matron; they are to deliver the effects immediately of such soldiers as die in Hospital to the Ward-Master, who is to be accountable for the same: All attempt to steal from, conceal the effects of, or otherwise defraud the patients . . . will be severely punished.[42]

The pay scale that Congress established in 1777 for hospital staffs also confirms the limited status ascribed to women and the weakness of their bargaining position. Early in the war, Washington had begged for pre-

42. George Washington to Congress, Sept. 14, 1776, Papers Cont. Cong. (M-247), Roll 166, Item 152: II, 553–554; "Rules and Directions for the Better Regulating the Military Hospital . . . ," Feb. 6, 1778, ibid., Roll 103: 567. Matrons' jobs were not primarily medical; matrons were in effect the heads of housekeeping services: receiving supplies, supervising cooks, and ensuring "that the Nurses do their duty." It was a common complaint that convalescing soldiers drank too much and became uncontrollable. See, for example, Worthington Chauncey Ford et al., eds., Journals of the Continental Congress, 1774–1789 (Washington, D.C., 1904–1937), VII, 231–237. Military hospitals occasionally cared for women as well as soldiers; the Albany hospital report of Mar. 20, 1780, listed "nine Women & ten children Patients" who together drew 12 rations. The "Return of Patients in the General Hospital from August 20 to 27, 1778" included among the 62 patients Jane Herrin, "a woman in the Continent. army," who was convalescing from childbed fever (Papers Rev. War [M-246], Roll 135, Jacket 3).

mium pay for nurses, and Dr. William Shippen, desperate for nurses for the hospital at Perth Amboy, New Jersey, reported that he had "been obliged to deviate from the regulation of the honorable Congress and allow them 10/per week instead of 3/9. The most ordinary woman here is able to earn much more, as there are so few women and so many men to work for. . . . the sick must suffer much unless well nursed and kept clean."

But as the hospital system was regularized, Washington's and Shippen's strictures were forgotten, and matrons and nurses were paid less well than stablehands. At a time when senior surgeons received four dollars per day and were entitled to six rations of food, matrons got only one-half dollar, and nurses' pay ranged from twenty-four cents to ninety cents per day, and one ration each. Wartime inflation drove up the salaries of physicians and surgeon's mates, but at the end of the war, when surgeon's mates got fifty dollars a month, matrons' salaries remained fifty cents a day.[43]

Had hospitals been staffed up to their full authorized strength, they would have provided employment to hundreds of women. The general plan for a coordinated military hospital establishment that Shippen and Dr. John Cochran drafted, and which was passed by Congress in April 1777, provided that a matron be hired for every hundred sick or wounded to see "that the provisions are properly prepared; that the wards, beds, and utensils be kept in neat order, and that the most exact economy be observed in her department." Nurses were to be hired in a ratio of one to every ten sick or wounded and were to be under the direction of the matrons.[44]

The realization of an efficient hospital system remained largely wishful

43. William Shippen to Congress, Sept. 19, 1776, Papers Cont. Cong. (M-247), Roll 102: XX, 55–58, Roll 20, Item 22: 61–62; George Washington to Congress, Sept. 14, 1776, *ibid.*, Roll 166, Item 152: II, 551–554. There was a little more flexibility in food supplies; women who had young children with them apparently did draw more rations. See "Return of Officers belonging to the General Hospital Northern Department," Mar. 20, 1780, Papers Rev. War (M-246), Roll 135, Jacket 3. (I am indebted to George Chalou for this reference.) The report of the General Hospital for the Northern Department, at Albany, for 1780 shows that the only people drawing more than one ration were those who had children with them. They included the carpenter, who drew rations for his wife and three children (the five of them received only three and one-half portions), four nurses, and the matron (*ibid.*).

44. Apr. 7, 1777, Ford *et al.*, eds., *Jours. Cont. Cong.*, VII, 231–237. The plan for establishing military hospitals of Feb. 27, 1777, provided for 1 nurse to every 15 sick or wounded. See "Report of the Committee on the Hospital," Feb. 1777, Papers Cont. Cong. (M-247), Roll 30, Item 22: 10.

thinking. Hospitals were usually dirty; the sick were not sufficiently separated from the wounded, who thereupon caught fevers and diseases.
Convalescents wandered off the premises; the drunken disorder of convalescing men gave hospitals a bad reputation. And there never were
enough staff. Lachlan McIntosh's report for the general hospitals in the
Pennsylvania area in 1778 claimed 571 men hospitalized and another
615 who had been admitted but died or deserted in the course of the
year. According to the official staff ratios, that number of patients would
have authorized employing seventy-nine nurses and ten matrons. But
reports of personnel do not indicate that hospital staffs ever approached
authorized levels. There was only one matron and one nurse to care for
133 patients at William Shippen's hospital in Philadelphia in 1779; four
nurses cared for over 100 sick at the general hospital in Hillsborough,
North Carolina. When a tally of hospital staff was prepared at the end of
the war, it listed only seven matrons and thirty nurses divided between
seven hospitals. No hospital had more than one matron, and the ratio of
one nurse to fifteen patients was rarely approached.[45]

One of the readiest ways for women to earn money had long been to
run a boardinghouse. This employment had the advantage of making use
of the form of capital that a widow or spinster was most likely to control
and of requiring a relatively slight form of readjustment; one continued
to live where one always had lived. Becoming a landlady might imply a
lowering of status, but not perhaps so radical a fall as that suffered by a
woman working for wages. The landlady remained self-employed while
she did the work that was traditional for women to do. Self-supporting
women were frequently found as landladies.

And as landladies they were affected by the war. The influx of delegates to the Continental Congress meant a large number of respectable
boarders for the boardinghouse keepers of Philadelphia. Sometimes landladies were paid for their services directly from the national treasury or
by local committees of safety, which rented rooms to house officers and
soldiers, employed women to cook meals for militia, and commandeered
supplies from boardinghouse cellars. The double purposes of the medi-
eval hotel—to care for the sick as well as to care for the traveler—had

45. "Report of the General Hospitals," Apr. 26, 1778, Papers Rev. War (M-246), Roll
135, Jacket 3. Often the lists of personnel do not include matrons and nurses at all. Surgeon's mates often handled the nursing duties. Women were not perceived as regular members of the staff. See also Papers Cont. Cong. (M-247), Roll 46: III, 395, Roll 102, Item 78:
XX, 586, Roll 30, Item 22: 61–62.

not yet fully disintegrated. Sick and wounded might be sent to private lodgings, and women were paid for their care.[46]

Boardinghouses had political complexions. Members of Congress vied with each other to stay with Mary House. James Madison was a regular boarder and maintained a private correspondence with Mrs. House and her daughter after he had returned to Virginia. Eliza House married Nicholas Trist and became part of nationalist political circles in Virginia. When Rachel Farmer established a lodging house in Philadelphia in 1781, she argued that Congress owed her patronage because of what she had risked during the war: "Your Memorialist, did for many years keep a Respectable Tavern In New Brunswick, which Business she Resolved to Quit, at the Begining of the War; but for the well Accommodateing the Gentlemen of our Army, & by the Solicittation of a Number of Gentlemen of Character, I Continued to keep a Publick House—the Consequence of which was, when the British took possession of that place, your Memorialist, had her House Burnt, & her Valluable Furniture Destroyed, & Rendered unable to prosecute Business."[47]

In 1783 when the Continental Congress, threatened with civil uprising in Philadelphia, was searching for a convenient place to move, it was flooded with petitions of invitation. The people of Princeton, "desirous to testify their Respect for the supreme Legislature of America" and willing "to furnish the best in their power," sent an invitation signed by six women and thirty-six men. Mrs. Rock and Mrs. Know indicated that their accommodations were not good enough for members of Congress, but that they would take attendants; Mrs. [Richard] Stockton offered "the whole House in which she lives, stables"; Mrs. Berrien offered "1 Room, 2 Beds, 2 Break & Dinners." A similar petition arrived from Trenton, though with fewer names and a caveat from five men who wished, reasonably enough, "to be excused from providing Dinners, as Congress do not dine at common Family hours."[48]

Wartime also created another group of less cordial boardinghouse

46. Ford *et al.*, eds., *Jours. Cont. Cong.*, XI, 801, IV, 237, VIII, 430, IV, 294; Browne *et al.*, eds., *Md. Archives*, XII, 96, 293, 234, 534.

47. Rachel Farmer's petition, Mar. 29, 1781, may be found in Papers Cont. Cong. (M-247), Roll 49, Item 41: 244. Characteristically, Congress ordered it to "lie upon the table."

48. Oct. 13, 1789, *ibid.*, Roll 60: 123. Congress did go to Princeton and was emphatically miserable. See Hutchinson, Rachal *et al.*, eds., *Papers of James Madison*, VI, 230–231, 256–258, 296, 352, 411. For Trenton, see Papers Cont. Cong. (M-247), Roll 103, Item 78: XXII, 283.

keepers—women who unwillingly housed soldiers during military occupation. Although the Americans paid for the services they commandeered of their own population, these payments were irregularly tendered, and the fees set by the Army.[49] The British came in the role of conquerors, and so they had less compulsion to pay for services rendered; even people of loyalist sympathies hesitated before offering room to foreign soldiers. The British preferred to maintain as long as they could the fiction that they were welcomed voluntarily into women's homes.

The process of negotiation was carefully detailed by Elizabeth Drinker, a Philadelphia Quaker woman. Her politics were pacifist, but she was generally sympathetic to the British. When her husband, Henry, along with nineteen other Quaker men, was exiled by the patriots to Virginia, she was left alone in her home. She was there with four young children and several servants when the British entered the city at the end of September 1777. Not long after the battle of Germantown, she was repeatedly visited by a British officer who asked her to "take in a Sick or wounded Captain," but she was able to "put him off" by arguing that her husband was already a martyr and that she was all alone. But being alone also made her vulnerable; soldiers simply marched into her house to take what they needed. On the fifth of November a soldier came to ask for blankets. "Notwithstanding my refusal," she wrote, "he went up stairs and took one." On November 25, she was deeply frightened by "an enraged, drunken Man . . . with a sword in his hand, swearing about the House, after going 2 or 3 times up & down the Entry." Finally a male visitor, Chalkley James, disarmed the man and sent him on his way. When a courteous and respectable young officer called a few weeks later, looking for quarters and arguing "that it was a necessary protection at these times to have [an officer] . . . in the House," his words had some plausibility. She put him off by saying that she had to think about it, but he returned the next day and the next to ask again. "I told him that my sister was out [consulting their friends for advice] . . . that I expected that we who were at present 'lone women, would be excus'd he said he fear'd not, for tho I might put him off . . . yet a great number of Foreign Troops were to be quartered in this Neighbourhood, he believed they might be

---

49. In 1776 Jesse Hollingsworth forwarded the petition of Mrs. Trepolet to the Maryland Council of Safety. She was "uneasy about her Howses Takken by Capt. Edwin Smith and Ramsey last winter for barraks. . . . the houses are much abused. . . . they are very carles and shee thinks they will burn her and all she has by their neglect. . . . she has cactch them with larg fires again the walls on the out side." The council did order that damages be assessed and rent paid (Browne et al., eds., Md. Archives, XII, 497).

troublesome; we had a good deal of talk about the mal Behaveour of the British officers, which he by no means justify'd."

Major Cramond promised her "early hours and little Company"; he threatened that there were few other officers who would make a similar promise. She was aware of that. Her friend Mary Eddy could not "make use of her own Front Door" because "her officer required the family to go up and down the Alley"; Mrs. Eddy had come to ask Elizabeth Drinker "to go to A. James with her and to desire him to accompany her to some Head officer to make complaint of the Insolence of one who has quarter'd himself, on her, and a woman who he calls his wife, but Mary thinks otherwise, he has insulted her, and behav'd very abusive."

"I am straitend how to act, and yet determin'd," Elizabeth Drinker wrote. "I may be troubled with others much worse, for this man appears much of the Gentleman, but while I can keep clear of them, I intend to do so." But she really had no options, and Major Cramond moved in. With relief, she decided he was a "thoughtful sober young man." But she quickly discovered that the major did not come alone. "Cramond has 3 Horses 3 Cows 2 Sheep and 2 Turkeys with several Fowls in our Stable. He has 3 Servants 2 white Men and one Negro Boy call'd Damon, the Servants are here all day, but away at Night. He has 3 Hessians who take their turns to wate on him as messengers or order men." He entertained a great deal, inviting eleven or twelve officers to dine with him on January 5 and eight more on January 8. Despite Cramond's initial promise, his company stayed up late (on February 1 until midnight). Cramond expanded his possession of the house: "Our officer mov'd his lodgings from the bleu Chamber to the little front parlor, so that he has the two front parlors, a chamber up two pair of stairs for his bagage, and the Stable wholly to himself, besides the use of the kitchen." By the spring he had occupied even more territory. "Our Major took it into his Head to dine to day in the Summer House with another officer, he had 2 or 3 to visit him while they set there, so that when the House is kept open, I suppose we shall have them passing and repassing, which has not been the case hitherto; they behave well and appear pleas'd—but I don't feel so." She expressed no sorrow, therefore, when May 22 found the major packing to leave with the British (though other Quaker women of loyalist sympathies, like Sally Logan, were much distressed).[50]

50. Diary of Elizabeth Drinker, Oct. 6, 25, 1777, Nov. 5, 25, 1777, Dec. 19, 21, 31, 1777, Jan. 1, 5, 19, 1778, Mar. 20, 1778. In 1781, the Americans tried to billet a French officer on the Drinkers. But Henry Drinker was back at home then, and his delaying tactics were effective; the Frenchman lodged elsewhere (*ibid.*, Jan. 25, 1781). For an anguished ac-

Jails were also scarce, and both British and Americans were likely to place prisoners, especially officers, under loose house arrest. Thus Catherine Heydshaw was paid £114 "for lodging, firing, candles and for dieting Hessian officers and soldiers" for a month in 1777, and Rachel Stille sent accounts for well over £300 to the Continental Congress for boarding British officers who were prisoners. American officers captured by the British were quartered with individuals on Long Island. When the war was over, those who had boarded the prisoners refused to return them until the cost of their lodging had been paid. The accounts of Abram Skinner, Commissary General of Prisoners, report some £800 paid to twelve women who had boarded American officers; women were perhaps 5 percent of the claimants.[51]

The detailed letters of one prisoner enable us to reconstruct the ambience of one of these homes-turned-prison. When the patriots returned to Philadelphia in 1779, they tried and jailed Samuel Rowland Fisher, a merchant of well-known British sympathies who persisted in quoting prices in sterling rather than in dollars and who refused to accept Continental currency in trade. Fisher was sent to a small jail presided over by Stokely Hossman, "a very rough, hard hearted Man [who] . . . seems to have as strong a delusion of the present times as any person I have ever met," and his wife, "a kind, affectionate Woman" of whom Fisher thought well and who always treated the prisoner "with respect." Fisher was kept there from the summer of 1779 to the summer of 1781, and he was regularly visited by Friends who came to pray with him and to chat. Women were among his most regular visitors: Rebecca Chambers, Susanna Lightfoot, Ann Moore, Edith Sharpless, Rebecca Moore. These women would no doubt have explained that they were engaged in a politically neutral act of religious consolation, but they could not help but be aware that there was a political dimension to all they did. On the

---

count of the occupation of a tory household by patriot troops, see H.O.H. Vernon-Jackson, "A Loyalist's Wife: Letters of Mrs. Philip Van Cortlandt, December 1776 to February 1777," *History Today*, XIV (1964), 574–580.

51. See N.Y. *Commissioners for Detecting Conspiracies*, II, 621; Browne *et al.*, eds., *Md. Archives*, XI *passim*; Ford *et al.*, eds., *Jours. Cont. Cong.*, VI, 877, IV, 305, VIII, 479; and "Account of Debts incurred by sundry American officers during their captivity . . . ," Aug. 5, 1782, Papers Rev. War (M-246), Roll 135, Jacket 4. Timothy Bishop of Guilford, Connecticut, applied to the state legislature on behalf of his wife, who had been employed by the selectmen of Durham "to nurse and tend two of the prisoners from New York sick with the small-pox." She herself came down with fever, which prevented her return home for more than three weeks, and "which cost the memorialist for her boarding, tending, nursing, doctoring . . . £8.6.4." The assembly instructed the Committee of the Pay Table to pay Bishop what they thought reasonable. See May 1777, *Conn. State Recs.*, I, 289.

eleventh of April, 1781, Mr. Hossman took special precautions. "All the Women who came in to see us in our room being obliged to leave their Cloaks & Bonnetts with him, for that he had good information that some person in our room intended to dress & go out in the appearance of a plain Woman friend. . . . I afterwards found Sam'l. Chapman had offered Wm. Bomberger, One of the Turnkeys, Money to let him pass out in such dress."[52]

Most of the civilian women who worked for the American cause, sometimes without pay, sometimes on a free-lance basis, did so unofficially. It is difficult to retrieve them, except anecdotally. Perhaps one of them, for whom the future chief justice John Marshall and other officers of the Virginia Continental Line organized a subscription, is as appropriate an epitome as we can find. The officers thanked

> Mrs Hay and her Daughter for their great attention and Tenderness to our Brother Officers, Prisoners in the City of Philadelphia. . . . they have come out at different times purely to serve the distressed at the risque of their Lives, and have actually assisted some officers in makeing their escape, besides nursing the sick & takeing particular care of the affects of the Deceased. Mrs Hay is a poor Widow, & any Little matter that Gentlemen chuse to contribute, can't fail of being acceptable and will be considered as a greatfull acknowledgement on their part for the Voluntary and Benevolent part she has acted.[53]

The influence women exerted on the war effort of both whigs and tories is difficult to evaluate. Following Elizabeth Ellet's nineteenth-century anecdotal accounts, it has been traditional to assume that what women had to offer was moral support—emotional validation of the choices their men had independently made. But the shrill tone of public instructions to women—Washington ineffectively trying to keep them in line, economic planners anxiously seeking their cooperation—suggests both that women had significant services to render if they would and that their cooperation could not be taken for granted. The diaries that remain are decidedly not diaries of clinging vines. "I did not feel half so frighten'd as I expected to be," wrote fifteen-year-old Sally Wister. "'Tis amazing how we get reconciled to such things. Six months ago the bare idea of being

52. "Journal of Samuel Rowland Fisher, of Philadelphia, 1779–1781," *PMHB*, XLI (1917), 153, 424.

53. Marshall contributed 15 shillings; the total amount collected was £50. See Herbert A. Johnson *et al.*, eds., *The Papers of John Marshall*, I (Chapel Hill, N.C., 1974), 13–14.

within ten, aye, twenty miles, of a battle, wou'd almost have distracted me. And now, tho' two such large armies are within six miles of us, we can converse calmly of it." During the grim fall of 1776, Abigail Adams told her husband, "We are no ways dispiritted here, we possess a Spirit that will not be conquerd. If our Men are all drawn off and we should be attacked, you would find a Race of Amazons in America."[54] Women discovered that they could be devious. The Quaker widow Margaret Hill Morris shielded a prominent loyalist refugee by tricking a patriot search party: "I put on a very simple look & cry[e]d out, bless me I hope you are not Hessians—say, good Men are you the Hessians? Do we look like Hessians? Ask[e]d one of them rudely. Indeed I dont know. Did you never see a Hessian? No never in my life but they *are Men*, & you are Men & may be Hessians for anything I know."[55]

Women gathered around each other for moral and emotional support. Elizabeth Drinker's prewar life had had a large share of calls and visits between friends, but during the dark days of her husband's exile and the British occupation, perhaps six women gathered around her virtually every day. The wives of the exiles formed what we would now call a mutual support group. They did the same in Wilmington, North Carolina, where, as we have seen, patriot wives were able to extrapolate from their own experience a sympathy for wives of their opponents. Those who were inclined to write wrote variants of the traditional phrase "Politics is not my affair" over and over again, but like it or not, politics had invaded their households. The "dreadful fruits of Liberty" were on every dinner table.

54. "Journal of Miss Sally Wister," *PMHB*, IX (1885), 463–464; Abigail Adams to John Adams, Sept. 20, 177[6], *Adams Family Correspondence*, II, 129.

55. "Private Journal of Margaret Morris," Dec. 13–16, 1777, in Larry R. Gerlach, ed., *New Jersey in the American Revolution 1763–1783: A Documentary History* (Trenton, N.J., 1975), 283–287.

Chapter 3

"WHAT HAVE I TO DO WITH POLITICKS?": THE MEANING OF FEMALE PATRIOTISM

The time is arrived to display the same sentiments which animated us at the beginning of the Revolution, when we renounced the use of teas. . . . we placed former necessaries in the rank of superfluities, when our liberty was interested; when our republican and laborious hands spun the flax, prepared the linen entended for the use of our soldiers; when [as] exiles and fugitives we supported with courage all the evils which are the concommitents of war.

—*Sentiments of An American Woman* (1780)

EXPLA

I America fitting on that quarter of the globe with the Fl
of the United States displayed over her head; holding
one hand the Olive branch, inviting the ships of all natic
to partake of her commerce; and in the other hand fu
sporting the Cap of Liberty.

II Fame proclaiming the joyful news to all the world,

America Triumphant and Britannia in Distress, from *Weatherwise's Town and
Country Almanack* (1782). Independent America is closely associated with
economic prosperity; in triumph she invites all nations to trade with her.
Courtesy The Colonial Williamsburg Foundation, Williamsburg, Virginia.

ION.

itannia weeping at the loss of the trade of America, atten-
with an evil genius.

ae British flag struck, on her strong Fortresses.

nch, Spanish, Dutch, &c. shipping in the harbours of America.

lew of New-York, wherein is exhibited the Trator Arnold, taken
remorse for selling his country, and Judas like hanging himself.

THAT WOMEN SERVED the patriot war effort is clear. What these women thought of their actions and of wartime politics is not. It is difficult to find women activists who justify their patriotism in political terms; for example, the pamphlet with the promising title *Women Invited to War* by "A Daughter of America" is in fact a religious homily.[1]

Any attempt to assess women's political consciousness must take into account the deep skepticism toward political behavior shared by the entire culture. Even those men who built successful political careers and displayed what by any measure would have to be called extraordinary ambition rarely acknowledged what they were doing, even to close friends; often they did not acknowledge their political drive to themselves.[2] As Hannah Griffitts wrote of Benjamin Franklin:

> To Covet Political fame,
> In Him, was degrading ambition
> A Spark, that from Lucifer Came,
> And kindled the flame of sedition.[3]

If coveting political fame was degrading even to the class of people who had always been seeking it, why should women be encouraged to take up this unsavory practice?

Participation in the national military forces during the war seems to have served as a bonding experience for many future political leaders since it widened men's allegiance from their colony to the nation. It is by no means clear that shared hospital service performed a similar politicizing function for army nurses and matrons. Most of the women who furthered the patriots' military purposes did not do so in an institutional context; as cooks, washerwomen, laundresses, private nurses, and renters of houses or of rooms, they served as individuals, sometimes along with their husbands and children. They did not change their domestic identity

---

1. [Hannah Adams], *Women Invited to War, or A Friendly Address to the Honourable Women of the United States. By A Daughter of America* (Boston, 1787).

2. Americans' skepticism toward political ambition has been subtly evaluated in Douglass Adair, *Fame and the Founding Fathers: Essays by Douglass Adair,* ed. Trevor Colbourn (New York, 1974), and in Charles S. Sydnor, *Gentlemen Freeholders: Political Practices in Washington's Virginia* (Chapel Hill, N.C., 1952). For John Adams's explanation of his ambition as an attempt to deserve posthumous fame, see Peter Shaw, *The Character of John Adams* (Chapel Hill, N.C., 1976). When Alexander Hamilton said the same, he was considered ambitious.

3. Nov. 1776, Hannah Griffitts Papers, Box 7422, Lib. Co. Phila.

(though they put it to a broader service), and they did not seriously challenge the traditional definition of the woman's domestic domain.

The career of one army nurse, for whom we have unusual anecdotal evidence, suggests the dual elements of the wartime experience. We see Mary Waters only through the eyes of Benjamin Rush, who scribbled notes for her biography in 1791. Was the nurse's life an appropriate subject? "Why not?" Rush asked rhetorically. "Her occupation was a noble one—and her example may be interesting to thousands—Only a few men can be Kings—& yet Biography for a while had few other subjects." Rush respected Mary Waters as a professional, and it is clear from his comments that she saw herself that way. She was bored by simple cases: the sicker the patient, the more she welcomed the challenge. "She dislikes nursing *lying in women*—as well as all sick persons as *are not very ill*. Nothing but great danger rouses her into great activity and humanity." His account also verifies that she was regarded as a medical professional by the staffs of the military hospitals where she served. But this professionalism had little postwar significance. What Rush most admired in her service following the war was that despite all her experience, she remained deferential to doctors, and she did not steal patients. "She was once sent for to prescribe for a lady in a consumption, for her skill was known to many people. Before She went, She found Out whose patient this lady was, and upon being complimented by her when she entered the room She said 'Indeed madam I know nothing but what I learned from Dr. ＿＿＿ (mentioning the name of the physician who attended her) in the military hospitals.' This at once . . . renewed [the lady's] confidence in her physician." Rush implied that Mary Waters, at least, did not use her wartime experience to increase her independence and her professional autonomy, and he thought this to her credit.[4]

The notion that politics was somehow not part of the woman's domain persisted throughout the war, expressed even by women whose own lives were in fact directly dependent on political developments and who had a sophisticated understanding of political maneuver. We have already noted that Anne Hooper and her friends paid obeisance to this tradition of female passivity before demanding that the North Carolina government refrain from harassing tory wives.

Grace Growden Galloway also reveals this cluster of contradictory

4. Benjamin Rush Papers, n.d., 1791, Lib. Co. Phila. Elizabeth Drinker noted Waters's death: "Heard today of the death of Nurse Mary Waters who has been gone for some weeks past" (Diary of Elizabeth Drinker, Jan. 8, 1800, Hist. Soc. Pa.).

traits and is worth considering at some length. She was a formidable woman, and not surprisingly her biographers tend to describe her as "imperious." She was the daughter of one of the wealthiest and most powerful men in colonial Pennsylvania, and she married another, Joseph Galloway, Speaker of the Pennsylvania Assembly for the decade before war broke out and refugee behind British lines after it began. He returned temporarily when the British occupied Philadelphia, but left again, taking the Galloways' only daughter with him when the American troops returned in June 1778. His wife grimly stayed on in occupied Philadelphia, hoping by her presence to maintain her claim to the property she stood to inherit from her father. She began a diary when her husband and daughter left with the British. It is a marvelously opinionated document in which she registered her emotions as well as the weather and the names of her visitors. Despite her open scorn for the patriot cause, which she did not trouble to conceal, she did not expect to be evicted from the Galloways' confiscated house, and she was highly indignant when Charles Willson Peale came to evict her. Mrs. Galloway refused to leave voluntarily.

> I told them Nothing but force shou'd get me out of My house Smith said they knew how to Manage that & that they wou'd throw my cloaths in the street. . . . I told [Peale] . . . I was at home & in My own House & nothing but force shou'd drive me out of it he said it was not the first time he had taken a Lady by the Hand. . . . [I] said pray take Notice I do not leave my house of My own accord or with my own inclination but by force & Nothing but force shou'd have Made Me give up possession Peel said with a sneer very well Madam & when he led me down the step I said now Mr. Peel let go My Arm I want not your Assistance.[5]

As litigation to recover her property continued, her scorn for whigs was as vigorous and emphatic as any patriot castigation of the loyalists. "Nothing reigns here but interess," she wrote of Philadelphia. But despite her pride and her assertiveness, she continued to define herself in private terms. "I . . . laughed at the whole wig party," she wrote in her diary on April 20, 1779. "I told them I was the happiest woman in town for I had been striped and Turn'd out of Doors yet I was still the same and must be

5. Raymond C. Werner, ed., "Diary of Grace Growden Galloway, Kept at Philadelphia . . . ," *PMHB*, LV (1931), 51–52.

Joseph Galloways Wife and Lawrence Growdens daughter and that it was not in their power to humble Me."[6]

Grace Galloway was a resentful woman to the end. The war seemed an intrusion into a private—and luxurious—world in which she had expected to enjoy her inheritance safely. She did not particularly love her husband, but she proudly claimed his identity. Though she made no secret of her hostility to the patriots or her admiration for the crown, she failed to comprehend why she—a woman—should be expected to account for her views or why her views had any more public significance than a preference for silver over pewter. She was not a stupid woman, but she failed to recognize that her political gestures went beyond merely private behavior, and she never came to terms with the invasion of the political world into her private life.

Philadelphia Quaker women varied greatly in the extent to which they understood that their private choices had political dimensions. Sarah Logan Fisher, for example, vigorously supported the refusal of Quakers to accept Continental currency, but professed herself shocked at the subsequent exile of Quaker leaders. Congressmen were, she said, "the ravenous wolves and lions that prowl about for prey, seeking to devour those harmless innocents that don't go hand in-hand with them in their cruelty and rapine."[7]

The patriot circles also held politically conscious women. Among them were Sarah Livingston Jay and Catharine Livingston, who, as daughters of the wartime governor of New Jersey, had been raised in political households and ultimately married strongly political men. Sarah Jay felt herself deeply committed to independence. In forsaking her child Peter in order to accompany John Jay on his ministry to Spain, weathering a transatlantic voyage that threatened shipwreck, and suffering the death of a newborn infant once on the Continent, Sarah Jay clearly had earned the right to claim that she had made the deepest of personal sacrifices for the patriot cause. Observing Spanish society, she was moved to an increased appreciation of her own and to vigorous support of the war. "Where is the country (Switzerland excepted)," she wrote in 1780,

6. *Ibid.*, 75–76, 88. In the late summer of 1779 she was in a despairing mood: "I am wrapped in impenetrable Darkness; . . . Can it ever be removed & shall I once More belong to somebody. . . . Now I am like a pelican in the Desert" (Werner, ed., "Diary of Galloway," *PMHB*, LVIII [1934], 164).

7. Diary of Sarah Logan Fisher, Sept. 21, 1777, Hist. Soc. Pa., Philadelphia. See also *ibid.*, Jan. 4, Sept. 4, 1777.

James Sharpless, *Sarah Livingston Jay and Her Children.*
Courtesy The Frick Art Reference Library, New York City, and the John Jay Homestead
State Historic Site, New York State Office of Parks and Recreation. On loan from Mrs.
David Cromwell.

"where Justice is so impartially administered, industry encouraged, health and Smiling plenty so bounteous to all as in our much favored Country? And are not those blessings each of them resulting from, or matured by freedom, worth contending for?" But that came close to a call to arms, and she stopped herself short. "But whither, my pen, are you hurrying me? What have I to do with politicks? Am I not myself a woman, and writing to Ladies? Come then, the fashions to my assistance!"[8] She did not say that moving from politics to fashion was to move from the sublime to the ridiculous, but she certainly implied that sentiment in the cynical tone of her transition.

Sarah Jay sent home confidential and detailed disapproving reports of her brother Henry Brockholst Livingston's political behavior. She also directed criticism beyond her family circle to people to whom she was not related, especially those she saw as self-serving adventurers in federal service. Occasionally she felt she needed to mumble an apology: "I've transgress'd the line that I proposed to observe in my correspondence by dipping into politicks, but my country and my friends possess so entirely my thoughts that you must not wonder if my pen runs beyond the dictates of prudence."[9]

Sarah's younger sister Catharine, who was perhaps even more consciously political, could also admit to a sense of inadequacy when dealing with politics. After a long letter to her future husband, Matthew Ridley, in which she delineated in some detail an attack on financier Robert Morris and the campaign to censure him, she concluded, "I should fancy I hear'd you exclaiming what a rage this girl has for politics. I wish she would not so mistake her province and talents—but still I will give her credit for the wish she evinces of informing me of what I appear to her to have an interest in." The terms of her apologia are carefully chosen; she has spoken politically out of a desire to please Ridley by speaking of his interests, not because she had her own "rage for politics." She admitted that she might be mistaking "her province." She might have had in mind

8. Sarah Jay to Catharine Livingston, Mar. 1780, Richard B. Morris, ed., *John Jay: The Making of a Revolutionary* (New York, 1975), 692.

9. Complaints about Brockholst appear in Sarah Jay to William Livingston, June 24, 1781, John Jay Papers, Rare Book and Manuscript Library, Columbia University, New York. For her apology, see Sarah Jay to Catharine Livingston, July 16, 1783, *ibid*. Her aunt Margaret commented that though she acknowledged that exiling the loyalists was probably a wartime necessity, it was "a heart-hardening Subject, too much so, for women to deal with" (Margaret Livingston to Susan Livingston, July 1788, Ridley Papers, Mass. Hist. Soc.).

a letter Ridley had sent her the year before: "Politics I have done with, were they ever proper to entertain you with."[10]

Though Catharine Livingston was careful to set her comments in a deferential context, her letters are usually full of political news and often of shrewd political criticism. For many years she maintained a correspondence with Gouverneur Morris and with her brother-in-law John Jay, and the news they exchanged was not limited to family gossip. "I know your bent for Politics," her brother Henry Brockholst Livingston wrote to her from Spain in 1781, "and how little you value a Letter in which a few pages are not taken up with news."[11] She was very friendly with the daughters of Samuel Vaughan, who were similarly sensitive to political nuance. Sarah Vaughan, for example, perceived with real annoyance that the French Minister François Barbé-Marbois always happened to pay her a visit when dispatches from Europe were expected. "Neither am I disposed to have my brains picked for news," she wrote with displeasure.[12] Kitty Livingston and her circle were scornful of the marriage market, and they liked having Congress meet in Philadelphia because that body provided interesting conversational companions, not romantic ones. "Every body is bewailing the loss of Congress," Rebecca Vaughan wrote to Kitty late in 1784. "The only cry you hear is what are we to do for Beaux we [her own family] are not so much distressed about it; Beaux are not so necessary to our happiness."[13] Others were distraught: "Mr. Chew is in despair he said the other day before a great many people he knew not what he should do with his daughters now Congress were gone he believed he must *sell* them how very indelicate even the thought and much worse publishing it."[14]

Examples of this awkward juxtaposition of the political and the domestic can be easily multiplied. Ann Gwinnett, the widow of the president of Georgia, wrote to warn the Continental Congress that the rank and file of the Georgia troops were loyal but that the officer corps was riddled with tory sympathizers. But she was careful to conclude her intensely political comment on a humble note: "These things (tho from a Woman, & it is not our sphere, yet I cannot help it) are all true."[15] When

10. Catharine Livingston to Matthew Ridley, [May 1785], Ridley Papers; Matthew Ridley to Catharine Livingston, n.d., 1784, *ibid.*
11. Henry Brockholst Livingston to Catharine Livingston, May 19, 1781, *ibid.*
12. Sarah Vaughan to Catharine Livingston, Mar. 28–31, 1785, *ibid.*
13. Rebecca Vaughan to Catharine Livingston, Dec. 1784, *ibid.*
14. Rebecca Vaughan to Catharine Livingston, Jan. 18, 1785, *ibid.*
15. Ann Gwinnett to John Hancock and the "other Members of the Grand Continental

the wife of an exiled tory tried to get Governor Alexander Martin's special permission for her husband to return to North Carolina, she argued theories of citizenship at some length and with great precision, maintaining that because her husband had never been a citizen of the state, he had never owed it any obedience. But first she placed herself on familiar grounds: "It is not for me, unacquainted as I am with politics and the laws, to say with what propriety this was done."[16] "You know I am nothing of a Politician," Catherine Read wrote on the eve of the Quasi-War with France. In some detail she went on to decry the prowar spirit: "For us Southern people to rejoice at a war is a species of madness." She insisted that she did not "always think it necessary" to think as her husband did.[17] Shortly after the Revolution, Abigail Adams's niece Elizabeth Palmer wrote to an English relative about the need for "a good commercial treaty"; then she explained self-consciously, "I verily believe this is the first Sentence of Politicks that ever Crep^d into a letter of mine —whether 'tis *orthodox* or not I dare not determine—for I'm very ignorant of these matters."[18]

In the absence of an established tradition of female public political behavior, many women may have found it difficult to explain precisely their actions outside their private circles. Perhaps the formulaic, ritualized apologies with which they prefaced their political comments were their way of acknowledging that they were doing something unusual. A very few women did begin to develop a structured rationale for their actions, however, and the most interesting of these theorists is Mercy Otis Warren, the dramatist and historian. Her comments on female politicization were enriched as her experience changed.

Like Grace Galloway, Mercy Otis Warren was the daughter of one prominent man and the wife of another. She lived her entire life in intensely political circles. Her brother was the ardent patriot James Otis, who argued the Writs of Assistance case in 1761; her husband was the Massachusetts legislator James Warren. For many years her closest female friend was Abigail Adams. Their letters to each other are often highly political: when John Adams complained about the famous teasing

Congress," [Aug. 1777?], Papers Cont. Cong. (M-247), Roll 87, Item 73: 135, Natl. Archives.

16. Mrs. McLean to Alexander Martin, Dec. 11, 1783, Governor's Letterbook, V, 612, State Department of Archives and History, Division of Archives and History, Raleigh, N.C.

17. Catherine Read to Betsey Read Ludlow, July 15, [1798], Read Papers, S. Caroliniana Lib., Univ. S.C., Columbia.

18. Elizabeth Palmer to John Cranch, Oct. 12, 1784, Boston Public Library.

Mather Brown, *Abigail Adams* (1785).
Courtesy New York State Historical Association, Cooperstown.

reminder to "remember the ladies" in drawing up the laws of the Confederation, it was Mercy Otis Warren to whom Abigail Adams turned for a sympathetic ear. Both women admired Catharine Macaulay immensely. Mercy Warren was inspired by Mrs. Macaulay's accomplishments, and after the war wrote at least one political pamphlet and her own multivolume history of the American Revolution.

In their letters to each other, Mercy Otis Warren and Abigail Adams were obviously comfortable with their shared political sensibility. They discussed politics without apology. When the crown asserted the right to make direct appointment of the Massachusetts Council in 1774, Warren wrote, "I think the appointment of the new counsel is the last comic scene we shall see Exhibite'd in the state Farce which has for several years been playing off. I fear the Tragic part of the Drama will hastely Ensue, and that Nothing but the Blood of the Virtuous Citizens Can repurchase the Rights of Nature, unjustly torn from us by the united arms of treachery and Violence." Abigail Adams wrote Warren in February 1775, "I would not have my Friend immagine that with all my fears and apprehension, I would give up one Iota of our rights and privilages. . . . we cannot be happy without being free, . . . we cannot be free without being secure in our property, . . . we cannot be secure in our property if without our consent others may as by right take it away.—We know too well the blessings of freedom, to tamely resign it."[19]

John Adams relied explicitly on his wife for local political news, and he expected her to keep his political fences mended. "What a politician you have made me," she wrote on July 5, 1780. She was easily able to conceive of the possibility of voting and came close enough to the political process to assist at the polls. "If I cannot be a voter upon this occasion, I will be a writer of votes. I can do some thing in that way."[20]

The barrier between the male political world and the women's domestic domain eroded in the years of the war and its aftermath. Mercy Otis Warren did not seriously apologize for writing her postwar history. When John Adams was president, Abigail Adams handled some of his correspondence openly. When Elbridge Gerry was appointed to negotiate with France in 1797, she wrote the new ambassador: "The president knowing how sincere an interest I had taken in the result of your deliberations,

19. Mercy Otis Warren to Abigail Adams, Aug. 9, 1774, *Adams Family Correspondence*, I, 138; Abigail Adams to Mercy Otis Warren, Feb. 3[?], 1775, *ibid.*, 184.

20. Abigail Adams to John Adams, July 5, 1780, L. H. Butterfield *et al.*, eds., *The Book of Abigail and John: Selected Letters of the Adams Family, 1762–1784* (Cambridge, Mass., 1975), 264.

communicated to me your Letter this morning received, and I do assure you, Sir, that it gave me great pleasure. I had anticipated many of your reasons, and arguments of a publick nature, and I did flatter myself that you would not decline so important an Embassy." By the War of 1812, Abigail Adams could not only report, she could openly criticize political events: "It seems as if every Naval victory was to be balanced, by some disgracefull defeat upon the Land. . . . I know not how to express my grief and chagrin at these repeated and stupid enterprises so unskillfully conducted."[21]

Abigail Adams and Mercy Otis Warren could not help knowing that they were unusual among their contemporaries, especially in the years before the war. One of Mercy Warren's friends, Hannah Lincoln, evidently wrote to her on the question of whether it was appropriate for women to address themselves to politics, implying that her own husband disapproved. Hannah Lincoln invited guidance.

The terms of Mercy Warren's reply, in the tense spring of 1774, are instructive. She was aware that women were vulnerable to criticism if they addressed themselves to politics, and in response she began to construct a rationale for women's interest in politics that was justified in terms of their right to free speech and self-expression. "I know not why any gentlemen of your acquaintance should caution you not to enter any particular subject when we meet," she wrote guardedly to Hannah Lincoln. "I should have a very ill opinion of myself, if any variation of sentiment with regard to political matters, should lessen my esteem for the disinterested, undesigning and upright heart; and it would argue great want of candour to think that there was not many such (more especially among our own sex) who yet judge very differently with regard to the calamities of our unhappy country . . . though every mind of the least sensibility must be greatly affected with the present distress; and even a female pen might be excused for touching on the important subject; yet I will not undertake to give a full answer to the queries proposed by my friend; for as the wisest among the other sex are much divided in opinion, it might justly be deemed impertinent or rather sanguine for me to decide." She would not get into an argument with Benjamin Lincoln. She did admit that politics was "a subject . . . much out of the road of female attention," but she began to construct a rationale that would permit women to attend to political matters without abandoning their

21. Abigail Adams to Elbridge Gerry, July 14, 1797, and Abigail Adams to William S. Smith, Feb. 18, 1813, Boston Pub. Lib.

domestic responsibilities, as men did. "But as every domestic enjoyment depends on the decision of the mighty contest, who can be an unconcerned and silent spectator? Not surely the fond mother, or the affectionate wife who trembles lest her dearest connections should fall victims of lawless power, or at least pour out the warm blood as a libation at the shrine of liberty."[22]

Mercy Warren argued that women's hearts and minds responded as accurately and as sensitively to public challenge as did men's, that women's duty to their own families required them to sort out public information accurately and to take a political position. Their political position— which they were to arrive at by informed discussion with men and women outside their families—could ultimately be expressed within the family and justified in terms of service to and protection of husbands and sons. Thus she counseled Hannah Lincoln to resist her husband's constraints on her political conversation, and at the same time assured her that a politically minded woman was not necessarily a threat to family politics. By 1797, when the Quasi-War threatened, Warren had no hesitancy in thinking of herself as a politician. She wrote to her son, "I dread it as a Woman, I fear it, as a friend to my country; yet think (as a politician) I see it pending over this land."[23]

For the most part, women confined their politics to their portfolios and their diaries. "July 4, Anniversary of Independence, 19 years," Elizabeth Drinker wrote in her diary in 1795. "General Orders in News-paper this forenoon, for a fuss and to do. I think, orders for peace and quietness, would be more commendable and consistant, in a well regulated Government or State." Hannah Griffitts wrote private poetry:

> The glorious fourth—again appears
> A Day of Days—and year of years,
>   The sum of sad disasters,
> Where all the mighty gains we see
> With all their Boasted liberty,
>   Is only Change of Masters . . .[24]

Abigail Adams wrote to her friends and her husband, not for publication. Kitty Livingston and Sarah Jay wrote within the broad Livingston

22. Mercy Otis Warren to Hannah Lincoln, Sept. 3, 1774, Mercy Otis Warren Letterbook, Warren Papers, Mass. Hist. Soc., Boston.
23. Mercy Otis Warren to James Warren, Jr., June 4, 1797, *ibid.*, 232.
24. Diary of Elizabeth Drinker, July 4, 1795; Hannah Griffitts Papers, 1785.

political network, but did not venture outside it. They brought public perceptions to their private world.

It has been common for historians to regard this evidence of hesitancy as evidence of a sort of false consciousness.[25] The implication is that these women ought to have been openly, frankly political. Because they were not, they are accused of mincing and simpering, of stupidly not seeing what was before their very eyes or of seeing the realm of politics but denying its existence. But these women deserve more than this contemptuous dismissal. Their culture had pointedly established that politics was not a female province. The daily lives of women in a preindustrial society *were* largely spent in a domestic circle, a confinement impossible to ignore. But politics did intrude into the women's world during the trauma of the war and the Confederation, and as it did women acknowledged its presence and responded to it. The North Carolina women would not let their neighbors be deported without contest; Kitty Livingston would not refrain from scrutinizing the politicians she met. To ask what they might have done had they lived instead in a world that allowed political concerns to be women's concerns is to ask an unanswerable question. To criticize them for not acting as if they lived in such a world is pointless.

In a culture that refused women the technical machinery of political expression, there remained available a most archaic mode of political behavior. With the biblical Esther as role model and a strong English constitutional tradition for justification, women were most likely to express their relationship to political enterprise through a petition. The petitioner is inherently a prepolitical being. The formulation of a petition begins in the acknowledgment of subordination; by definition the petitioner poses no threat. The rhetoric of humility is a necessary part of the petition as a genre, whether or not humility is felt in fact. Occasionally the restiveness of the petitioner peeps out from the smothering rhetoric, and the petition approaches the broadside.

Women petitioned Revolutionary governments and local committees of safety for permission to cross enemy lines to join husbands or other family members, to claim property left behind, to reach ports from which they might embark for Europe. These petitions were frequently an irri-

25. See, for example, Lawrence J. Friedman, *Inventors of the Promised Land* (New York, 1975), 148–155, and Lawrence J. Friedman and Arthur H. Schaffer, "Mercy Otis Warren and the Politics of Historical Nationalism," *New England Quarterly*, XLVIII (1975), 194–215.

tant. The committees of safety that handled them often had far more momentous—sometimes desperate—concerns than the movements of individual civilians. But the committees could not afford to ignore these petitions. If a petition were granted, the committees were at least doing a disservice to the patriot cause by facilitating the reunion of families and thus improving enemy morale. But the effects could be much worse—they might unwittingly be permitting the passage of a spy or a smuggler. On the other hand, if they denied a petition, they risked burdening their own charitable facilities with women and children who could not support themselves and missed the opportunity to rid themselves of a possible fifth column.

As we have seen, there were many women who did not wish to leave patriot territory and who were expelled by their neighbors. But if a woman had little or no property to protect and knew where her husband was, she might be better off, both psychologically and financially, with him. The Pennsylvania Assembly, for example, received petitions from women whose husbands had gone to New York with the British. There was Mary Munn, who found herself "unable in these hard and inclement times to support herself and sick babe, having neither provision, Clothing or fuel, and no friends to assist her with any"; there was Abigail Ott, whose husband had gone to New York "leaving your Petitioner quite unprovided for. . . . your Petitioner all this time has struggled hard for a living Under severe sickness and four small Children one suckin at the Breast"; and Sarah Engle, who was "not . . . able to hold out any longer." Patriot governments were most likely to look favorably on the plea that unless women left they would become public charges. It was common for women to insist that they could not support themselves without their husbands and to avoid political statements entirely. But the fear that the women had political purposes to serve persisted, occasionally stirring vigorous debates.[26]

26. Mary Munn to Pennsylvania Council, Jan. 6, 1778, Papers Cont. Cong. (M-247), Roll 83, Item 69: II, 109; Abigail Ott to Pennsylvania Council, *ibid.*, Roll 83: II, 347; Sarah Engle to Pennsylvania Council, *ibid.*, Roll 83: II, 355. For a particularly heated argument that involved Benedict Arnold in Rachel Levy's request to pass to New York, see *ibid.*, Roll 83: I, 587 and *passim.* For requests to pass to New York City from upstate New York, see *N.Y. Commissioners for Detecting Conspiracies,* I, 252, where Mrs. Sarah McMichael is given permission because her son, who supports her, is already there. Other permissions are readily found in *N.Y. Commissioners for Detecting Conspiracies, Conn. State Recs.,* and *The Acts and Resolves, Public and Private, of the Province of Massachusetts Bay . . .* (Boston, 1869–1922). From May 1777 to Apr. 1779, the Massachusetts General Court granted, without exception, every petition requesting permission to pass behind the enemy lines; 35 requests were from men, 30 from women. The court occasionally

As the war continued, the Continental Congress began to receive petitions directly from individuals. In a society with few formal elements of poor relief apart from workhouses, those who owed their economic desperation to their sacrifices for their country thought it only fitting that their government should respond. Perhaps 5 percent of the petitions received by Congress were from women. They included a few who had served the army directly, among them Nonhelema, or Catherine the Grenadier, an Indian woman who had relieved Americans besieged at Fort Randolph, on the upper Ohio, by driving forty-eight head of cattle into their stockade.

Most petitioners were widows who had been left destitute. Their pleas are among the saddest artifacts left from the war. The real needs of the women as well as the constraints of the rhetorical form ensured that petitions would emphasize economic necessity, weakness, and despair. But many also testified to a strong belief that the widows had made real sacrifices to the state, and that the political system owed them something in return.

"To the Honorable Congress I Rachel do make this Complaint," wrote Rachel Wells of Bordentown, New Jersey. "Who am a Widow far advanced in years and Dearly have occasion of the Intrust for that Cash I Lent the States. . . . I was a sitisen in the jearsy when I Lent the States a considerable Sum of Moneys & had I justice done me it mite be suficant to suporte me in the Contrey." She had moved away from Bordentown temporarily after her widowhood "to Phila to try to git a Living" because she "could Doe Nothing in burdentown"; but that move had apparently put her title to her claim in jeopardy. "Now gentelmen is this Liberty had it bin advertised that he or she that moved out of the state should Louse his or her Interest you mite have Sum plea against me. But I . . . Suspectd no trick. I have Don as much to Carrey on the warr as maney that Sett Now at the healm of goverment." She did not expect the principal back, but she did want the interest, and urged the Congress to think of her plight this way: "If She did not fight She threw in all her mite which bought the Sogers food & Clothing & Let them have Blankets."[27]

---

forbade the petitioner to take along "any papers" (*Acts and Resolves of Massachusetts Bay*, xx and *passim*).

27. Petition of Rachel Wells, May 18, 1786, Papers Cont. Cong. (M-247), Roll 56, Item 42: VIII, 354–355. Rachel Wells claimed that she was owed £300 and that "one of our Chaplens to our armey I believe has Robd me of one hundred & Eighty Six pounds." She estimated that she had lost £2,805 "hard cash" by British depredations: "This I can barr but to be Robd by my Contrey men is verey trying." Rachel Wells was the sister of Patience

Petition of Rachel Wells, May 18, 1786, from Papers of the Continental Congress.
Courtesy The Library of Congress, Washington, D.C.

355

ask Doct: Rogers & generall MackDugell Mr. Hancock Cornell Sloss
Mr. Shearman Mr. Adams & Number Doct: Franklond with whom She
was Intimate & gave him Intiligence as She could git accounts where
he not they Cond not goe as She was Takeing peoples Licknesses in wax
they Talk on politicks & c c

I think gentelmen that I Can ask for my Intruste as an
individual on Hir acount Now She is no more) I onley want my
one) Cant there be order given to our asembley that the widow
Rachel Wells in and of the jarsey State may have the Intruste of her
Cash that She Lent of Estates in 1798 & Not maketion that Law
mad in Eighty three tho I hartely pity others that ar in my Case that Cant
Speak for themselves may god Convict you their is bred Enough & to Spair
god has Spred a plentifull Tabel for us & you gentelmen or y Carvers
for us pray forgit Not the Poor weaklings at the fut of the Tabel
if poor Sogers has got Sum Crumbs that fall from their mostens
tabel Sum 1/6 Sum 2/3 in y pound why Not Rachel Wells have a littel
intruste if She Did Not fight She threw in all her mite which bought
y Sogers food & Clothing & Lett them have blankets & know that She
has bin oblig'd to Lay upon Straw & glad of that

And as to my Creraradors ask Doctr Rogers
& generale MackDugell
Mr william goforth
Mr John Mersey
Mr Laffard
Jeames bond
Zebell Robins
I am no Stranger in york or was not before the war
But Number of my ob frind are Sene Dead
& I Doe Expect to hear Simithing to my Satesfaction Very Soon
That I may Lay before I Leave this world that the State Did me
justice tho Never Expect to See the principall
is the prayer of your humbel Sarvent Rachel Wells

Copy

Bordenton may 18th 1786

Eliz Town November 19 1779

July 17th being Sent for by genrl Patterson Suspooted
For helping the americans prefeners to make their
Escape gorge Hebley Coming from your Excelence the
Weak before and Cared out Mager van Burah Captn
Crain Lt Lee who Mad ther ecape from the guard on
Long Island Gorge Higby Brought a paper to me from
your dole Deuelled to Col Mc garr on Long Island he the sd
gorge Higly being taking up and Confined in the provoft
Guard his Wife told genrl Patterson that he Cared out
Two hundred americann prefeners for Me for Witch Reafon Known
My Self guilty Did hide My Self for two weeaks
in New york underftanding genr Patterson had
Offerd a bounty of two Hounded pounds for taking me
he Keps a guard five days at my houfe Leting no
body Come in oullt thin throu the half of Friends
got on Long Island and ther Staid five Weeaks Then
William Scudder Came to Long Island in wale boat
And I Maid My Efcape With him wee being Chafed
by two Boats half way the Sound then got to New
Englan and Came to Philadelphia Then I got a pafs of
The Bord of War to go to Eliz Town to try to get My
Children from New york Witch I oblained in three or four
Weeks but Could not get My Clofe or any thing But
My Children When application waf Made by mr John
Franckling My Clofe & Furniture thay Should be Sold
And the Money be giving to the Loyler

Petition of Elizabeth Burgin, November 19, 1779, from Papers of the Continental
Congress.
Courtesy The Library of Congress, Washington, D.C.

I am now Sir very Desolate without Money without
Close or friends to go to I Mean to go to philadelphia Whir
god know How I Shall Live a Cold winter Coming on
For the Throuth of the above your Excellence Can inquir
Mager John Stuart or Col Thomas Thomas I Lived opsicd
Mr John Franklings and by their desir make this
Application if your Excellence pleiasd you Can diwet
Mr Thomas Frankling in philadelpis Whir I Can be found
If the gener thinks proper I should be glad to Drow provisions
for My Self and Childrens in Phaladelphia Whir
I Meain to Remain helping our poor prisoners Brought
Me to Want Whith I dont Repent

       Elezebeth Burgin

Elizabeth Burgin, whom the British had accused of directing the smuggling of two hundred American prisoners out of New York and on whose head the British had placed a bounty, was reduced to begging directly of George Washington: "I am now Sir very Desolate without Money without Close or friends to go to. I Mean to go to philadelphia Whir god know How I Shall Live a Cold winter Coming on. . . . If the gene^r[al] thinks proper I should be glad to Draw provisions for My Self and Childrens in Philadelphia. . . . helping our poor preseners Brought Me to Want Whitch I dont Repent."[28] Elizabeth Gaudin's husband had died in Boston, "defending the rights of america," but his prize money had never been paid. "I am sorry to say I think myself ill-used," Elizabeth Gaudin wrote. "Shall a widow that Lost her Husband Suffer and want?"[29]

The litany of women's petitions fell on unresponsive ears. The only military group with any lobbying power to speak of was the Continental Line, and when pensions were ultimately provided, they went only to the widows of Continental officers. Not until 1832, fifty years after the close of fighting, were the widows of enlisted men included in pension legislation. The most obvious legislation for women that the Revolutionary generation might have provided would have been pensions for war widows; that it had the lowest of priorities was one result of the exclusion of women from the political system.[30]

Without clear legislation, widows of enlisted men, even women who had themselves worked for the army, were reduced to begging and hu-

---

Wright, the famous waxwork sculptor and American spy. Wells herself made wax models for physicians and seems to have transmitted some of Wright's messages. Her close association with the spy increased Wells's sense of anguish: "My dr Sister wright wrote to me to be thankfull that I had it in my Power to Help on the war which is well enough but then is this to be Considerd That others gits their Intrust & why then a poor old Widow to be put of who am thus Stript" (ibid.). Patience Wright's intriguing career is described in Charles Coleman Sellers, *Patience Wright: American Artist and Spy in George III's London* (Middletown, Conn., 1976).

28. Elizabeth Burgin to George Washington, Nov. 19, 1779, Papers Cont. Cong. (M-247), Roll 170: VIII, 312 and *passim*.

29. Petition of Elizabeth Gaudin, Mar. 7, 1787, *ibid.*, Roll 54: III, 301. The Commissioners of Accounts could not find her husband's name on their rolls and concluded he must have served "in some Private Ship." Benjamin Walter to Charles Thomson, Apr. 2, 1787, *ibid.*, Roll 38, Item 31: 163. See also Petition of Lydia Wallingford (signed by Amos Cogswell on her behalf), *ibid.*, Roll 56, Item 42: VIII, 379; the denial of Wallingford's petition, Apr. 16, 1787, *ibid.*, Roll 151: II, 483; and Petition of Ann Ledyard, read Aug. 14, 1787, *ibid.*, Roll 54: IV, 430.

30. See Gustavus A. Weber, *The Bureau of Pensions: Its History, Activities and Organization* (Baltimore, 1923). The last surviving Revolutionary War widow did not die until 1906.

miliation. Eleanor Healy wrote that she "underwent the Severity of Cold and heat in the Service of her Country—besides A Greater, which was the loss of her Husband, who was killed. . . . your Petitr (tho not of an envious temper) thinks herself Intitled to the priviledges, allowed the Widows and Orphans belonging to the army, as A number of flaunting women who have no Children. . . . your Petit[r] has lost the use of her Arm in the service and has two Orphans, the support of which puts [her] . . . very often in dispair and Confusion." Finally she received a letter from George Washington introducing her to General Henry Knox. When she presented this document to the general, "he ordered your Petitr to call next day, which your Petitr Conformed to, when at the same time Genl Knox was steping into his Carriage," leaving her to see only his clerk, who of course could do nothing.[31] George Washington occasionally sent cash donations directly to women whose pleas for help were especially touching, but that sort of assistance simply pointed out the weakness in the general plan.[32]

Widows who could get no help from the federal government turned to the states, where occasional cases of hardship were relieved by a private bill. However, state legislatures, already deeply troubled by war debts, hesitated to embark on a general commitment. When Phoebe Norwood, whose husband had died in the Continental service, asked the South Carolina legislature for help, she found sympathetic ears in the senate, which having satisfied itself "that Congress provides for the Soldiers wounded in the Continental Service, but not for the Widows of Soldiers who have died in the said service," authorized an annuity of five pounds a year. But the lower house, unmoved, refused to concur. Occasional pensions of similar magnitude were granted on a case-by-case basis as a matter of hardship, not as a matter of right.[33]

One other form of petition remained: the personal plea in the manner of Esther. The personal encounter was the most traditional: it guaranteed the petitioner would be very deferential, it did not require literacy, and it took advantage of the chivalric responsibilities of the male-female relationship. But this form of appeal also challenged the petitioner's persuasive gifts and placed her directly in contact with people who wielded

31. Petition of Eleanor Healy, Feb. 16, 1785, Papers Cont. Cong. (M-247), Roll 50, Item 41: IV, 252.

32. See, for example, George Washington to Elizabeth Neil, Apr. 27, 1777, Fitzpatrick, ed., *Writings of Washington*, VII, 482.

33. Petition of Phoebe Norwood, Dec. 1, 1795, Manuscript House Journals, South Carolina Department of Archives and History, Columbia, S.C.

Elizabeth Sandwith Drinker, unknown artist.
Courtesy Historical Society of Pennsylvania, Philadelphia.

power. Local committees of safety in New York, Connecticut, and elsewhere were regularly besieged by wives pleading for the exchange of their imprisoned husbands. The wives and friends of Quakers who were jailed as suspicious neutrals regularly petitioned the leaders of the Pennsylvania government. When Samuel Rowland Fisher was imprisoned for refusing to accept Continental currency, his sisters were eventually successful in asserting his innocence to Philadelphia patriot leaders.[34]

Elizabeth Drinker carefully recorded the experience of carrying a personal petition. Her husband, Henry, was a Philadelphia Quaker who repeatedly refused to sign a loyalty oath to the rebel government. Early in September 1777 he and nineteen other Quaker men were seized and held at the Masonic Lodge in what his wife declared to be "an illegal unpredesented manner." The suspects were permitted to receive their friends, wives, and children, who swarmed to the lodge "in great number" to write political protests and to spend their last night together before the prisoners' exile. Through it all the Drinkers' young son Henry was very sick "with a vomiting and disordered Bowels. . . . he voided . . . 3 large worms." Elizabeth Drinker dosed her child and worried about him as her husband was making preparations to leave. On his father's last night home, little Henry had "a constant fever."[35]

Elizabeth Drinker went to see Henry off, despite her discomfort because there were so "few women" in the crowd, and then she maintained her family and managed her household through the winter of Howe's occupation. Prices and political tension rose; Major Cramond and his household staff insinuated themselves into the household. The absence of her husband was increasingly "hard to bare," and by February Mrs. Drinker had ceased to feel sorry for herself and was beginning to feel guilty. "I have been much distress'd at times, when I have thought of my being still here, when perhaps it might be in my power to do something for my dear Husband."[36]

The women's petition that she eventually helped present was initiated by men as well as women in the close-knit community of Philadelphia Quakers. The idea was first presented to Mrs. Drinker by Mary Pemberton, who showed Elizabeth "a Letter from her Father; intimating something of the kind to her Mother and herself." Other women were "full of the notion of going to Congress," but not until news of the ill health of some of the exiles was coupled with the failure of a delegation of other

34. "Diary of Samuel Rowland Fisher," *PMHB*, XLI (1917), 433 and *passim*.
35. Diary of Elizabeth Drinker, Aug. 20, 21, 1777, Sept. 3, 9, 10, 1777.
36. *Ibid.*, Oct. 16, 1777, Feb. 6, 1778.

Quakers to Congress did the wives of the exiles commit themselves to a petition. It is not fully clear who wrote the final draft. On March 31, Mrs. Drinker went to Mary Pleasants's home. "She showd me a paper drawn up to send or take to Congress, she had drawn it up, and her mammy had added something to it. Nic[holas] Waln had also made out one for us. . . . in the afternoon O[wen?] Jones came to desire I would meet the rest of the Women concern'd at 6 oclock at M: Pembertons, which I did, they were all there except R. Hunt, Hetty Fisher T Afflick's wife." There were five men there too. Nicholas Waln "read the address, and the women all signed it." Whether Waln, who was a lawyer, read his own draft or the one prepared by Mary Pleasants and her "mammy" is impossible to say. But it was Waln who came by two days later with a fresh copy for Mrs. Drinker to sign. "Mary Pemberton had copy'd it afresh with some small addition." The group decided that Susan Jones, P[olly?] Pemberton, Mary Pleasants, and Elizabeth Drinker ought to carry the petition to General Washington, then camped on the outskirts of Philadelphia. Mrs. Drinker confided in her diary, "I wish I felt better both in Body and mind for such an undertaking."[37]

It seems to have been assumed that the women would need a male escort, but Elizabeth Drinker was most hesitant in accepting the company of Israel Morris, who had his own cause to plead with Washington. Apparently fearing that the women's plea would in effect be merged with Morris's, she agreed to travel with the petitioner only after he had promised not to appear with the women when they made their request. They all left Philadelphia by coach (accompanied by "two Negroes who rode Postilion") on April 5 and spent the evening with the Roberts family, ten miles out of town. That evening an American scouting party came by, and "2 of their officers came into the House saying that they had heard there was Ladys from Phila.ᵃ" The next morning the women crossed the American lines, receiving a pass and guards who led them to the American headquarters, where they arrived at 1:30 P.M.

---

37. *Ibid.*, Feb. 6, 14, 1778, Mar. 21, 31, 1778. The petition was signed by 18 women, "the afflicted and sorrowful Wives, Parents and near Connections of the Friends in Banishment." It read "We firmly believe these dear Friends are clear and innocent of the Charges alledged against them. . . . This application to you on this interesting Subject is intirely an Act of our Own, we have not consulted our absent Friends on the occasion, hoping and believing, it will not be of Disservice and request you will take no offence at the freedom of Women, so deeply interested as we are in this Matter" (Quaker Collection, Haverford College Library, Haverford, Pa.).

> We . . . requested an audience with the General—set with his wife (a
> sociable pretty kind of woman) untill he came in; a number of
> officers there, who were very compliant, Tench Tillman [Tilghman]
> among the rest, it was not long before GW. came and discoarse with
> us freely, but not so long as we could have wish'd, as dinner was
> serv'd in, to which he had invited us. There was 15 of the officers
> besides the Gl and his Wife. Gen Green, and G. Lee we had an
> elegant dinner, which was soon over when we went out with the
> Genl wife up to her Chamber, and saw no more of him. he told us,
> he could do nothing in our busyness further than granting us a pass
> to Lancaster, which he did, and gave.

Thus the custom of separating the ladies from the gentlemen was
carefully used by Washington to limit his dealings with the importunate
Quaker women. The general was passing the buck, though not without
some justification; three weeks before the women arrived, formal control
of the exiles had been transferred from Congress to the Supreme Executive Council of Pennsylvania. The Revolutionary government of Pennsylvania was meeting in Lancaster, and to Lancaster the women headed,
finding "the roads exceeding bad." After a two-day trip, they arrived in
Lancaster, where they "drove directly to Thos. Whartons door, . . . were
admitted to him and a number of others, but desird to speak to him by
himself—[they] had about 1/2 hour conversation with him, not very
satisfactory." On April 10 Elizabeth Drinker reported, "We paid a visit to
3 of the Councilors, vixt Coll. Hart, Edgard, Hoague. . . . After the council had set some time, T. M. [Timothy Matlack] came for our address,
which was sign'd by all the Women concern'd. he say'd he would come
for us, when it was proper, but after above an hour waiting he inform'd
us, that our presence was not necessary, and put us off in that way."[38]
The women stayed with friends outside Lancaster, and each day went
into town over roads washed out by spring floods to speak to whomever
they could find who might be influential: "In our journey today, we
found the roads so bad, that we walkd part of the way, and climbd 3
fences." Elizabeth Drinker hardly even noted in her diary that the council
finally agreed to permit the exiles to return because the ideological issue,
the Quakers' refusal to take the test oath, was not settled. The men
reached Lancaster on April 25, but the joy of reunion was dampened
by the knowledge that the council would not give them "a proper dis-

38. Diary of Elizabeth Drinker, Apr. 5, 6, 7, 8, 10, 1778.

charge." It was, Mrs. Drinker said, "a sham release." The entire party returned to Philadelphia on the last day of April to the welcoming cheers of the Philadelphia Quaker community, who flooded the Drinker home for weeks after.[39]

It is not clear what impact the women's petition had on the course of events. One man had died in exile, which was very embarrassing to the patriots; others were sick, and the Congress and council had apparently decided that the men ought to be restored to their families before the women had set out. The women's petition expressed the hope that Congress would "take no offense at the freedom of Women" and put the case squarely in terms of the need of their families for the men's assistance. When Washington gave them permission to return to Philadelphia through his lines, he commented that "humanity pleads strongly in their behalf."[40] It may be that the case was given more human resonance through the women's presence.

In her matter-of-fact way, Elizabeth Drinker made no further comment in her diary. Although she had repeatedly voiced doubts and prayed for strength before engaging in the undertaking, it was clear that once on the way she and the other women were never inhibited by the fear that what they were doing was inappropriate or unwomanly. What they did was justified by their function as wives and mothers; they seem to have assumed that they had a special claim to the attention of the Revolutionary government. Mrs. Drinker, in particular, was extraordinarily straightforward about the politics of her actions. For the rest of her life she maintained a skeptical and critical attitude about government. She would be more critical of Republicans than of Federalists, but she never gave either party unguarded admiration.[41]

Whatever their form or their goal, women's petitions shared the characteristic of being individual expressions of opinions. Only rarely do we find petitions with multiple signers, and it is even more rare to find a consistent effort to organize a female constituency.

One such unusual example of a women's petition with multiple signers was submitted to the South Carolina General Assembly in 1788 by "sundry seamstresses of the city of Charleston." Few of the petitioners knew how to write; thirty-four of the sixty-six signers used their mark,

39. *Ibid.*, Apr. 13, 24, 25, 27–30, 1778.
40. See Robert F. Oakes, "Philadelphians in Exile: The Problem of Loyalty during the American Revolution," *PMHB*, XCVI (1972), 322–324. See also Hannah Griffitts's poem "To my worthy (Banish'd) friends in Virginia," [Mar. 1778], Hannah Griffitts Papers.
41. See, for example, Diary of Elizabeth Drinker, July 4, 1795.

and the others had trouble spelling and forming letters. But they knew that the war had made them widows, and they were not without an understanding of the economic significance of the political choices that lay before their legislators.

> Your petitioners have reason to believe their want of employment is occasioned by the great importation of ready made Clothes such as shirts, and breeches, that your petitioners can make here, and which are exported in great quantities to this place by a nation whose policy it is to employ their own industrious poor rather than give bread to foreigners.
> Your petitioners therefore humbly pray that a much larger duty be laid on the above articles, which will have a tendency to give employment to your petitioners and increase the revenue as they are bulky articles that cannot be easily smuggled.[42]

The right of petition these women surely had. But they had no control, and little influence, over what happened to their petitions once submitted. Petitions that fell into traditional categories, for which the machinery of government was prepared, were often handled with dispatch; the common request by mothers for permission to alienate some inherited property in order to provide support for children was usually answered in the affirmative. When women from well-known families petitioned for preservation of certain property rights, they found sympathetic listeners. Mary Brewton Motte of the prominent South Carolina family, for example, successfully sought to prevent the establishment of a ferry route through her land, which "would absolutely render her said Plantation useless to her."[43] But petitions like that of the seamstresses of Charleston, which did not fit the usual pattern and which lacked lobbyists' support, sank without a trace. Legislatures simply had no will to deal with them. Their impotence suggests the political barrier against which women pressed.

The best-known organized political action by American women is the campaign of the female patriots of Philadelphia to collect funds for Washington's troops. Organized and led by Esther De Berdt Reed (in her role as wife of the president of Pennsylvania) and Benjamin Franklin's daugh-

42. Petition 19, General Assembly Petitions, 1788, S.C. Dept. Archives and Hist. The petition was tabled.
43. Petition 35, *ibid.*

Charles Willson Peale, *Esther De Berdt Reed*.
Courtesy The Frick Art Reference Library, New York City. In the collection of Mrs.
David Middleton.

John Hoppner, *Sarah Franklin Bache* (1797).
Courtesy The Metropolitan Museum of Art, Wolfe Fund, 1901.

ter, Sarah Franklin Bache, the campaign gained much publicity because its leadership included "the best ladies" of the patriot side. "Instead of waiting for the Donations being sent the ladys of each Ward go from dore to dore and collect them I am one of those, Honourd with this business. Yesterday we began our tour of duty and had the Satisfaction of being very Successfull," wrote Mary Morris. Collecting contributions door-to-door implied confrontation: "Of all absurdities," the loyalist Anna Rawle wrote to Rebecca Rawle Shoemaker, "the ladies going about for money exceeded everything; they were so extremely importunate that people were obliged to give them something to get rid of them."[44]

By July 4, 1779, Esther Reed was writing to George Washington that "the subscription set on foot by the ladies of this City for the use of soldiery" had resulted in some three hundred thousand paper dollars. When Washington suggested that the funds be directly deposited in the Bank of the United States, and in that way be united "with the gentlemen," Esther Reed replied coolly that it had not been the women's intention to give the soldiers "an article to which they are entitled from the public," but rather some special item that obviously came from an unusual source. The women wished to change the paper into hard specie and to give each soldier two dollars "to be entirely at his own disposal." Washington turned that down, claiming "a taste of hard money may be productive of much discontent, as we have none but depreciated paper for their pay." He also feared that the men would use specie to buy liquor. In the end the money was used to buy linen for making shirts. When Esther Reed died in the fall of 1780, the organization was taken over by Benjamin Franklin's daughter, Sarah Franklin Bache. In December, Sarah Bache sent Washington 2,200 shirts, with the wish that they "be worn with as much pleasure as they were made." If the women did not get their wish to provide each soldier with hard cash, they had at least managed to supply something distinctly from the ladies of Philadelphia; they had not merged their money into the common fund.[45]

Attempting to duplicate this project, New Jersey women organized a similar fund-raising drive. Wives of prominent politicians were given charge of soliciting contributions in each county, though the center seems to have been Trenton. Eventually Mary Dagworthy transmitted $15,488

44. Mary Morris to Catharine Livingston, June 10, [1780], Ridley Papers; Anna Rawle to Rebecca Rawle Shoemaker, June 30, 1780, William Brooke Rawle, "Laurel Hill and Some Colonial Dames Who Once Lived There," *PMHB*, XXXV (1911), 398.

45. William B. Reed, *Life and Correspondence of Joseph Reed*, II (Philadelphia, 1847), 264, 265, 270, 429–449.

—without the Philadelphians' skepticism—directly to George Washington, to be used as he thought proper; wartime inflation was so bad that he found it provided only 380 pairs of stockings for New Jersey troops.[46] A smaller donation came from the women of Maryland, sent by Mary Lee, the wife of the governor; this money was used to buy shirts and stockings for the men of the southern army. Martha Washington seems to have suggested that the Philadelphia women's project could be imitated, and on her suggestion Martha Jefferson contacted the wife of the president of the College of William and Mary. "Justified by the sanction of her [Martha Washington's] letter in handing forward the scheme," Martha Jefferson wrote to Sarah Tate Madison, "I undertake with chearfulness the duty of furnishing to my countrywomen an opportunity of proving that they also participate of those virtuous feelings which gave birth to it." But Martha Jefferson was no activist and felt she could only promote the proposed drive "by inclosing to . . . [Mrs. Madison] some of the papers to be disposed of." Following this vague commitment, the scheme seems to have petered out.[47]

Many historians of women in the Revolution have admired the Philadelphia project excessively. "A noble Example!" cried Ezra Stiles. Benjamin Rush, whose wife was an enthusiastic participant in the campaign, wrote, "The women of America have at last become principals in the glorious American controversy."[48] But they were not principals, of course, they were fund raisers, and only for a brief time and in a single city. Nor were the female patriots principals in the controversy to the extent that being a principal implies emergence from the women's private domain, and they were not above teasing and flirting to get contributions, remind-

46. Mary Dagworthy to George Washington, July 17, 1780, Fitzpatrick, ed., *Writings of Washington*, XIX, 72. See also *ibid.*, XXI, 77.

47. George Washington to Mary Lee, Oct. 11, 1780, *ibid.*, XX, 158; Martha Jefferson to Mrs. James Madison, Aug. 8, 1780, Private Collection #634.1, State Dept. Archives and Hist., Raleigh, N.C. Benjamin Franklin's sister, Jane Mecom, was briefly tempted to spread the effort to Rhode Island: "I have, as you sopose heard of yr Ladies Noble and generous Subscription for the Army and honour them for it," she wrote to Sarah Franklin Bache, "and if a harty good will in me would Effect it we would follow your Example but I fear what my Influence would procure would be so Deminuitive we should be ashamed to offer it, I live in an obscure place have but Little Acquaintance and those not very Rich, but you may [say?] a mite has been Accepted and may be again but that was a time when there was more Relidgon and less Pride" ([Fall, 1779?], Carl Van Doren, ed., *The Letters of Benjamin Franklin and Jane Mecom* [Princeton, N.J., 1950], 202).

48. July 5, 1780, Dexter, ed., *Literary Diary of Ezra Stiles*, II, 442; Benjamin Rush to John Adams, July 13, 1780, L. H. Butterfield, ed., *The Letters of Benjamin Rush*, I (Princeton, N.J., 1951), 253.

ing those who were unenthusiastic that it was rude to refuse anything to pretty women.

Yet we ought to hesitate before dismissing this effort as short-lived philanthropy. Broadsides that accompanied the drives provided an ideological justification for women's intrusion into politics that would become the standard model throughout the years of the early Republic. The Philadelphia manifesto was entitled *The Sentiments of an American Woman*; the one circulated in New Jersey was called *The Sentiments of a Lady in New Jersey*. The two are differently phrased, but share many of the same themes.[49]

The Philadelphia version first stated that American women were "born for liberty, disdaining to bear the irons of a tyrannic Government" and claimed that "if the weakness of our Constitution, if opinion and manners did not forbid us to march to glory by the same paths as the Men," women would be found at least equal, and perhaps stronger, in their convictions and their loyalty to the Republic.

The broadside then presented a list of historical role models, examples of politically active women: Deborah, Judith, Esther. "Rome saved from the fury of a victorious enemy by the efforts of Volumnia. . . . famous sieges where the Women have been seen . . . building new walls, digging trenches." Some of their choices of "Sovereigns . . . who have held with so much splendour the scepter of the greatest States" revealed only their lack of historical information; they claimed to admire "the Elizabeths, the Maries, the Catherines, who have extended the empire of liberty." But they also remembered "the Maid of Orleans who drove from the kingdom of France the ancestors of those same British, whose odious yoke we have just shaken off, and whom it is necessary that we drive from this Continent."[50] The New Jersey variant eschewed classical role models

---

49. *The Sentiments of an American Woman* (Broadside), Philadelphia, June 10, 1780. The broadside of the Ladies of Trenton appeared in the *N.-J. Gaz.* (Trenton), July 12, 1780; a portion is reprinted in Gerlach, ed., *N.J. in the Revolution*, 348–349.

50. *Sentiments of an American Woman*. The analogy between French resistance to the English in the 15th century and the American resistance to the English in the 18th had been made forcefully by Thomas Paine in the first Crisis paper, which referred specifically to Joan of Arc and added the wish "that heaven might inspire some Jersey maid to spirit up her countrymen, and save her fair fellow sufferers from ravage and ravishment!" (*The American Crisis* [Dec. 23, 1776], in Philip S. Foner, ed., *The Complete Writings of Thomas Paine*, I [New York, 1945], 51.) In John Daly Burk's play *Female Patriotism* (New York, 1798), act 4, sc. 1, Joan of Arc repeatedly expresses a vision of the Republic: " 'Tis not to crown the Dauphin prince alone/That hath impell'd my spirit to the wars,/For that were petty circumstance indeed;/But on the head of every man in France/To place a crown, and thus at

and substituted contemporary female martyrs: "[The British have] even waged war against our sex. Who that has heard . . . of the tragical death of Miss M'Crea, torn from her house, murdered and scalped by a band of savages hired and set on by British emissaries, of the melancholy fate of Mrs. Caldwell, put to death in her own house . . . but would wish to avert from themselves, their kindred, their property, and their country in general, so heavy misfortunes."

The place to display female political consciousness would be, naturally enough, on their own turf, at home, in the woman's domain. We understand, the activist women said, that if we live in safety, it is because the army protects us. In the words of the New Jersey broadside, women in the Revolution "have born the weight of the war, and met danger in every quarter. . . . they have with Roman courage and perseverance suffered." It was time, the Philadelphians said, "to display the same sentiments which animated us at the beginning of the Revolution, when we renounced the use of teas, . . . we placed former necessaries in the rank of superfluities, when our liberty was interested; when our republican and laborious hands spun the flax, prepared the linen entended for the use of our soldiers; when exiles and fugitives we supported with courage all the evils which are the concommitents of war." For all its limits, this call to action was a novel formulation. Western political theory had provided no context in which women might comfortably think of themselves as political beings. The major theorists of the Enlightenment, the Whig Commonwealth, and the republican revolution had not explored the possibility of including women as part of the people. The *man* of Enlightenment theory was literal, not generic. The only reference to women in *The Federalist Papers* would be to the dangers that the private intrigues of courtesans and mistresses pose to the safety of the state.[51]

Despite this traditional blindness to women's political activity, a vision

---

once create/A new and mighty order of nobility/To make all free and equal, *all men kings*/Subject to justice and the laws alone."

51. *Sentiments of an American Woman; Sentiments of a Lady in N.J.* See also [Alexander Hamilton, John Jay, and James Madison], *The Federalist; A Commentary on the Constitution of the United States . . .* , with an introduction by Edward Mead Earle (New York, 1937), No. 6, 28–29: "Pericles, in compliance with the resentment of a prostitute, at the expense of much of the . . . treasure of his countrymen, attacked, vanquished, and destroyed the city of the *Samnians*. . . . The influence which the bigotry of one female [Madame de Maintenon], the petulance of another [Duchess of Marlborough] and the cabals of a third [Madame de Pompadour] had in the contemporary policy, ferments, and pacifications, of a considerable part of Europe, are topics . . . generally known."

of female patriotism did emerge from the war. There are subtle differences in the ways men and women habitually handled the concept. As
George Washington described female patriotism, it was passive, admir-
ing, and quietly suffering; it was, he wrote to Anne Francis and other
Philadelphia contributors, "the love of country . . . blended with those
softer domestic virtues."[52]

Shortly after the Philadelphia broadside was circulated, the College of
New Jersey at Princeton held its annual commencement. One standard
feature of college commencements was the formal dialogue, and this one
examined the conditions of American political culture. One of the young
men looked forward to leadership in laying "the foundations of this
mighty fabric" of a new republic. He promised he would not lose his love
of freedom in the process, he would not become a Caesar: "Nay, by the
sacred flame of liberty! . . . I had rather be a woman—I had rather be
Lucretia, that glorious woman, than all the Caesars that ever wore the
imperial purple." It is true that the speaker considered Lucretia glorious
—but only as an alternative to a tyrant. The more typical female patriot
was simply expected to suffer, to admire the military, and to maintain
her innocence.

> No mean merit shall accrue to him who shall justly celebrate the
> virtue of our *ladies*, or the sufferings of virgin and of matron
> innocence. Shall not their admiration of military virtue; shall not
> their generous contributions to relieve the wants of the defenders of
> their country, supply a column, to emulate the Roman ladies,
> stripped of their jewels, when the publick necessities demanded
> them? What honours shall be conferred on him who shall weep, in
> the most moving strains, over the violated innocence of the
> daughters of New-Jersey, and melt into tears the sympathetic
> theatre?[53]

Other men would ring changes on this theme, a constant in patriotic
addresses for at least a generation. Thirty years later, when Congregational minister Solomon Aiken gave the Fourth of July Address in New-
buryport, Massachusetts, he was still calling up images of tenderness and
concurrence as the characteristic forms of female patriotism. The soldiers

---

52. Feb. 13, 1781, Fitzpatrick, ed., *Writings of Washington*, XXI, 221.
53. The speech was delivered in 1780; it is reprinted in *N.J. Archives*, 2d Ser., V, 31–35.

Woodcut from "A New Touch on the Times. . . . By a Daughter of Liberty, living in Marblehead" (1779). This wartime woodcut of a female partisan grimly gripping a musket contrasts sharply with the young women in the following illustration who demonstrate their loyalty by strewing flowers before the republican hero.
Courtesy The New-York Historical Society, New York City.

J. L. Morton after Thomas Kelley, *Washington's Reception on the Bridge at Trenton.* As Washington passed through Trenton in 1789 on his way to the inauguration, he was led under a triumphal arch inscribed with the sentiment "The Hero Who Defended the Mothers Will Protect the Daughters." A chorus of

girls, dressed in white, sang a song of welcome that stressed their passive role:
"Virgins fair and Matrons grave,/Those thy conquering Arms did save."
Courtesy The Library of Congress, Washington, D.C.

of the Revolution, he declared, "were stimulated by the fire of *female patriotism*; which unlocked the arms of the fair, from the most tender embraces . . . saying 'go! go . . . and save our country.' "[54]

The version of female patriotism described in women's broadsides is not quite so bland. Classical allusions were used not simply to illustrate, but to legitimize women's fortitude in the face of disaster. While the male version of female patriotism described the virtue as completely passive (to sacrifice luxuries, to give up husbands and sons who had made their own political decisions), the broadside variant was somewhat more assertive. It continued to praise sacrifice, but sought it actively; it brought politics into the domestic circle and found ways to make it relevant to the conditions of daily living. The political woman who solicited contributions for needy soldiers, and, subsequently, who took responsibility for needy widows and orphans, was a more emphatic patriot than the woman who contented herself with the display of "those softer domestic virtues."

A female patriotism in which men had little interest was elaborated in a pamphlet written by the historian Hannah Adams in 1787. She addressed *Women Invited to War* to the "worthy women, and honourable daughters of America." "It is our lot," she wrote, "to live in a time of remarkable difficulty, trouble and danger; a time wherein we have heard the confused noise of the warrior, and seen garments rolled in blood: yet blessed by God, we have had the honour and favour of seeing our friends and brethren exert themselves valiantly in the defence of life and liberty." But the war to which she invited American women turned out to be one against Satan, an "enemy" who "has done more harm already, than all the armies of Britain have done or ever will be able to do." It was a war in which the "superiority of the Male" was acknowledged, but since men ignored their responsibilities there was nothing to hinder "the Female from being either the first engaged, or more zealous and courageous."[55]

In a few brief paragraphs Hannah Adams had moved from the contemplation of women in war emergencies to the arguments that women ought to conduct their wars against enemies different from those of men, that women's challenges were spiritual and not political, and that women's energies ought to be directed at their private worlds. This pam-

54. Solomon Aiken, *An Oration Delivered Before the Republican Citizens of New-buryport, and Its Vicinity, July 4, 1810* (Newburyport, Mass., 1810), 13.
55. [Adams], *Women Invited to War*, 3, 10–12.

phlet is as good an example as we have of the deflection of women's patriotism into benevolence. It may be that patriotism required translation into charity and service before it could be made plausible to the millions of women whose lives were defined by their domestic responsibilities.

The postwar years saw the initiation of a score of women's service and reform societies, their constitutions roughly similar to the Philadelphia one of 1780, their charity now directed at widows and orphan girls. Among the many were the Female Association of Philadelphia for the Relief of Women and Children in Reduced Circumstances, the Newark Female Charitable Society, and the Boston Female Asylum. They too had their board of manageresses and their treasuresses, and often collected substantial sums of money. Because of the danger that property held by a married woman would be swallowed up in her husband's estate, the treasuress was often required to be a single woman—spinster or widow.

All organizations provided a milieu for female collective behavior, although their aims differed. Many were primarily religious in tone and associated closely with churches. It was common, for example, for the major fund-raising effort to be an annual sermon by a sympathetic minister, at which the beneficiaries of the organization's charity would be lined up in the front pews as a demonstration of the worthiness of their cause. Others were primarily social, like the Ladies Stocking Society of New York, which knitted stockings for soldiers in the War of 1812 and raised perhaps six hundred dollars for military uniforms, but which flirted with activism in the context of upper-class sociability. In their own limited ways, however, women's associations could not help but enlarge women's political horizons. John Adams's niece Nancy Cranch was a founding member of the Ladies Missionary Society in Washington, D.C. She had a sense that she was part of a broad movement: "Ladies everywhere shew their zeal in the great cause." And she thought of what she was doing as a sort of public service: "Tho' I cannot become a preacher of the gospel in public—why may I not at least endeavor to increase the knowledge of God & religion in my little circle."[56] These "little circles," first formed as a wartime response to a wartime challenge, represented a significant stage in women's political education and formed a base for nineteenth-century abolitionist and reform movements.

56. Diary of Nancy Cranch, Apr. 22, 1819, July 4, 1819, Cranch Papers, Library of Congress. This theme has been extensively explored in Nancy F. Cott, *The Bonds of Womanhood: "Woman's Sphere" in New England, 1780–1835* (New Haven, Conn., 1977).

Within a generation after the Revolution, the women who wished to communicate with government had developed a variant of the individual petition. The image of the political woman provided by the Philadelphia broadside of 1780 represents the beginning of a female political role that integrated the traditional domestic domain into the political world. It was no accident that a generation later, when John Quincy Adams rose in Congress to defend the right of women to petition Congress and to attack the Gag Rule (which was, after all, specifically aimed at their petitions), he found himself recapitulating the reasoning of the Philadelphia broadside. He too insisted that women might be patriots and that their political feelings were to be respected. He sneered at those who thought it " 'discreditable' for women to take any interest or any part in political affairs." He insisted that women had "political rights," and he let himself come close to asserting that women might well claim the right to vote. Like the women of Philadelphia, John Quincy Adams offered a pantheon of heroines to support his case: Miriam, who had as clear opinions on what constituted the welfare of Israel as did Moses and Aaron; Deborah, prophetess and judge; Queen Esther, "who, by PETITION, saved her people and her country"; Isabella of Castile, "the patroness of Columbus, the discoverer. . . . Did she bring discredit on her sex by mingling in politics?"

Finally he insisted that the woman's domestic domain might properly be integrated into the political one; the women of Philadelphia had in fact done so during the Revolution, and the abolitionist women of Massachusetts were doing the same in his own generation. "Why does it follow," Adams demanded, "that women are fitted for nothing but the cares of domestic life? for bearing children, and cooking the food of a family . . . to promoting the immediate personal comfort of their husbands, brothers, and sons? . . . I admit that it is their duty to attend to these things. . . . But I say that the correct principle is, that women are not only justified, but exhibit the most exalted virtue when they do depart from the domestic circle, and enter on the concerns of their country, of humanity, and of their God . . . when it is done from purity of motive, by appropriate means, and towards a virtuous purpose."[57]

The women's bazaars of the abolitionist campaign were an example of collective action hinted at by Esther Reed's fund raising, and the women's abolitionist petitions that flooded Congress in the 1830s and

57. *Speech of John Quincy Adams . . . upon the Right of the People, Men and Women, to Petition . . .* (New York, 1969 [orig. publ. Washington, D.C., 1838]), 66, 74, 76, 70, 67–68.

forced confrontation of the slavery issue were the lineal descendants of Esther Reed's broadside. Women's associations justified themselves in terms of women's domestic and religious obligations. Before women could join John Adams's political republic, many of them had first to enlist in the ranks of Hannah Adams's spiritual army.

Chapter 4

"SHE CAN HAVE NO WILL DIFFERENT FROM HIS": REVOLUTIONARY LOYALTIES OF MARRIED WOMEN

Can we believe that a wife, for so respecting the general understanding of her husband as to submit her own opinions to his . . . should lose her own property, and forfeit the inheritance of her children? Was she to be considered as criminal because . . . she did not, in violation of her marriage vows, rebel against the will of her husband?

—Theodore Sedgwick

Joseph Strutt after R. E. Pine, *To Those who wish to Sheathe the Desolating
Sword of War* . . . (1778). The imagery in this engraving is largely female:
"America kneels beside an obelisk which commemorates the war heroes. In the
background a city burns, fences and walls lie in ruins. . . . A female figure,
probably Peace, brings an olive branch from the sky. Heroic Virtue comes to
America presenting Liberty who is attended by Concord, Industry, and Plenty.

Virtue is a noble savage clothed in skins carrying a club. Liberty carries a liberty cap and a staff. Concord wears flowers in her hair. Industry holds a bundle of wood and a bee hive. Plenty carries a cornucopia and is surrounded by children and animals."

THE EXPERIENCE OF the Revolution provided evidence that women could indeed display political behavior. Would their patriotism become the basis for a new vision of women's relationship to the state? Could the Republic devise a way of accepting women into the political culture of the new nation?

Women's political support had been demanded by the warring parties; this support had been given. But republicans and loyalists alike defined it as a free gift, self-evidently justified, for which no recompense was necessary. When the war was over, heroines like Elizabeth Burgin were again reduced to the political status of ineffectual petitioners.

Although the war itself did not create a new ideology of women's patriotism, it did place women in unfamiliar positions, where they found old ideologies less and less useful. During the war the practical problem arose in the law of determining whether married women might be expected—or even required—to make political decisions at odds with those of their husbands. The statute law of the early Republic reveals where male Americans believed women belonged in the political culture, and the very limited extent to which they were prepared to accommodate women.

When lawmakers chose coverture over independence, and dependence over autonomy, they set down clear limits on the transformation of the political culture. Women pressed against these limits, making emphatic use, for example, of the law of divorce when it was available to them. Conservative politics triumphed in the early Republic; but before it triumphed it was challenged by adversaries, and sometimes an adversary was female.

Although the Revolution was the occasion for a radical reappraisal of the laws by which they lived, Americans had no intention of relinquishing the entire British legal tradition. Many early state law codes specifically reenacted large portions of the common law and of equity practice. Most features of the British law of domestic relations were so retained.

In English practice, "Baron and Feme" was the law of domestic relations. The very wording implies a political relationship: lord and woman, not husband and wife. One party had status as well as gender; the other had only gender. As "Baron," husband stood to wife as king did to baron. Wives were expected to accept "moderate" physical chastisement. Traditionally the slaying of wife by husband was simple murder, while the slaying of husband by wife was "petit Treason." This feature of English law, with its clear intent of vicious punishment for the murderer (such as death by burning), was largely a dead letter by the eighteenth century. But the old tradition of treating baronicide as treason reveals many of the basic English assumptions about a wife's political identity. It could not be simpler: her husband was her king. The implication that there was a political, as well as a private, feature to a woman's relationship with her husband persisted in the colonies and surfaced in the treason and confiscation legislation of the Republic. The familiar notion that the family circle was a woman's state was not a simple figure of speech, but a deeply rooted assumption of the English legal tradition, gone but not forgotten.

The details of the relationship between husband and wife traditionally rested on the concept of coverture, the assumption that woman's identity became submerged, or covered, by that of her husband when she married. A married couple became a legal fiction: like a corporation, the pair was a single person with a single will. The fictive volition of the pair was always taken to be the same as the real will of the husband.

Political and economic implications were commingled in the notion of coverture. Because husband and wife shared a single will, they could not testify against each other. All property possessed by the wife was vested in her husband, "who might use and dispose of it without her consent." The definition of women's status embraced an illogical syllogism: A married pair might express only one will to the outside world—the husband's; therefore a married woman had no independent control of her property. Since republican theory emphasized that the right to participate in the management of a political unit stemmed from ownership of property, the denial of political rights to women seemed quite natural.[1] But what of unmarried adult women? By republican logic, the *feme sole* ought to have met no impediment in the expression of her political choices. In practice, while the *feme sole* clearly had property rights that she might vigorously protect, she was not permitted to exercise the political rights that theoretically accompanied them.

---

1. The notion that husband and wife are one person in law was popularized by Sir William Blackstone in his *Commentaries on the Laws of England* (London, 1765), which circulated widely in America. Blackstone is a useful guide to interpretations that were familiar to American lawyers, but should be used with caution as a guide to common law itself. In their magisterial *History of English Law before the Time of Edward I*, 2d ed. (Cambridge, 1968), Frederick Pollock and Frederic William Maitland scorn Blackstone's interpretation and argue that the origins of the law of Husband and Wife lie in "the *mund*, the profitable guardianship, which the husband has over the wife and over her property" (*ibid.*, I, 485). See also *ibid.*, II, 399–406. Zephaniah Swift, *A System of the Laws of the State of Connecticut*, I (Windham, Conn., 1795), 183–212, is the basic contemporary American treatise.

Coverture, in short, was inconsistent with the most basic maxims of republican theory. The married woman, "covered" by her husband's political identity, became politically invisible. Charles Brockden Brown wrote a simple formulation of fundamental republican maxims. Each one included the implied phrase "except women." "All power is derived from the people. Liberty is every one's birthright. Since all cannot govern or deliberate individually, it is just that they should elect their representatives. That every one should possess, indirectly, and through the medium of his representatives, a voice in the public councils; and should yield to no will but that of an actual or virtual majority."[2] Woman's will was not part of the General Will.

As the colonies drifted into war with England, everyone was forced into a new relationship to the government. Individual states moved swiftly to demand oaths of allegiance and to force hesitant individuals to make a choice between the empire and the rebels. Initially women could avoid the issue, since loyalty oaths were generally required only of adult males.[3]

There was no question, however, that women—married or unmarried —could commit treason. Even before the Declaration of Independence, a treason statute was passed by the Continental Congress that carefully avoided the use of the generic *he* in declaring that "all persons abiding within any of the United Colonies, and deriving protection from the laws of the same, owe allegiance to the said laws, and are members of such colony."[4] State statutes defining treason often used the explicit "he or she." A loosely drawn New York statute, for example, provided that anyone who came out from the enemy's lines to "secretly lurk" could be considered a spy, and that "he or she" might be put to death after court-martial.[5]

2. Charles Brockden Brown, *Alcuin: A Dialogue* (New York, 1971), 30–31.

3. See, for example, "An Act to Oblidge every Free male inhabitant of this state, above a certain age [16] to give assurance of Fidelity and Allegiance," in Thomas Cooper, ed., *The Statutes at Large of South Carolina*, IV (Columbia, S.C., 1838), 147.

4. Bradley Chapin, *The American Law of Treason: Revolutionary and Early National Origins* (Seattle, Wash., 1964), 37; Ford *et al.*, eds., *Jours. Cont. Cong.*, V, 475–476.

5. *Laws of N.Y.*, June 30, 1780, Mar. 30, 1781, I, 282, 370. When Mary Fairchild of New Milford was charged with having "knowledge that Samuel Brinkwater Junr was then using his Influence to persuade the Subjects of this State to Give aid comfort & assist the Enemies of this and the United States," special notice was sent to her husband, James, "that he may appear if he See cause to Defend his said wife." There is no evidence that he did; she was tried before the Connecticut Superior Court in Feb. 1779 and pleaded not guilty. She was judged guilty, fined £20 and two months in Litchfield jail, and required to pay the heavy costs of prosecution, £73 15s. 4d. (Record Book 19 and Miscellaneous Papers, Confiscated Estates and Loyalists, Connecticut State Library, Hartford).

Punishments that seemed appropriate for men presented a problem when applied to women. The penalty for New Jersey men convicted of treason, for example, was death without benefit of clergy—with the option that the condemned person might receive a pardon if he enlisted in the Continental Navy. Women, however, were not welcome in the navy. For them, the law had to provide alternative punishment: a fine up to three hundred pounds and imprisonment for up to one year. No provision was made for men's second offenses since enlistment in the navy and confinement on ship were expected to make it impossible for a man to cross back into enemy lines. The legislature could, however, imagine that released women might indulge in a second offense, and it explicitly provided that a woman's second act of treason was a capital felony for which she was to suffer death without benefit of clergy.[6]

The effort to enact treason statutes, which in the eyes of the whigs was accomplished with statesmanlike deliberation, was perceived by loyalists as a mad rush to force the issues. Loyalists and civilian neutrals in areas disputed by the opposing armies wanted as much time as possible before committing themselves politically. The extreme version of their position was this: since it could not be known whether the new government would in fact be established until a peace treaty acknowledging independence was signed, the patriots ought not to demand oaths of allegiance until the war was successfully concluded. Margaret Livingston, herself a patriot, could sympathize with the position of friends who clung to their neutrality, though she conceded that their arguments were politically "trivial." " I am not so unfeeling a patriot as not to Suffer exceedingly for the many families, who are now Leaving us, on their refusal to take the Oath to the State the tendering of which they Say, Should have been delay'd till we are, what we Stile ourselves & which we have never yet been, our Independence to which they are to swear, being Still contested by a Large army in our Country."[7]

"Probably the most common treason of the Revolution," Bradley

6. "Act for Constituting a Council of Safety," Sept. 1777, in *Acts of Gen. Assembly of N.J.*, 87. The only woman we know of who was jailed for "high treason" was Esther Marsh of Morristown, N.J. See *Minutes of the Council of Safety of the State of New Jersey*, Jan. 14, 1778 (Jersey City, N.J., 1872), 189.

7. Margaret Livingston to Susan Livingston, [July 1778], Ridley Papers, Mass. Hist. Soc. James Kettner emphasizes that the concept of volitional allegiance was a new one and that the undecided were given some time to make up their minds: "No treason prosecutions were instituted against civilians until after the states passed treason laws" ("The Development of American Citizenship in the Revolutionary Era: The Idea of Volitional Allegiance," *Am. Jour. Legal Hist.*, XVIII [1974], 226).

Chapin has written, "was going over to the enemy." Apparently by common consent, a married woman who did so openly, in an effort to join her husband, was not treated as a traitor. She needed only to petition the sitting legislature, or the active committee of safety, for permission to join her husband. Her petition had to explain why she wished to go, at what point she wished to cross the enemy lines, and what she wished to take with her. Permission to pass was invariably granted, although the supplies and household goods she might take with her were often substantially reduced, and usually she was not permitted to take servants. Almost all these petitions specified that the woman wished to join a husband or other family member and implied or made explicit that she needed her husband's economic support. Legislatures do not seem to have been inhibited by the consideration that in permitting women to join their husbands they were contributing to the morale of the enemy.[8] In granting these women's requests, the Revolutionaries were freeing themselves of economic dependents, and they were gaining abandoned property without a struggle. But they were also sanctioning the idea that these women had no political obligations to the state.

Of course the patriots believed that the husbands of these women *did* have political obligations. The most common way of punishing absenteeism was by seizing the property left behind.[9] If the absentee were married, his property was a complex amalgam of the property he owned in his own right and the property his wife had brought into their marriage, which he had the right to alienate so long as coverture continued. Normally his wife claimed a dower right to a life estate in one-third of his landed property after his death. Was the property of the absentee's wife properly subject to seizure? Ought her dower rights to be ignored? If he adhered to the enemy, and in doing so put his property at risk, did it automatically follow that she had done the same?

Just as there was a degree of variation in the treason statutes passed by the states, there was variation in the confiscation acts—and in the explicitness with which these acts dealt with the wives of absentees. The confiscation acts had a double purpose. The first was to provide legal grounds for seizing vulnerable property and for using it to support the

8. Chapin, *American Law of Treason*, 75. Between Mar. 1777 and Oct. 1778 the New Jersey Council of Safety forcibly removed many wives of tories behind enemy lines. But when women petitioned to leave, force was not required. In those 18 months, permission was granted to 26 women, with their children under 12 and often their servants. Only six men received such permission. See *Minutes N.J. Council of Safety, passim.*

9. Chapin, *American Law of Treason*, 75.

rebels' cause. The second purpose was implicit: to inhibit the undecided from joining the enemy by placing a high price on what they stood to lose if they left. The threat of confiscation in effect challenged neutrals and loyalists to consider whether their political commitments outweighed their desire to protect their property. What price did they put on their allegiance?

The Massachusetts legislature framed this second purpose in an extraordinarily radical way: it explicitly encouraged the wife of the absentee to break from her husband, to declare her own loyalty to the Republic, to set herself at risk for the Republic, and in doing so to protect her property. The General Court of Massachusetts passed two similar statutes on April 30, 1779: one a bill of attainder, confiscating the estates of twenty-nine highly placed loyalist officials (Thomas Hutchinson, the Mandamus Councillors, the Commissioners of the Customs, Samuel Quincy, Harrison Gray); the other a general act for "confiscating the Estates of certain Persons commonly called Absentees," providing for the confiscation of the estate of anyone who had levied, or would in the future levy, war against the United States or who had withdrawn from his usual place of habitation to seek protection of the king's forces. Thus far the legislation resembled other states' confiscation acts. But both Massachusetts statutes also contained the following section:

> Where the wife or widow of any of the persons afore described, shall have remained within the Jurisdiction of any of the said United States, and in Part under the Actual authority thereof, she shall be entitled to the Improvement and Income of One Third-Part of her husband's Real and Personal Estate, after Payment of Debts, during her Life and Continuance within the said United States; and her Dower therein shall be set off to her by the Judges of Probate Wills, in like Manner as it might have been, if her husband had died intestate, within the Jurisdiction of this State.[10]

The Massachusetts treason statute, passed earlier that year, had provided for the confiscation of the estates of executed traitors, but with the traditional proviso that their wives' dower rights would be preserved.[11] The absentee statutes were less generous. They did not require women to

10. *Acts and Resolves of the State of Massachusetts*, chap. 73, Apr. 30, 1779, 1055, chap. 74, Apr. 30, 1779, 1059.
11. *Ibid.*, chap. 71, 1777, 1051.

take loyalty oaths, but they did insist that if a woman wished the Republic to preserve her property rights in her husband's estate, she must make her own political commitment. The Republic promised to protect her property only if she remained in America, dissociated herself from her husband, and declared her own political allegiance. As the American jurist Nathan Dane would point out in 1824, this was a radical departure from the long-standing English rule that dower would be turned over to the wife only upon the *real* death of her husband, not upon his "civil death."[12]

The absentee statutes also included a threat: should a woman accompany her husband into exile, patriots would assume that she was making her own political choice, and they would therefore treat her property as forfeit. In distinguishing between the tory wife who stayed and the tory wife who left, the Massachusetts statute encouraged the separation of families and the making of political decisions. The woman who remained in order to protect her portion of the family property was at the same time demonstrating, at real personal risk, a conviction that the rebel government would live up to its promises. The wife who followed her husband into exile did not share that trust. The Virginia statute of forfeitures similarly provided for the reservation of the dower right only for wives and widows "residing within the state." Virginia also exempted the full estate from forfeiture if a child remained in the state.[13]

Some women in other states acted as though the Massachusetts statute represented the common sense of the matter, even though their own state's confiscation statutes had not been equally explicit. Mary Hoyt of Danbury, Connecticut, could not have been clearer in insisting on a distinction between her husband's politics and her own. Her husband, "being an enemy to his country, went off and joined" the British when they passed through the town. She agreed that "he did justly forfeit all his estate both real and personal" and did not question the right of

---

12. Nathan Dane, *A General Abridgement and Digest of American Law*, IV (Boston, 1824), 704; and A. W. B. Simpson, *An Introduction to the History of the Land Law* (Oxford, 1961), 65–66.

13. For an example of a Massachusetts woman who made use of this law, see the account of Ruth Atkins Gay, who remained in Hingham after her husband, Martin, fled with the British and who succeeded in having the probate court set off her dower third of the real estate of her absentee husband, in Crary, ed., *The Price of Loyalty*. See also "An Act concerning escheats and forfeitures from British subjects," May 1779, in William Waller Hening, ed., *The Statutes at Large; Being a Collection of All the Laws of Virginia . . .*, X (Richmond, 1822), chap. 14, 71, and *ibid.*, 74.

the selectmen of Danbury to seize it. But she protested "that she has ever been a true friend to the rights of her country," and the action that deprived her of "the necessaries of life" was unjustified. She wanted her dower right immediately, and the General Assembly of Connecticut agreed, giving her "the free use and improvement of one third part of all the real and personal estate of her said husband during the pleasure of this Assembly."[14]

The South Carolina confiscation statutes (of which there were many revisions) did not specifically reserve dower rights. They did, however, attend in part to the matter of separate support for wives and families by providing that the commissioners who supervised the sale of confiscated property might allocate part of it "for the temporary support of such of the families of the persons mentioned . . . as shall appear to them necessary." Permanent provision was left to the discretion of the legislature; relatives of loyalists would have to petition individually for maintenance.[15] North Carolina reserved to the wife and children of absentees "so much of the estate of such absentee as [they] . . . might have . . . been allowed, if such absentee had died intestate," and paid special, sympathetic attention to their elderly parents. "It may happen," the North Carolina statute of 1779 concluded, "that many absentees from the state may have left fathers or mothers in an advanced age, and whose sole dependence for their subsistence has been upon the property and filial attention of their children." The statute implied that it was too much to expect that traitors would show filial affection, and so encouraged these aged or infirm parents to apply to the district superior court, which "is hereby empowered to set off and allot to such aged parent such part of portion of the estate of the absentee as such aged person hath heretofore been accustomed to receive and enjoy, and as much more as shall be necessary."[16]

The position that the *feme covert* agreed with her loyalist husband

14. Memorial of Mary Hoyt, wife of Isaac Hoyt (late of Danbury), May 1777, *Conn. State Recs.*, I, 299–300. The Connecticut statute of confiscation did not specifically mention reservation of dower right. Land was to be sold under the direction of judges of probate, after a review of claims on the estate. Presumably this review could be interpreted to include the claim of dower. See *Acts and Laws of the State of Connecticut* (Hartford, Conn., 1976), 172–173.

15. "An Act for Disposing of Certain Estates and Banishing Certain Persons," Feb. 1782, in Cooper, ed., *S.C. Statutes*, IV, 51. Other modifications were passed in Mar. 1783 (*ibid.*, 55–56) and Mar. 1785 (*ibid.*, 666–667). After the war, many did petition for maintenance from the state.

16. Henry Potter *et al.*, eds., *Laws of the State of North Carolina . . .*, I (Raleigh, N.C., 1821), chap. 139, 1779, 372.

unless proven otherwise, and that she ought to pay the price of that political commitment, was a radical position. It was more generally assumed that she had no political opinions unless she could be accused of some overt act. For example, the New York law of attainder, requiring the forfeiture and sale of the property of persons who had adhered to the enemy, listed fifty-six men by name, but only three of their wives.[17]

The question of what loyalty married women owed to the state reappeared after the war, when widows of exiled loyalists tried to claim their dower rights. Occasionally sons of loyalists sought to claim confiscated property inherited through their mothers. Four of these claims are particularly instructive.

South Carolina's confiscation statute had left the burden of proof on the wife who did not share in her husband's disloyalty. The indignant petition that Florence Cooke submitted to the General Assembly of South Carolina in 1783 spelled out the implications of confiscation for the woman who was unlucky enough to be married to a convicted tory. The Cooke family had been in Charleston during the British occupation. Intimidated, Mr. Cooke had signed the oath of allegiance to the king and was forced into exile when the patriots approached the city. His wife's petition is rich in quotidian detail.

> She is informed that herself is deprived of her right of Dower, and her child a Daughter of Twelve years of age, of all future claim on the inheritance of her father. This law she humbly thinks the more severe as her Child received early & strong impressions of real Attatchment to the liberty of her Native Country; with a Confirmed aversion to our Enemies; principally inculcated by yr Petitr who if providence had blessed her with a number of Sons, would have thought herself happily engaged in employing all the influence & Care of a Mother, to render them fit for the defence and Support of their Country. Conscious of this, she the more regrets that her self and Child should be put out of the protection of the former Laws of this State, with respect to her own Dower, and her Daughters right

17. *Laws of N.Y.*, Oct. 22, 1779, I, 173. It is not fully clear why these three women should have been singled out for attainder. A century later, in an unforgivingly loyalist history of New York, Thomas Jones maintained that it gave the state an excuse to seize "large, and valuable real estates" that their husbands held "in right of their wives." Jones was a biased observer and insisted on having it both ways. The woman who had not permitted her property to be fully "covered" during her marriage discovered, logically enough but perhaps to her surprise, that she had left it at political risk (*History of New York during the Revolutionary War . . .*, II [New York, 1879], 271).

of future succession to her fathers inheritance: a property that has been earned, *not more by the hard industry of her husband, than by her own Domestic toil, frugality and attention.*

Your Petitioner is not only inocent of any crime, but if a sincere affection for the independence and freedom of her Country, avowed and testified in the worst of times, be any Merit, she flatters herself she has some to plead. With regard to her banished husband, She has but little to say. Being a laborious hardworking man in a Mechanic employment, and not versed in the knowledge of publick troubles, it is not likely he could do any political good or harm. The change that happened in Charles Town was too powerful for his Situation and Circumstances to withstand; he might have said an Idle thing, but your petitioner believes he had neither inclination nor influence to execute any mischievous one. . . . She makes this application to the members of the legislature as her Country men & fellow Citizens. Humbly entreating, to allow her husband & the father of her Child, to return and have a hearing, if he has Commited any Crime. If he be acquited as she trusts he will, she Pledges herself that she will Exert all the ascendency of a Wife & friend to make him a Good man and useful Citizen.

And lastly she humbly implores of this honorable house, that she may not be deprived of the only resource for herself and the maintenance & Education of her Daughter, who must otherwise be turned into the world, without friend or protector, exposed to that Misfortune and affliction, which Seldom fail to pursue an unhappy female fallen from affluence to poverty.

Florence Cooke asserts her claim to dower on her own patriotism, her own citizenship, and her own "Domestic toil," which has made an economic contribution to her husband's estate. She does not regard dower as a gift to a helpless female; she assumes that she has a right to the equal protection of the laws and resents the situation in which she has been placed. It is her husband who was insufficiently sophisticated, "not versed in the knowledge of publick troubles," and too weak to "do any political good or harm." She has no doubts about her own political competence, her own ability to shape her daughter's mind, or her ability to raise patriotic sons. Though a petitioner, she had not lost her pride; even the final reference to the danger of her daughter's descent into a life of prostitution is an abstract recognition of social pressures on all who find themselves in a similar situation. If she is given the tools to resist these pressures—that is, if she can give her daughter an education—she has no doubt that she can and will resist them.[18]

Occasionally claims for dower rights made their way to the courts. In 1789, for example, the widow of Mr. Pendarvis, one of the men who had been affected by the South Carolina confiscation law of 1782, demanded her dower in his estate. The state attorney general, Alexander Moultrie, had no sympathy: "The common law goes upon the idea, that husbands are oftentimes influenced and governed by the sentiment and conduct of their wives. If, therefore, they do not exert this influence, by example and dissuasion, they are considered in the law, as having incurred such a degree of guilt, as to forfeit every right or claim under their husbands." Moultrie insisted that when Mr. Pendarvis forfeited his property, his wife had also lost her dower right in it; confiscation was thus tantamount to an attainder for treason. He went on to say that if the legislature had intended to reserve the right of dower, it would have done so, just as it had made special provision for the temporary support of wives and children. To open the door to dower claims would risk calling into question all resold confiscated property and "would be productive of endless demands against the state."[19]

Moultrie's argument had something in common with the rationale for the Massachusetts absentee confiscation act of 1777. The attorney general claimed that married women did bear political responsibility, and if they did not exercise that responsibility, they would have to accept the

18. Florence Cooke to the General Assembly, Jan. 21, 1783, Petition 37, General Assembly Petitions, 1783, S.C. Dept. Archives and Hist. Italics added. Another claim of dower in confiscated property is that of Mary Stuart, *ibid.*, 1783, signed with her mark. In 1791 Catherine Carne was granted £200 sterling "in lieu of dower" in response to her petition (Petition 118, *ibid.*, 1791, and Committee Report 139, 1791, S.C. Dept. Archives and Hist.). For a lawsuit in which an exiled loyalist wife sued for her dower right to her husband's confiscated estate, see Margaret Leake's commission to attorney James Watts to "bring an action of Dower . . . for the especial Purpose of recovering my Rights of Dower" (Dec. 13, 1792, Leake Papers, N.-Y. Hist. Soc., New York City). The habit of ascribing to women the political opinions of their nearest male relatives caught two widows of patriots in a cruel bind. Hannah Deveaux Ashe and Margaret Deveaux Ashe, who were sisters as well as sisters-in-law, complained that the legislature had mistakenly ascribed to them the loyalist identity of their father and deprived them of their patrimony by the acts of amercement and confiscation. They implied that they deserved the chance to identify the male relative whose politics they supported (Petition 24, General Assembly Petitions, 1795, S.C. Dept. Archives and Hist.).

19. Mongin and Wife, late Pendarvis, against Baker and Stevens, Apr. 1789, in Elihu Hall Bay, *Reports of Cases Argued and Determined in the Superior Courts of Law, in the State of South-Carolina, since the Revolution* (Charleston, S.C., and New York, 1798–1811), I, 76–78.

consequences. The common law tradition was based on the faith that fear of leaving behind penniless widows and children would dissuade men from crime and that their wives would reinforce this fear. But this argument was weak. Political responsibility could not be directly exercised by a dissident wife; in order to save her property, not only did she have to be a patriot, but she had also to persuade her loyalist husband to be one, or at least to conceal his loyalism. Moultrie's reasoning was made even weaker by the recent adoption of the federal Constitution, which narrowly defined the crime of treason and made it impossible to maintain that all whose property had been confiscated during the war had been traitors and were subject to the most severe penalties of the treason law. In fact the general drift of American judicial thinking was to narrow the grounds of treason, not to widen them to include people whose sole crime had been failure to save someone else from treason.

Federalist attorney Henry William DeSaussure had little difficulty in persuading the court that Moultrie was wrong. He emphasized that "acts of *attainder* were generally looked upon with a jealous eye," that Pendarvis had never actually been tried for treason, and that "constructive treasons and attainders, are the most dangerous, the most pernicious doctrines ever introduced among mankind." Mrs. Pendarvis's right to dower, he said, "could not be taken away from her, but by some act of her's, amounting to forfeiture." Since *she* had not, by her own acts, forfeited her right to dower, the property seized by the state was in fact encumbered by her claims. The commissioners might sell the confiscated estate, but they could not by right seize more than two-thirds, and they could not sell what they did not have.[20]

The question of the vulnerability of dower rights did not appear before the federal Supreme Court until the case of *Kempe's Lessee* v. *Kennedy et al.* in 1809. Because the Court denied jurisdiction on a technicality, there is no clear account of judicial reasoning on the matter. The best record we have of the legal issues involved comes from the arguments of the opposing attorneys.

Grace Kempe had been the wife of John Tabor Kempe, the king's attorney general for New York City. She had brought New Jersey lands

---

20. *Ibid.*, 74–76. Seven years later DeSaussure argued the other side of the issue, defending a creditor against the claim of a tory widow for her dower. But the argument he had made in 1789 held too well, and the court impatiently upheld Mary Wells's claim to her dower, making specific reference to the Mongin case. Judge Bay did not even bother to detail the arguments for the court, complaining that "they were very long and uninteresting" (*ibid.*, II, 20–23).

with her into their marriage; when her husband was attainted, these lands had been confiscated and sold by the state of New Jersey. When John Tabor Kempe had died in exile in England, Mrs. Kempe claimed that she had not been a proper target of the wartime confiscation laws, and she sought to recover the estate. The case was originally tried in the Inferior Court of Common Pleas for Hunterdon County, which found against her claim, and then came to the Supreme Court on appeal.[21]

Grace Kempe's lawyer, Richard Stockton, began by portraying the Kempes as passive victims of the Revolution; when the British occupied New York City, "they did not go to the enemy, but remained at their own homes, and the enemy came to them." This was a hard position to maintain. As king's attorney, John Tabor Kempe had made no secret of his commitment to the crown; indeed his entire sense of self-respect hinged on his loyalty to the oath he had taken and to his appointment. Stockton backed away from developing a defense of John Tabor Kempe and moved to a defense of Grace Kempe on the grounds that as a *feme covert* she had been even more passive than her husband. "She simply *remained with her husband*, without affording any aid to the enemy. Such a person is not within the purview of this section, and therefore, though the forfeiture perhaps operated on the interest of the husband, it did not reach the estate of the wife." The confiscation act, Stockton argued, had been directed at those who voluntarily went within the enemy lines or aided the enemy's war effort. "It supposes a *free will*, a *volition*, an election to go or stay; but a *feme-covert*, in the presence of her baron, has no will; and on the subject of residence, she can have no will different from his. She is bound by law to live with him if he required it. . . . as freedom of will is of the essence of all crimes, a woman cannot commit a crime of this sort, not even this species of treason, by obeying her husband." He cited English precedent to the effect that even if she knew her husband to be a traitor, remaining loyal to him was not treason. Stockton was certain that the American legislature had not intended, even in the crucible of revolution, to break with English precedent: "They did not mean to legislate against the most important duties of social and domestic life, to cut asunder the bands of matrimonial union, to compel a wife to abandon her husband or forfeit her estate."[22]

---

21. *Kempe's Lessee v. Kennedy et al.*, 5 Cranch (U.S.) 173–187 (1809).

22. Stockton acknowledged that the act referred to the confiscation of "his or her" property, but he was sure that "the word 'her' in the last clause . . . may be satisfied by restricting its sense to single women." In passing, he tossed off the opinion that a *feme covert* "cannot properly be called an inhabitant of a state. The husband is the inhabitant. By the constitu-

Kempe's Lessee was the only case of this nature to appear before the Supreme Court. On February 20, 1809, Chief Justice John Marshall announced that Grace Kempe had not brought the right form of action. New Jersey statutes had clearly defined the crime of treason, clearly prescribed the punishment, and accurately identified the final tribunal in which judgment should be sought. Appeals from the state court of common pleas ought to go up through the state court system, not directly to the Supreme Court. Marshall did permit himself a few elliptical obiter dicta strongly suggesting that his sympathies lay with Stockton and that he believed the inferior court's judgment to be "erroneous."[23]

In arguing *Kempe's Lessee*, both contending attorneys referred repeatedly to *Martin v. Commonwealth*, a complicated case that worked its way slowly up through the Massachusetts judicial system until it was decided by the state supreme court in 1805. *Martin v. Commonwealth* occasioned the fullest and most elaborate discussion of the political responsibility of women to the state.[24]

As noted earlier, the Massachusetts confiscation statute passed on April 30, 1777, and reenacted with only minor variations in 1779, did not mention wives who left with loyalist husbands. But it promised wives of loyalists who chose to remain in the United States that their dower rights would be protected during confiscation and that their portion of the family estate would be immediately set off and reserved to them in the event of seizure and sale.

William and Anna Martin were loyalists who had fled with the British to Halifax and then to New York under British occupation before removing to England. Their abandoned property was confiscated and rented out or sold by the state of Massachusetts in 1781. Twenty years later, the Martins' son William returned to claim his deceased parents' property. He petitioned the Inferior Court of Common Pleas to the effect that a series of errors had been made; the crucial one was that William Martin, Senior, had only a life interest in the family lands, and that "the fee simple thereof belonged to . . . Anna Martin." William Martin, Junior,

---

tion of New-Jersey, all inhabitants are entitled to vote; but it has never been supposed that a *feme covert* was a legal voter. Single women have been allowed to vote, because the law supposes them to have wills of their own" (*ibid.*, 175–178).

23. *Ibid.*, 176–178, 186. Marshall explicitly affirmed his judgment that the court of common pleas had erred in his opinion in *Ex parte Watkins*, 28 Peters (U.S.) 201–205 (1830).

24. *Martin v. Commonwealth*, 1 Mass. 347–397 (1805). The file papers that enable the reader to follow the slow progress of appeal are in the Clerk's Office, Supreme Judicial Court, Boston, Mass.

claimed the properties as *her* son and heir and argued that because his mother had been a *feme covert*, she had never been "liable to have her estates confiscated."

Martin's counsel was the well-known Federalist attorney Theophilus Parsons, who the next year would be raised to chief justice of the court in which the case appeared. Parsons had first come to political prominence as an organizer of the Essex Result, a protest against the first draft of the Massachusetts state constitution in 1778; he had been a pillar of the conservative Federalists ever since.[25] Parsons could not have stated more bluntly the position that the court ultimately took: Martin deserved the return of his property because it had been unfairly seized from his mother. As a married woman Anna Martin had "no *political* relation to the *state* any more than an alien." Parsons had never shrunk from extreme statements. This certainly was one. That married women were in effect political aliens was traditional theory with a vengeance.

Parsons then carefully analyzed the working of the Massachusetts confiscation statute, which referred to every "*inhabitant and member* of the state." Parsons distinguished between the two categories and explained that *femes covert* might be inhabitants, but they were not members. Had the legislature intended to include women it would have merely said "inhabitant." He pointed out that the law demanded an oath of allegiance, but "a *feme-covert* was never holden to take an oath of allegiance." The statute went into great detail on the services that a state may require of its members, always identified with the male pronoun. "How much physical force is retained by retaining married women? What are the *personal services* they are to render in opposing *by force* an actual invasion? What *aid* can they give to an enemy?" Women were not of service in the defense of a country; in fact, they were rather a clear impediment to that defense.

The solicitor general for the state was Daniel Davis, a Republican who found Parsons's argument to be nonsense.[26] Women were both inhabi-

---

25. For Parsons's career see Theophilus Parsons, Jr., *Memoir of Theophilus Parsons* (Boston, 1859), and David Hackett Fisher, *The Revolution of American Conservatism: The Federalist Party in the Era of Jeffersonian Democracy* (New York, 1965), 254. Fisher argues that Parsons's property law decisions made it clear that he thought of property as an "'alienable right,' subject to the will of rulers and the needs of the state." Parsons's decision in *Martin v. Commonwealth*, however, does not conform to his general pattern of thinking.

26. Daniel Davis (1762–1835), an Antifederalist lawyer from the Maine District, acted as solicitor general from 1802 to 1832, when the office was abolished. Little is known about him, though he published a useful work, *A Practical Treatise upon the Authority and Duty of Justices of the Peace in Criminal Prosecutions* (Boston, 1824). See William T. Davis, *History of the Judiciary of Massachusetts . . .* (New York, 1974 [orig. publ. Boston, 1900]), 284–285.

tants and members of the state. "Surely a *feme-covert* can be an inhabitant in every sense of the word. Who are members of the body politic? are not all the *citizens*, members . . . ?" It was, Davis thought, ridiculous to abandon the generic *he*. "The same reasoning would go to prove that the *constitution* of the commonwealth does not extend to women— secures them no rights, no privileges; for it has no words in the feminine gender; it would prove that a great variety of crimes, made so by statute, could not be committed by women, because the statutes had used only the words *him* and *his*. . . . Cannot a *feme-covert* levy war and conspire to levy war? She certainly can commit treason." Davis had no doubt that a *feme covert* could withdraw herself from the state into part of the British dominions. The absentee act's special provision to protect dower rights of wives who did *not* accompany their husbands into exile showed that *femes covert* could make political decisions. Wives could choose to stay with the rebels; if they did, the rebel government would treat their husbands as dead and act to protect their dowries. If they went off with their husbands, that too was a political choice, and the rebel state owed them nothing. A wife's implicit claim on a portion of her husband's property was nullified by absenteeism, and the claims were confiscated along with the property.

Davis went further. He argued (and it was a view that flew in the face of English tradition) that "where the husband has abjured the realm, the relation is dissolved between the husband and wife." William Martin had abjured the realm and forfeited his property, which then passed to Anna Martin. But she too had abjured the realm, "which is in itself treason; which a *feme-covert* can certainly commit, and by which she forfeits her estate." If Anna Martin had forfeited her estate, there was nothing left for her son to claim.

Davis was undercutting coverture. The politicized woman did have "a will of her own" for which she was responsible and for which she could be punished. The implications of Davis's argument pushed Parsons into spelling out the political implications of coverture as clearly as they would ever be spelled out in post-Revolutionary America. "The real question is," said Parsons, "whether the statute was intended to include persons who have, by law, no wills of their own. The statute extends to persons who have *freely* renounced their relation to the state. Infants, insane, *femes-covert*, all of whom the law considers as having no will, cannot act *freely*. Can they freely renounce? The statute meant such, and such only as could." Then in a series of rhetorical questions, the answers to which he thought his audience would find obvious, Parsons returned to the crucial issue of the duties the state owed to women and women owed to the state. "Is the state entitled to the *personal* services of a *feme-covert* to defend it in war? Can she render any? What aid and comfort can she give to an invading enemy? Had she control of property? Is she ever required to take the oath of allegiance?"[27]

Federalist judges upheld the Federalist lawyer. Each of the four judges offered an opinion, but the longest and most carefully drawn was Theodore Sedgwick's, the conservative whig who had become a pillar of the right wing of the Federalist party.[28] There was only a single substantive issue, Sedgwick thought, and that was whether the forfeiture of land for levying war against the United States and adhering to the king of Great Britain had properly been charged against both husband and wife. Granting that William Martin had been properly libeled and exiled, was his wife also attainted?

Sedgwick was unambivalent, and his words had important implications for the political theory of women and the state. He began from the standard common law assumption that married women were not guilty of "actions performed jointly by them [husband and wife], unless of the most heinous and aggravated nature." For example, a married woman was not charged with a theft committed with her husband "because she is viewed in such a state of subjection, and so under the control of her husband, that she acts merely as his instrument." This subjection was implicit in the vow of obedience a woman took at marriage. "Can we believe that a wife, for so respecting the general understanding of her husband as to submit her own opinions to his, on a subject so all-important as this, should lose her own property, and forfeit the inheritance of her children? Was she to be considered as criminal because she permitted her husband to elect his own and her place of residence? Because she did not, in violation of her marriage vows, rebel against the will of her husband?"[29]

The last question was the crucial one. The Revolution had implicitly

---

27. *Martin v. Commonwealth*, 1 Mass. 368, 376, 370, 381, 383–393 (1805).

28. For Sedgwick, see Richard E. Welch, Jr., *Theodore Sedgwick, Federalist: A Political Portrait* (Middletown, Conn., 1965).

29. *Martin v. Commonwealth*, 1 Mass. 391–392 (1805). For a case in which a loyalist wife successfully demanded her dower in a confiscated estate, see *Esther Sewall v. Benjamin Lee*, Oct. 1809, in Dudley Atkins Tyng, ed., *Reports of Cases Argued and Determined in the Supreme Judicial Court of the Commonwealth of Massachusetts*, IX (Boston, 1853), 363–370. Now chief justice, Theophilus Parsons delivered the court's opinion in this suit brought by the widow of the colonial solicitor general, Jonathan Sewall. She had fled with her husband to New Brunswick, and his properties were rented out to Benjamin Lee. Parsons argued that the legislature had intended to preserve dower rights of loyalist wives: "It would

challenged all to rebel against familial rule. In a metaphorical sense, Americans had rebelled against father king and mother country. The son of a loyalist father was explicitly encouraged to rebel against his father's will. Thomas Paine had rested the most widely accepted ideological justification for the Revolution on the argument that it was natural for sons to shake loose from familial direction.

But even for republican ideologues, it remained unnatural for daughters to reject familial direction, unnatural for women to reject their husbands. Sedgwick was horrified at the thought that the Revolutionaries might be thought to have asked a woman to "rebel against the will of her husband." It was a "horrid alternative" to force women to choose between disobeying their husbands and losing their property. Sedgwick was certain that the Revolutionary legislatures had never intended as much, and that they had been willing to pay the small price of the loss of women's loyalty and support. Faced with a choice between encouraging a woman's support for the Revolution and her loyalty to a tory husband, even some Revolutionaries insisted that she choose loyalty to her husband. Faced with a choice between coverture and independence, the Revolutionary chose coverture. Even after the Revolution, the family circle remained a woman's state.

---

be a construction extremely hard to admit that the legislature intended to punish these offenders with greater severity than that with which traitors and felons are punished" (*ibid.*, 368).

Chapter 5

"DISABILITIES . . . INTENDED FOR HER PROTECTION": THE ANTI-REPUBLICAN IMPLICATIONS OF COVERTURE

I fear there is little reason for a compliment to
our laws for their respect and favour to the
female sex.

—St. George Tucker

Enoch G. Gridley after John Coles, Jr., *Pater Patriae* (1810). When Washington died, a static image of him became part of the political iconography of the Republic. He was Father of his country, an emblem of reliability in a revolutionary world where nothing seemed stable. He was often juxtaposed, as he is in this engraving, with Columbia and Minerva, who are less abstract and more vigorous.
Courtesy The Henry Francis du Pont Winterthur Museum.

COVERTURE, the common law tradition that interposed husbands between their wives and the civic community, held the attention of legislators and jurists after the war when allegiance was no longer a primary issue. Often justified as protective rather than restrictive in nature, this definition of the married woman's identity continued to shape American public law and private psychology, even while some of its more unfair consequences disappeared in the Republic. The protective interpretation of coverture derived from the belief that married women, lacking independent economic power and therefore also lacking the ability to make free and independent political judgments, were vulnerable to the influence of their husbands. A married woman, however free she might appear, could never be a fully independent "free dealer"; she was always subject to some degree of covert manipulation and open intimidation. For her own good, it was thought, she ought not be permitted to place herself in a situation in which her husband might take unfair advantage of her frailties. Moreover, community policy ought not be influenced by the votes of "unfree" persons. Both the constraining and the protective aspects of coverture retained their vitality in the early Republic, confirming the traditionally held assumptions of the role of women in the civic order and in the family.

Many specific legal limitations on women's behavior that had been part of the common law were weakened by the British system of equity jurisprudence. As Richard B. Morris showed in his path-breaking study of early American law, equity jurisprudence was widely available in the colonies and was often used by women to their advantage. Through equity procedures, wives *could* sue husbands, and judges were not bound by the rules of coverture.[1] Morris's claim of women's success in equity courts was extended by Mary Beard, who criticized nineteenth-century feminists for overstating their history of female subjugation. "Leaders [of the feminist movement] took Blackstone's metaphorical words about the civil death of the married woman . . . to heart and advertised it throughout the Western world," she complained. "Not content with attacking legal discriminations against women in detail," she argued, "they adopted

---

1. The best introduction to equity jurisprudence remains William S. Holdsworth, *A History of English Law* (London, 1903–[1966]), I, 395–468, V, 278–338. See also Richard B. Morris, *Studies in the History of Early American Law* (New York, 1930), chap. 4, and John Demos, *A Little Commonwealth: Family Life in Plymouth Colony* (New York, 1970), 82–99.

a myth and made a frontal assault on that."[2] But in her quest to defend women from the image of complete suppression, Mary Beard tended to discount the constraints of the common law in the early Republic and to exaggerate the advantages of equity jurisprudence.

It is certainly true that in America the law of "Baron and Feme" was interpreted flexibly and modified significantly. Some constraints on women, however, remained in force, for although common law was modified, it certainly was not killed. Nor was equity invariably the friend of women.

William Blackstone's *Commentaries on the Common Law*, published in 1771, continued to enjoy wide usage in the early Republic despite its famous arrogant paragraph on coverture: "Even the disabilities, which the wife lies under, are for the most part intended for her protection and benefit. So great a favourite is the female sex of the laws of England."[3] The distinguished Virginia jurist St. George Tucker, who protested that he was "not so much in love" with the common law "as to be inclined to leave it in possession of a glory which it may not justly deserve," was still willing to annotate and reprint Blackstone's work in 1803, increasing its circulation and its reputation. As Tucker worked his way through the chapter on the law of Husband and Wife, he found himself complaining of occasions when women were improperly treated under American law. One injustice he found particularly distasteful was that the most effective claim for damages for rape was the legal fiction that a daughter was her father's "servant, and that by the consequences of the seduction, he is deprived of the benefit of her labour."[4] A more general problem, Tucker wrote, was that women experience "taxation without representation; for they pay taxes without having the liberty of voting for representatives." These and other provisions of English law were unchanged by the great wave of American constitution making that accompanied the Revolution. "I fear," Tucker concluded, "there is little reason for a compliment to our laws for their respect and favour to the female sex."[5]

2. Mary R. Beard, *Women as Force in History* (New York, 1946), 114–115.

3. St. George Tucker, ed., *Blackstone's Commentaries: with Notes of Reference, to the Constitution and Laws, of the Federal Government of the United States; and of the Commonwealth of Virginia*, II (Philadelphia, 1803), 445.

4. *Ibid.* Although it is usually assumed that these grounds were not argued in America, see *Samuel Mott v. Calvin Goddard*, Sept. 1792, Connecticut Superior Court Records, New London District, Record Book 25, Conn. State Lib., Hartford. The victim of rape is described as "the plaintiff's daughter and servant"; by being made pregnant, she had been rendered "unfit for service."

5. Tucker, ed., *Blackstone's Commentaries*, II, 45.

Coverture could be, and often was, outwitted by women who had property to protect and a fair degree of legal foresight. It was possible, for example, for a woman to settle a prenuptial contract that specified the property that she brought into the marriage and set constraints on its use and alienation by the future husband.[6] A prenuptial contract was a settlement in equity, rather than in law, upheld in a court without a jury. The system of equity jurisprudence offered courts willing to entertain those suits that common law courts could not, including lawsuits by wife against husband for the enforcement of a prenuptial contract. And yet despite equity courts' flexibility, they tended to construe these contracts quite narrowly. The argument of the defense in a South Carolina equity case of 1791 reveals the ideological implications of prenuptial contracts and the dangers thought to arise from considerable limitations on the husband's control of the wife's property: "Marriage settlements are . . . deviations from the fixed laws of the land, and should not be carried to extremes. They will become dangerous instruments of domestic unhappiness. . . . The separation of interests between husband and wife, produced by marriage settlements, is calculated to produce many mischiefs, discords, loose morals and other ill effects. It relaxes the great bond of family union, and should not be favoured."[7] The implication is that coverture, or more specifically the power of the husband over his wife's property, is "the great bond of family union."

Marriage settlements were most likely to be challenged in court after a husband's death, by the husband's creditor who wished full repayment of debts or by the widow who wished to retain the property that had been settled on her. The courts were biased toward creditors and against debtors. As the South Carolina equity court openly admitted, "That creditors ought to be and are always favoured in this court there can be no doubt."[8] Even carefully drawn deeds of gift might not be enough to secure a widow's property. Mary Haig's father had made a gift of several slaves "to the only use and behoof of my said daughter, her heirs and assigns," but the South Carolina equity court ruled in 1793 that "this being a direct gift of personal property to the wife, the legal estate im-

---

6. The parties to a prenuptial contract normally included adult male relatives of the woman, who were in effect authorizing her to bring family property into her married state and therefore ensuring that the property would remain in the family.

7. *Winifred Wilson v. John Wilson*, Aug. 1791, in Henry William DeSaussure, *Reports of Cases Argued and Determined in the Court of Chancery of the State of South Carolina, from the Revolution, to [June 1817]*, rev. ed. (Philadelphia, 1854), II, 232, 234, hereafter cited as *S.C. Equity Reports*.

8. *Lennox and Wife v. W. H. Gibbes*, June 1792, *ibid.*, I, 305.

mediately vested in her husband, and the marital rights attached absolutely," despite the phrase "to the only use."[9] The only safe method for securing a married woman's independent property was a trusteeship, in which the property at issue was vested not in the married woman but in a male adult other than her husband who could safeguard the property from seizure for the husband's debts. It followed that marriage settlements had to be drawn with the utmost care and with an expertise available only to the well-to-do or the legally sophisticated.[10]

Coverture had unexpected practical implications. The law of vagrancy, for example, was shaped by the custom of coverture to the woman's disadvantage. The willingness of towns and counties to provide for legal residents incapable of supporting themselves was accompanied by an extraordinary caution about entertaining poor strangers, a skepticism of vagrants, and an insistence that each person establish clearly his or her right to legal settlement. The careful and explicit enforcement of the law of settlement had direct implications for married women, whose right to settlement in a town (and whose implicit claim, therefore, on town charity) was far more vulnerable than the right of men.

In Connecticut, for example, even a person born in the state might be considered alien to a particular town, and the only ways to "gain a legal settlement" were "by vote of the inhabitants, by consent of the civil authority and selectmen, by being appointed to and executing some public office, or by acquiring in his own right in fee, real estate to the value of thirty pounds." A married woman could have no settlement separate from her husband—"her settlement is suspended during coverture"— nor could a husband claim a right of settlement from his wife: "If a woman marries a man who has a settlement in any other of the United States, she shall follow the settlement of her husband, tho she has never been there."[11] Nor could she, if she became destitute elsewhere, return to the town of her birth and throw herself on the town's charity: "If she be reduced to want during the continuance of her husband with her, she cannot be sent to the place of her settlement because as it is not the settlement, of her husband, he cannot be sent with her, and the law will

---

9. *Mary Haig* v. *Executors of Dr. George Haig*, June 1793, *ibid.*, II, 348.

10. Chancellor James Kent would comment that settling property on daughters through trustees meant "that half the property of England was vested in nominal owners, and it had become difficult to ascertain whether third persons were safe in dealing for fiduciary property with its trustee" (*Commentaries on American Law*, II [New York, 1827], Pt. iv, lecture 28, 148).

11. Swift, *System of Laws of Conn.*, I, 168–169.

not admit the separation of husband and wife. They must both be considered as vagrants wherever they are."[12] Only if the destitute husband were a foreigner, *and* he died or deserted her, might she return to her original residence and claim the right of settlement there for herself and her children. In short, the Connecticut rules of settlement severely limited a poor woman's freedom to travel if she seemed a potential burden on public charity (regardless of whether she actually sought relief). The constraint was more severe than the restraint on the rights of impoverished men.

Normally a married woman could not make a will; in part that was because she usually did not have property in her own name to convey. If she had made a prenuptial agreement, she might have retained property that she could convey in her lifetime, after separate examination before a magistrate. But a will she could not make according to the law of coverture. This constraint, too, was justified as a protective measure. "Exposed as they are," the Connecticut judge Oliver Ellsworth wrote of married women, "to coercions imperceptible to others, and dangerous for them to disclose—placed in the power of a husband, whose solicitations they cannot resist, and whose commands, in all things lawful, it is their duty to obey. Their wills, taken in a corner, and concealed from the world till they have left it, can afford but very uncertain evidence of the real wishes of their hearts."

Ellsworth's comments ended with an evaluation of a woman's "political" role in family government, a summary that clarified the normative assumptions about family life and the value of a woman's contributions that had shaped his opinion. Wills were instituted, he said, because they aid in the maintenance of orderly family relationships. But a woman's will could not have this effect, "because the government is not placed in her hands." Nor could a woman justify her will's "utility in stimulating to industry and economy; for her exertion adds nothing to the stock she

---

12. *Ibid.*, 169–170. If the dying or deserting husband had a settlement in any town elsewhere, the wife was required to throw herself on the charity of that town; she had no right to return to her original home. See *Willson et al.* v. *Hinkley et al.*, Nov. 1787, in Ephraim Kirby, ed., *Reports of Cases Adjudged in the Superior Court of the State of Connecticut . . .* (Litchfield, Conn., 1789), 199–202, an argument between two towns over the support of an Indian woman, Amy Caesar, and her two children. She had lived in Tolland until she was 22, thus gaining a legal settlement; she then married Timothy Caesar, an Indian servant in Coventry. After 18 months Caesar left Amy and her children, who sought relief. Coventry held that because the Caesars had been slaves, Amy had not gained residence as a *feme covert* and was not entitled to support. She then returned to her hometown of Tolland, which said she had lost her right of inhabitancy when she married and sent her back to Coventry. The court upheld Tolland's action and recognized the Caesars as servants, not slaves.

is to dispose of." Assuming that women contributed nothing to the family estate, Ellsworth concluded that extending the power to make wills to married women would only have the unfortunate effect of generating "endless teasing and family discord." A generation later, in 1827, the distinguished Chancellor James Kent restated the point in his *Commentaries on American Law*: the more the courts allow a married woman to operate as a *feme sole* in regard to her own property, the more they "unfortunately withdraw from the wife those checks that were intended to preserve her more entirely from that secret and insensible, but powerful marital influence, which might be exerted unduly, and yet in a manner to baffle all inquiry and detection."[13]

Although a husband gained direct control over his wife's personal property at marriage, he assumed the status of "tenant by courtesy" over her real estate only after the birth of a child. He then could rent out those lands, cut timber on them, and otherwise use them, but he could not alienate them. Thus one effect of coverture was to freeze possession of the lands that a woman brought into marriage until they could be passed to her heirs. This element of coverture operated most directly to keep women's property outside the normal operations of the market economy. It was also the device most easily justified in terms of its protective function. And so it may not be surprising that it was one of the earliest elements to be dissolved.

The practice of treating the husband as tenant by courtesy was better suited to a precapitalist, minimally speculative economy than to an America in which land speculation was a major source of economic mobility. The need for liquidity meant that the frozen nature of "covered" property could become a severe economic burden on families; it was easily conceivable that wives as well as husbands might wish to alienate their lands and so enjoy the immediate profits from them. On the other hand, if it were possible for women to alienate their property, the private pressures to which Ellsworth had alluded might well become intolerable.

13. *Adams* v. *Kellogg*, Nov. 1786, in Kirby, ed., *Cases in Superior Court of Conn.*, 195–198, 442–443. Judge Ellsworth used *Adams* v. *Kellogg* as an opportunity to comment on the continuing function of coverture in the Republic. He granted that the statute dealing with wills had not specifically included *femes covert*, but maintained that the category "otherwise legally incapable" included married women. "We have no statute," Ellsworth wrote, "to divest a feme covert of her personal estate; and yet nobody doubts but, by the act or condition of coverture, it becomes the husband's. nor have we any that she shall not contract and bind her person and estate, as a feme-sole may; yet she cannot do it" (*ibid.*, 438). Kent, *Commentaries on American Law*, II, 139.

Colonial statutes provided that husband and wife might sell the woman's property *if* she gave her separate consent to a deed of sale, which she signed alone before a judge. This private examination and signing procedure was supposed to offer some protection against duress, but it could not have offered much since the woman returned to coverture and to face her husband. She could not very well say that she was selling property against her will without putting her own security at risk.[14]

The practice of separate examination could easily drift into informality. When Elizabeth Drinker was needed to swear that she acted freely in divesting herself of property in 1795, the justice of the peace came to visit her at home—that is, the swearing took place on her husband's property, not on neutral ground.[15] In Pennsylvania the process came to be treated so informally that the separate deeds signed by married women might not even be registered. In 1764, for example, one claimant sought to overturn a deed signed by a *feme covert* by arguing that although she may have consented and signed separately, a formal writ had never been sworn out specifying that she had done so. Both the lower court and the Pennsylvania Supreme Court, to which the case was appealed, defended the informality. "For fifty years and upwards, it had been the constant practice and usage," argued the defense, "in cases where *baron* and *feme* have been desirous to settle, sell and dispose of the estate of the *feme*, for the *baron* and *feme* to join in a deed . . . and for the *feme* to go before some justice of the peace, in the county where the lands lie, out of court, and for the said justice to examine such *feme* in private and apart from her husband, respecting her signing and executing such deed, . . . with her full and free consent. . . . a great number of titles to valuable estates in this province, were held under, and did depend upon deeds executed by *baron* and *feme*, in the manner aforesaid. . . . the titles to such estates had never . . . been called in question."[16] Three years later the state supreme court reaffirmed its decision, claiming that to do otherwise would be "dangerous" because it could "impeach" a great number of estates held under informally arranged deeds.[17]

14. See *The Public Statute Laws of the State of Connecticut* (Hartford, Conn., 1808), 444–445, and Swift, *System of Laws of Conn.*, I, 195–196.

15. See Diary of Elizabeth Drinker, May 30, 1795, July 16, 1795, Aug. 1, 1795, Hist. Soc. Pa.

16. *Hugh Davey et ux.* v. *Peter Turner*, 1 Dallas (Pa.) 11–13 (1764).

17. *Lessee of Thomas Lloyd* v. *Abraham Taylor, ibid.*, 17 (1767). Separate examination occasionally slipped out of usage entirely. James Kent reported that in colonial New York it was not the custom to give separate examination to wives who wished to convey their lands (*Commentaries on American Law* [1854 ed.], II, Pt. iv, lecture 28, 135). Kent also reported

Another apparently protective device afforded by common law had been the assumption that the dower—the widow's life possession of one-third of her husband's real estate—was a primary right. It was not easily questioned—as we have seen, it was protected even in the face of treason. The widow's third was to be defined promptly and set off from the estate before other claims on the property were met. For example, a seventeenth-century Connecticut statute provided that a widow might complain to the judge of probate if she had not been allotted her share within sixty days of her husband's death.[18]

After the Revolution, however, courts and legislatures moved to free women's dower claims from their traditional protections. The North Carolina legislature was most explicit, framing its 1784 act in frankly political terms. In an effort "to promote that equality of property which is of the spirit and principle of a genuine republic," the North Carolina legislators intended to simplify the descent of real estate and to do away with entail. Their new law did not abolish dower, but it did encroach on the heretofore sacred "widow's thirds." If there were more than two children to inherit, the widow was to "share equally with all the children, she being entitled to a child's part."[19]

By including revision of dower rights in the general statute that revised the whole system of descents, the legislature placed the entire concept of dower in an unfamiliar context—and in jeopardy. Within ten years the dower law was challenged in the case of *Susannah Winstead v. The Heirs and Terretenants of Richard Winstead, deceased.* A few days before Richard Winstead's death, the county sheriff had levied an execution upon Winstead's land and had sold it to settle a lawsuit. Winstead's widow, Susannah, later contended that she was entitled to her share in that property. However, Judge John Haywood's decision in 1795 denied her dower rights on the strength of the new law.

---

that a similar custom prevailed informally in Massachusetts, citing Judge Trowbridge in the *American Jurist* #27 to the effect that joint deeds without separate examination of the wife could be upheld (*ibid.*, 136).

18. "An Act Concerning the Dowry of Widows," in *Pub. Laws of Conn.*, 239–240. For South Carolina's attempts in 1777 and 1778 to hasten the process of allocating the widow's share, see Cooper, ed., *S.C. Statutes*, IV, 385–386, 742–743.

19. "An act to regulate the descent of real estates . . . ," 1784, in Potter *et al.*, eds., *Laws of N.C.*, I, chap. 204, 470. In the next paragraph the drafters provided that estates were to be equally divided among sons, and go to daughters only "for want of sons." Not until 1795 was the statute rephrased to include daughters in the first division of property (*ibid.*, chap. 435, 780).

It was a principal object of this act to take off all restraints from the alienation of lands, to the end that this species of property might be accommodated to the purposes of individuals engaging in useful undertakings, and to the principles of a Republican government. This act destroys estates tail entirely, and in order to enable husbands to convey their lands, free from the incumbrances of the wife's claim of dower, it directs that this claim shall commence for the future, from the death of the husband . . . which plainly discovers the meaning of the Legislature to be, that with respect to fair conveyances, she was not entitled to dower—which point at once proves and establishes the doctrine, that dower at the common law is abolished; for by the common law, the widow was entitled to dower in all the lands the husband sold after the coverture; whereas now, she cannot claim dower in them if fairly sold.[20]

Other states were not as explicit as North Carolina, and the common law rule on dower rights seemed to prevail. But as Morton Horwitz has explained, that protection was increasingly eroded by court decisions. Many difficult questions brought dower cases before the courts: Was a widow entitled to one-third of the land held by her husband at any time during coverture or at the moment of his death? How could land values be measured precisely in a speculative market? How could improvements on land be evaluated? In *Conner v. Shepherd* the Supreme Judicial Court of Massachusetts denied a widow dower in unimproved lands and maintained that the right of dower "would operate as a clog, upon estates, designed to be the subject of transfer." "The conclusion seems inescapable," Horwitz argues, "that [Judge Isaac] Parker's central purpose . . . was to undermine the right of dower itself." Other state courts also moved to rid themselves of this hindrance to easy transfer and liquidity of estates; New York and Pennsylvania courts ruled that widows might not enjoy the advantages of gains in land prices or of improvements on land.[21]

The erosion of dower rights was the most important legal development directly affecting the women of the early Republic. That it occurred

20. *Susannah Winstead* v. *The Heirs and Terretenants of Richard Winstead, deceased,* Oct. 1795, in John Haywood, *Reports of Cases Adjudged in the Superior Courts of Law and Equity of the State of North-Carolina, From the Year 1789, to the Year 1798,* I (Halifax, N.C., 1799), 281.

21. Morton J. Horwitz, *The Transformation of American Law, 1780–1860* (Cambridge, Mass., 1977), 56–58. A study of dower is being written by Joan Hoff Wilson.

at all was masked both from contemporaries and from subsequent observers who assumed that the interests of husband and wife were always coterminous. This notion seemed to cover even occasions when alienation of land by the husband diminished the wife's dower. Cases that specifically argued the demise of dower, like *Winstead* v. *Winstead*, were rare and generally ignored.

In England there was a well-established tradition of respecting a married woman's commercial responsibility. In some American localities, especially commercial centers like New York, Nantucket, and Charleston, the English borough tradition of married female traders acting as though they were *femes sole* was secure, although it was necessary for husbands to recognize their wives' independent trading capacity.[22] In 1795 the South Carolina equity court ruled that a married woman, Ann Robertson, had in fact maintained *feme sole* status throughout her life and had in the process acquired property that her mother, as the sole heir of a childless marriage, was able to claim as an inheritance. Henry De-Saussure's account of this case provides a useful explanation of how *feme sole* status might be proved.

> John Robertson and Ann his wife lived together many years in Charleston. He carried on business, and acquired real and personal property, for which he took the titles and bills of sale in his own name. His wife also carried on a separate business, bought and sold property in her own name, and took the titles to the real estate, and the bills of sale for the personal estate, in her own name. There was no deed from the husband formally constituting the wife a sole dealer, nor any writing agreeing that the acquisitions of her industry should be her own separate property. But there was ample proof that she acted with her husband's privity, acquiescence and verbal permission; and she always claimed the property acquired by her as her own. Some of the witnesses proved he acquiesced merely for peace sake, as she was of a violent temper.

South Carolina courts consistently maintained that *feme sole* status could be granted implicitly by a husband's public acceptance of his wife's activities as a sole dealer. It was necessary to prove only that a husband

---

22. See Richard B. Morris, ed., *Select Cases of the Mayor's Court of New York City* (Washington, D.C., 1935), 21–26, and *S.C. Equity Reports*, I, 445–449.

had known of her activities and had done nothing to stop them. At the Robertson trial, the court pointed out that "there is no law here defining what is a sole dealer, and how a *feme covert* can be made a sole trader; nor is there in England. The custom of London authorizes it: and a clause in our attachment act recognizes the right in this country."[23] Three years later the South Carolina Superior Court upheld a creditor's claim against another *feme sole*, agreeing with the counsel for the plaintiff "that to suffer her at this day, to screen herself from responsibility, under the plea of coverture, when it was notoriously known that the husband was not worth a shilling, would in fact be enabling her to swindle the plaintiff out of the amount of the goods shipped to her." In this case Judge Elihu Hall Bay referred both to the laws of South Carolina and to the custom of London.[24]

If a husband were present, one could assume that he had consented to his wife's activities as a *feme sole*. The disruptions of the Revolution, however, and the resulting dislocations of families meant that deserted women might not be able to prove their husbands' consent to their trading activities. Shortly after the Revolution, Massachusetts passed a statute that made it easier for married women to act as sole dealers. "Whereas it sometimes happens, that husbands absent themselves from this Commonwealth, and abandon their wives, not making sufficient provision for their support, who may be thereby reduced to great distress, not being able to make any valid contracts or dispose of any estate of their own," the justices of the Supreme Judicial Court were authorized to

---

23. *Catharine McGrath v. Administrators of John Robertson and Ann Robertson*, Mar. 1795, in *S.C. Equity Reports*, 445–446, 448. The court rejected Charles Cotesworth Pinckney's argument for the defense that "acquisitions made by the wife enure to the husband. . . . she . . . must be considered a trustee for the husband." The court was satisfied with the evidence that John Robertson knew of his wife's activity and did not stop it: "The husband would sometimes caution her against bidding too much for property at auctions, but she repelled his interference, and said the money was her own, and she would do as she pleased with it; to which he replied that was no reason she should ruin herself" (*ibid.*, 446). The only question the court found difficult to decide was which property was hers and which her husband's.

24. *Newbiggin v. Pillans and Wife*, 1798, in Bay, *Cases in S.-C. Sup. Courts*, II, 163–165; *Martha Surtell v. Williams Brailford, ibid.*, 333–338. In the first case, the plaintiff's main concern was that "she had been very successful in trade, and had made a great deal of money; while, on the other hand, her husband had . . . made nothing; so that a verdict against him would have been of no use to her creditors, as he had nothing to pay them with" (*ibid.*, 163). This concern would be used to support married women's property acts later in the century. See Lawrence M. Friedman, *A History of American Law* (New York, 1973), 184–186.

license the sale of real estate by a married woman "in such cases where any married man has heretofore, or may hereafter absent himself from this Commonwealth . . . as if she was sole and unmarried."[25]

In most states a determined married woman had to petition for *feme sole* status by means of a private bill in the legislature, setting out the particulars of the transactions she wished to make. The grounds for such an application were usually that the husband had been absent for an extended period of time, or that he was ill in body or mind and therefore incompetent to manage the family's affairs. A revealing example of such a petition is one submitted to the Connecticut legislature in 1790 by Sarah Woodworth of East Windsor. She wanted the power to sell twenty-six acres of land and a small house "which was the Property of said Sarah before her Intermarriage." In order to get that permission, she first had to certify that her husband had "for a number of Years . . . been deprived of his reason" and remained "in a State of Insanity and wholly incapable to make any Provision for his Family," that she depended "on her own Industry and her Friends" for the support of the family, but that she had reached the point of desperation, "incapable to support herself & Children any Longer." The petition is a limited one. The assembly did grant her permission to sell her real estate as though she were a *feme sole*, but the permission covered only that single transaction. If she wished to engage in commerce again, she would need a subsequent grant. Another request came from Violet Pease, whose husband had abandoned her eight years before in order to live with another woman by whom he had several children: "Lately she has a small real Estate fallen to her by Descent which for the better support of herself & Family she wishes to Sell and give a good Title to but by reason of Coverture is unable." The legislature agreed that she might sell and convey her lands "in the same manner as if she was a *Feme Sole* . . . her Coverture notwithstanding."[26]

These bills for *feme sole* status seem rarely to have been contested, but

25. "An act authorizing the Justices of the Supreme Judicial Court to license the Sale of Real Estate by Married Women in certain Cases," Nov. 21, 1787, in *The Perpetual Laws of the Commonwealth of Massachusetts*, I (Boston, 1801), 404–405.

26. May 1792, *Conn. State Recs.*, VII, 412. Sarah Woodworth was petitioning for property she had brought into her marriage. Naomi Richards petitioned for the right to sell lands that she herself had held in fee simple before her marriage. Normally, this property could have been sold if she had submitted to separate examination before a judge; since her husband, Benjamin, was incapable of managing his affairs, she needed special permission to act alone. The assembly allowed that "such Conveyance . . . shall have all the effect and Authenticity that a Conveyance by the said Benjamin and Naomi would have had if said Benjamin were not insane" (Oct. 1791, *ibid.*, 344).

that lack of contest in Connecticut did not mean that the state was willing to abandon formal procedure, as Elizabeth White of Stafford discovered. Mrs. White's husband, William, had "for a long time been absent from his Family" when she complained to a Hartford justice of the peace that on the night of June 17, 1770, several of their sheep had been mutilated, killed, or driven away. She "vehemently" suspected that Nathaniel and Lucy Butler were guilty, and she brought her complaint because she thought herself to be "the Natural head of the said William White his Family and Interest During his the sd White's absence, and his the said Williams Natural Representative."

The Butlers did not deny outright that they had mutilated the sheep. But they did demand that the proceedings be "quashed . . . because . . . the Matters Complained of" were only a "Trespass for which Lucy being a *Feme Covert* cannot be liable," and more significantly, because Elizabeth, "being also a *Feme Covert*," had no "right by the rules of Law to bring forward an Action or Complaint either Civil or Criminal for anything done to the Person or Property of her husband." Justice Daniel Alden upheld Mrs. White: he granted her the £1 damages she had demanded and set £1 10s. 11d. court costs. He was so sure of his judgment that he denied appeal to the Connecticut Superior Court and insisted that the judgment be executed immediately. But the Butlers believed that Alden had "mistook the Law" and appealed to the Superior Court, which agreed with them. It ruled that Alden had been in "manifest error" when he assumed that a *feme covert* could sue on her own behalf in her husband's interest and thereby implicitly denied Elizabeth White's claim to being the "Natural head" of the family in her husband's absence.[27]

Courts seem to have insisted—as the Connecticut Superior Court had done—on maintaining a clear line between the status of *feme sole* and *feme covert* and were skeptical of those who wished to dismantle the barrier. There is of course no way of discovering how many women were inhibited by their lack of political sophistication or of legal advice from applying to the legislature for special permission. Because *feme sole* sta-

27. *Nathaniel and Lucy Butler v. Elizabeth White*, Mar. 1771, Conn. Sup. Ct. Recs., Hartford District, Rec. Bk. 17, and Connecticut Superior Court File Papers, Hartford District, Record Group 3, Box 96, Conn. State Lib., Hartford, hereafter cited as Conn. Sup. Ct. File Papers, Hartford Dist. It was prohibitively expensive to use the services of the Connecticut court system. White had asked for, and received, £1 10s. 11d. costs. When the case went to the Superior Court, the Butlers were awarded the damages and repayment of the lower court costs (£2 10s. 11d.) plus an additional £1 10s. 11d. for the Superior Court costs, and another 6s. 6d. in fees, leaving a total of £4 8s. 4d. that White apparently paid in Mar. 1771—more than four times her original suit.

tus was itself a legal gray area—in some places assumed to be satisfactorily established by custom, in others not—some women may well have *thought* they could act as sole dealers and may have applied for such status only after their right to it had been questioned. Northern courts could be very strict on the subject. Even a woman who had been granted a divorce on the grounds of desertion was regarded as under coverture during the time of the desertion, and was therefore unable to carry on a business or to collect her debts without special permission. Thus Mercy Honey, of Ridgefield, Connecticut, who was granted a divorce in 1792 from a husband who had deserted her eight years before, needed to petition for the right to "collect all Debts due her from any Person . . . for her Labour . . . in the same manner as she might have done by due Process in Law had she remained . . . a Single and unmarried Woman."[28] In 1805, John Cullins was accused of stealing ninety-eight handkerchiefs, but the Commonwealth of Massachusetts was not absolutely sure whether he should be charged with stealing them from Walter Healey, who had been last heard from in the East Indies six or seven years before, or from Healey's wife, Hannah, who had "for several years past . . . been in trade, and carried on business as a *feme sole.*" Mrs. Healey's attorney argued that it would be convenient if Cullins could be convicted of theft from her, because Cullins could then be required to restore the value of the goods stolen, and Mrs. Healey could make use of his work. But the Massachusetts Supreme Judicial Court ruled that since she had never specifically applied for or been granted *feme sole* status, she was still to be treated as though under coverture. She was still William Healey's wife, and the handkerchiefs were William Healey's property. Cullins was guilty on the second count of the indictment and was required to return the stolen property (or its equivalent) to the estate of the absent Healey, not to the wronged wife.[29]

Coverture was based on the assumption that married women had

28. Oct. 1792, *Conn. State Recs.*, VII, 532. In South Carolina, the equity court made it clear that debts owed to a man could not be paid to his wife without his express consent.

29. *Commonwealth v. John Cullins*, 1805, in Ephraim Williams, ed., *Reports of Cases Argued and Determined in the Supreme Judicial Court of the Commonwealth of Massachusetts*, I (Boston, 1866), 116–117. Occasionally courts were sufficiently impressed by the possibility of error if they clung too closely to *feme covert* status. While Mary Jones's husband, Robert, was away, Elias Weld entered the Jones property and stole Mary's clothes. Weld did not deny the theft, but claimed that in a trespass case a wife could not recover damages for a trespass on her husband's property. But the court held for Mrs. Jones (*Mary Jones v. Elias Weld*, 1775, Conn. Sup. Ct. Recs., Hartford Dist., Rec. Bk. 18).

neither independent minds nor independent power. The ease with which this assumption could be transferred to single women implies that it drew its strength not only from technical legal definitions, but from an ancient Western political tradition that defined all women as politically and legally irresponsible. By inhibiting the independent manipulation of property, coverture reinforced political weakness and was used to justify other elements of the traditional legal system that did the same.

One of these features of the Anglo-American legal system had not changed since Anne Hutchinson had gazed out on her judges: the courtroom remained a male domain. The exclusion of women from formal legal training meant that women were absent from the courtroom as attorneys, judges, or clerks. Because women were not thought to be political beings, they did not serve on juries; their absence meant that accused women did not receive a trial before their peers. Women were present in the courtroom only as plaintiffs, defendants, or witnesses—as recipients, rather than dispensers, of justice.[30]

The effects of this exclusion are difficult to measure, but they are not on that account nonexistent. Would juries that did not include women be more or less sympathetic to women defendants? In cases in which women were defendants, or which had strong emotional overtones—the common murder charge of infanticide, for example—it seems reasonable to expect that the presence of women on juries might have made a difference in outcome.[31]

30. Occasionally a woman acted as an attorney, pleading her own case or that of a family member, but this rare practice waned as the legal process became more technical and professionalized. See Joseph H. Smith, ed., *Colonial Justice in Massachusetts (1639–1702): The Pynchon Court Record* (Cambridge, Mass., 1961), 259, and Linda L. Angle, "Women in the North Carolina Colonial Courts, 1670–1739" (M.A. thesis, University of North Carolina, 1975). Most female attorneys argued cases in the informal courts that justices of the peace held in their homes or in local taverns. One rare 18th-century example is *Nathaniel Saltonstall v. Ephraim Wheeler*, Oct. 27, 1748, New London (Conn.) Justice Court Records, Record Group 3, Box 565, Conn. State Lib., Hartford: "The plaintiff appeared by his attorney Ms. Lucretia Saltonstall & produced sd note." The defendant did not appear, and Saltonstall won the case.

31. The first American women to qualify for jury service were citizens of Utah in 1898, but service did not become generally available until after the 19th Amendment. It has been common for states to exclude women from jury venire lists unless they specifically request to be placed on them. Not until 1975 did the Supreme Court rule that such jury lists do not permit the election of a jury that represents a fair cross section of the community (*Taylor v. Louisiana*, 419 U.S. 522 [1975]). The majority decision quoted a 1946 opinion of Justice William O. Douglas in response to a claim that an all-male panel drawn from all groups in the community would be representative. "Who would claim that a jury was truly repre-

Another effect of exclusion can only be surmised, not measured. In a premodern agrarian society, where information was communicated primarily by conversation, the county courthouse functioned as the central transmitter of political and practical information. Men gathered on court days to exchange local news and to observe the proceedings in court. They learned from travelers and legislators what had happened in distant cities. News from the capital was announced from the courthouse steps. During the war loyalty oaths were administered by the court. The courthouse was, in effect, the physical locale in which public political education took place.

Women were absent from this political culture. They appeared on its fringes: as keepers of taverns in court towns, as sellers of merchandise at the markets held in courthouse squares. But they had relatively little share in the crucial political rituals by which men were emotionally aroused into patriotic unity of purpose and, ultimately, into resistance to England.[32]

The claim that coverture was effectively negated in the United States seems, in conclusion, overstated. Despite its incongruity with republican doctrine, coverture was not abolished quickly or coherently. Nor did proceedings in equity fully counterbalance the disadvantages of coverture. It is true that equity law had some special advantages for married women and offered devices by which some of the implications of coverture might be evaded. Its procedures were somewhat simpler than those of courts of law, and equity courts may well have been perceived as more accessible, less overwhelming, than courts of law. But equity law remained judge-made law, independent of legislative direction, conservative in tone and intent. The British jurist John Selden's words, written in the seventeenth century, retained their force: "Equity is a roguish thing. For law we have

sentative of the community if all men were intentionally and systematically excluded from the panel? The truth is that the two sexes are not fungible; a community made up exclusively of one is different from a community composed of both; the subtle interplay of influence one on the other is among the imponderables. . . . The exclusion of one may indeed make the jury less representative of the community than would be true if an economic or racial group were excluded" (Justice Douglas, *Ballard* v. *U.S.* 329 U.S. 193–194 [1946]).

32. See Rhys Isaac, "Dramatizing the Ideology of Revolution: Popular Mobilization in Virginia, 1774 to 1776," *WMQ*, 3d Ser., XXXIII (1976), 357–385. As tavern keepers, of course, women were not insignificant; it is relatively easy to identify substantial numbers of women who ran taverns and to identify some of these as "political places" where committees of safety carried on their business. But it is difficult to distinguish between the service role played by the tavern keeper and the active choice of entertaining these political groups.

a measure. . . . [But] equity is according to the conscience of him that is Chancellor, and as that is larger or narrower, so is equity. 'Tis . . . as if they should make the standard for the measure a Chancellor's foot."[33]

Equity eroded slowly and erratically during America's first half-century. Dower rights, for example, were encroached upon long before the Revolution, but not until the 1850s could married women's property legislation be called a trend. The first half-century of the Republic was a time when it became ever harder for married women to control their own property. These were years during which trusteeships became more complex and access to equity courts became more difficult. Women were included in the marketplace so far as they could serve that marketplace; it became easier, for example, to attach a married woman's property for her husband's debts. But it was the unusual legislator who understood the married woman's lack of civil capacity to be not only an accidental remnant of feudalism, but also a threatening contradiction to republicanism. Reform would not come until it was part of the codification movement of the 1830s and 1840s. The arguments for married women's property legislation eventually opened the way to the assertion of a feminist demand for republican rights.[34]

33. Holdsworth, *History of English Law*, I, 467–468.
34. This theme has been extensively and usefully explored in Peggy Rabkin, "The Origins of Law Reform: The Social Significance of the Nineteenth-Century Codification Movement and Its Contribution to the Passage of the Early Married Women's Property Acts," *Buffalo Law Review*, XXIV (1975), 683–760.

Chapter 6

"DOMESTIC LIBERTY":

FREEDOM TO DIVORCE

That since Marriage was instituted for the
purpose of promoting the happiness of individuals and the good of society . . . when . . .
the purposes for which marriage was instituted
then entirely faile . . . the good of Society no
less than the well-being of individuals requires
that it should be disolved and that the parties
should be free to form such other domestic
connections as may contribute to their felicity.

—John Christian Smith to the South Carolina
    legislature, requesting a divorce

Britania and Her Daughter. A Song (1780). The language of family relationships was often used for political description. Tom Paine had argued that it was the common sense of the matter that the colonies, like a son reaching maturity, should wish for independence. This British broadside made a similar argument on behalf of a female personification of the colonies: "I'm a Woman full grown,/ and long for to keep a good house of my own." But the daughter moves from her mother to another sort of dependence; impatient with her parent, she must seek out a man "for to live with him."
Courtesy The Library of Congress, Washington, D.C.

WOMEN PARTICIPATED LITTLE in political ritual because they were thought to lack political responsibility. This exclusion was based on the familiar belief that they could be expected to have personal commitments to their families, but none to the public world. Ironically, then, a woman turned to the agencies of government when her private world was shattered and when her family structure was broken down. The *feme covert*, the invisible, "covered" married woman, was uncovered—notorious even—when she was divorced.

Divorce is possible in a variety of political cultures, ranging from the totalitarian to the democratic; it is of course experienced by both men and women. But at least since John Milton's divorce tracts, written in the context of the English Civil War, theoretical justification for divorce has been weighted with political implication. Milton linked the right of divorce to the existence of free self-expression: "Asking myself whether I could in any way advance the cause of true and substantial liberty . . . I observed that there are, in all, three varieties of liberty without which civilized life is scarcely possible, namely ecclesiastical liberty, domestic or personal liberty, and civil liberty, and since I had written about the first, while I saw that the magistrates were vigourously attending to the third, I took as my province the remaining one."[1]

Did the right to pursue happiness give one the right to be free of an unhappy marriage? During the American Revolutionary era, divorce came to be defended as a republican right of particular interest to women, because it was sought by them more frequently than it was sought by men. Wives' testimony to why they wished to be divorced tells us a great deal about the texture of their lives.

The divorce experience can be studied only in selected localities. In South Carolina it simply did not exist as a legal option. Jurists there in the late nineteenth century boasted that not a single divorce of any sort was granted until 1868. In colonies like New York and Virginia, which closely followed the English practice, full divorce was an ecclesiastical affair and rarely permitted. Legislatures in those states might grant divorces, but these were in effect only separations that did not permit remarriage. Only in New England, where Puritan tradition regarded marriage as a civil contract—which, like other contracts, could be broken

---

1. John Milton, "Pro Populo Anglicano Defensio Secunda," in Don M. Wolfe, ed., *Complete Prose Works of John Milton* (New Haven, Conn., 1953–), IV, 624. See also Milton's more famous essay, "Doctrine and Discipline of Divorce," *ibid.*, II, 220–356, and Harvey Couch, "Milton as Prophet: The Divorce Tracts and Contemporary Divorce Laws," *Journal of Family Law*, XV (1977), 569–581.

under certain circumstances—were statutes providing for final divorce part of the legal code. Because divorce was not permissible in England except by way of rare private bills in Parliament, colonial divorce statutes were in fact contrary to the law of England, and the colony that passed such a law was always vulnerable to reprisal. (It does not appear that the crown took advantage of this vulnerability, perhaps because the same colony could usually be attacked more easily on the grounds of violating the mercantile laws.) In 1773, on the eve of the Revolution, the Privy Council disallowed a Pennsylvania divorce act and sent instructions to all colonial governors to withhold consent from any provincial bill of divorce. Freedom to regulate colonial marriages, like freedom to regulate colonial taxation, became a Revolutionary issue.

Even in New England, where civil divorce was available, there was a substantial degree of variation among the colonies' laws. Massachusetts was the first to have a divorce statute, but the practice of granting separations (divorce *a mensa et thoro*, from bed and board) continued along with that of dissolving marital relations. In Connecticut, however, separation was the exception rather than the rule, and the colony's—and state's—experience with divorce is well documented.[2]

The General Assembly of Connecticut sat, as Parliament did, as a court of equity as well as a legislative chamber; in its role as an equity court, it undertook to entertain petitions for bills of divorce. The earliest known Connecticut petition is "the sad complaint of Goody Beckwith, of Fairefield," who reported in 1655 that her husband had deserted her. The assembly ruled that if she would appear in person before the magistrates at their next sitting as a court at Stratford, and testify on her oath, the magistrates were empowered to give her a bill of divorce "and sett her free."[3] A divorce was granted in 1657 to Robert Wade of Seabrooke, whose wife had deserted him; in 1660 to Sarah North, whose husband had been gone nearly seven years; and in 1662 to Bridget Baxter "upon good consideration and solid reasons and evidenc," though we are not

2. Nancy Cott has argued persuasively that the pattern of Massachusetts divorce cases suggests increasing demands by women for independence and autonomy after the Revolution ("Divorce and the Changing Status of Women in Eighteenth-Century Massachusetts," *WMQ*, 3d Ser., XXXIII [1976], 586–614). This chapter draws extensively on the court and legislative records of Connecticut, where divorce was long handled as a relatively normal procedure. See Henry S. Cohn, "Connecticut's Divorce Mechanism: 1636–1969," *Am. Jour. Legal Hist.*, XLIV (1970), 35–54.

3. J. Hammond Trumbull and Charles J. Hoadly, eds., *The Public Records of the Colony of Connecticut . . .* (Hartford, Conn., 1850–1890), I, 275.

told what these reasons were.[4] Certainly they were among those listed in Connecticut's divorce statute:

> It is ordered by this Court that noe bill of divorce shall be granted to any man or women lawfully marryed but in case of adultery, fraudulent contract, or willful desertion for three years, with totall neglect of duty, or seven years providentiall absence being not heard of after due enquiry made and certifyed, such party shall be counted as legally dead to the other party; in all which cases a bill of divorce may be granted by the Court of Assistants to the agreived party who may then lawfully marry or be marryed to any other.[5]

The negative rhetoric in which the statute was phrased ("no bill . . . shall be granted" except in certain cases) masked the leniency of several new options unavailable elsewhere in the British Empire. Passage of the statute entailed some political risk; it was an act that directly disregarded the laws of England. Those who jealously guarded the Connecticut charter were careful not to bring this statute to the attention of the crown; and the crown, for its part, rather carefully did not notice. It is not fully clear why the Privy Council indulged in such studied ignorance. One possible explanation is that the divorce statute was only one of several other Connecticut laws contrary to the laws of England; if the administration wished to challenge the colony's assertion of legislative independence, stronger cases might be made on the grounds of other unusual statutes. In 1706 two Quakers did make formal protest to the Board of Trade against eleven statutes that seemed to them to be contrary to the laws of England, including the divorce law. The lawyer for the crown, Francis Fane, explicitly agreed that the divorce law violated England's law and practice, but let the matter ride.[6]

A reorganization of the judicial system in 1711 transferred jurisdiction over most divorce petitions to the Connecticut Superior Court. Cases not precisely fitting the statute, usually cases of severe cruelty or with com-

---

4. *Ibid.*, 301, 362, 379. Sarah North's divorce was granted on the condition that her husband stayed away the full seven years. See also the petition of Hannah Huitt for divorce on the grounds of desertion, *ibid.*, II, 129.

5. *Ibid.*, II, 328.

6. Charles M. Andrews, *Connecticut and the British Government* (New Haven, Conn., 1933), 30.

plicated property settlements, continued to come directly to the legislature by petition.[7] The Superior Court was the highest court in the colony, and the reputations and social standing of its justices were formidable. The court rode circuit, usually sitting two times a year in each county; as the eighteenth century wore on and the number of inhabitants and counties rose, the court's work load increased substantially.

The option to divorce was obviously one shared by both men and women. But the extent to which people availed themselves of this option varied not only with the degree of their dissatisfaction with marriage (which in turn was dependent on their expectations from marriage), but also with their willingness to approach the Superior Court and press their claim. Even the simplest case required at least a formal petition drawn up by a court clerk according to a prescribed mode, signed with a signature or mark, and accompanied by written evidence from a minister or a witness that the petitioner had in fact been married on the date claimed. Often supportive testimony was furnished. Whether or not one pressed a divorce petition depended in part on one's political sophistication and civic competence.

A careful reading of the court records and file papers submitted with the petitions (scattered for most districts, but nearly complete for the Hartford District) offers insight into the lives of some of the unhappiest families in eighteenth-century Connecticut. Even so small a sample reveals much about the economic and emotional expectations that women had of their marriages, the levels of literacy among those who sought divorce, and the absence of privacy in the household.

Throughout the eighteenth century, the typical Connecticut divorce petitioner was a woman whose husband had deserted her, usually leaving her economically troubled, if not desperate. Few petitioners specified that they wished to remarry, as the seventeenth-century petitioners had, but that is surely one implication of the constantly repeated phrase "that she

---

7. Swift, *System of Laws of Conn.*, I, 74. See also Cohn, "Connecticut's Divorce Mechanism," *Am. Jour. Legal Hist.*, XLIV (1970), 35–54. The General Assembly of Connecticut, like Parliament, originally sat as a court of equity, and well into the 19th century it retained some equity jurisdiction. The assembly might grant a divorce on the grounds of cruelty; in other states this option was not available. In New York, in the early 19th century, it was decided "that the *husband* cannot sustain a bill for divorce on the ground of cruel treatment nor for desertion . . . the terms of the statute embracing only the case of the wife, and the common law having given the husband sufficient power over her to protect himself." Henry St. George Tucker, *Commentaries on the Laws of Virginia, Comprising the Substance of a Course of Lectures Delivered to the Winchester Law School*, I (Winchester, Va., 1831), 104.

may be free of the obligations of the marriage covenant." Distances between separated couples were often great and seemed even greater; the farther away from Connecticut the deserting husband, the vaguer the place to which he went. If to New York or Massachusetts, the town is usually given, but the "Jersies" then seemed far enough away that specific locations are rarely known. Sailors often set out for the West Indies and were never heard from again; a divorce petition was an efficient way of declaring a lost sailor missing and presumed dead.[8]

Although divorce was primarily a "woman's request," as time went on men were more likely to present claims also. When a Connecticut man petitioned for divorce before the Revolution, it was likely to be on the grounds of his wife's adultery; almost three-quarters of eighteen men's petitions submitted in the colony in the five years before the war were on that basis (and others on closely related grounds like premarital pregnancy by another man or bigamy). For the same period, only a few of the sixty-eight petitioning women made adultery their prime complaint. Throughout the eighteenth century, women were most likely to complain of desertion; roughly 80 percent of the Connecticut women seeking divorce in the five years before the war reported deserting husbands. After the war, men, who had earlier rarely complained of deserting wives, were finding desertion a problem, and it became a common ground for divorce. Between 1789 and 1793, fourteen of the forty men's petitions report a deserting wife. Simultaneously, women began to complain of their husband's adultery; between 1736 and 1740, only two of the thirty-seven women's petitions mentioned a husband's adultery; between 1789 and 1793, twenty-five of eighty-eight women's petitions made adultery the primary complaint.

These shifts in complaints suggest changes in expectations of marital behavior and, perhaps, some changes in this behavior itself. They may well imply that wives were less willing than they had been to tolerate their husbands' adulterous behavior. Desertion by women implies a growing degree of physical mobility in postwar New England, though since virtually none of the petitions reveals where the wife went (other than naming the man with whom she might be living), it is not possible to generalize about the opportunities these women perceived for themselves outside of marriage. All one can say, and perhaps it is enough, is that after the war women were physically moving out of their unhappy households, an action that, judging from the divorce literature, had been rela-

8. The Massachusetts statute explicitly provided this option.

tively uncommon before the war. And women were prepared to demand divorce from disloyal husbands—again, a demand rarely made before the war.

Divorce records reveal not only the causes and frequency of divorces, but also something of the texture of life in eighteenth-century New England, the expectations people brought with them to marriage, and the disappointments they found. Divorce petitions can serve, for example, as a source for measuring the prevalence of sign literacy, the minimal ability to sign one's name. One may be impressed, on first perusal, by the large number of petitions endorsed with signatures. Of twenty-eight petitions between 1735 and 1745, only four are signed with marks, all by women. But careful examination often reveals that what appears to be a signature is in fact in the handwriting of the clerk who drew up the petition. That the petitioner did not write the whole document and then sign it is often made clear by the appearance of the same hand in other notes on the sheet, including the official notice to the county sheriff that he summon the accused spouse to the next sitting of the Superior Court. Whether a transcribed signature means that the clerk was in haste, or that he did not think the petitioner could write, or that the petitioner was illiterate, or, finally, that the petitioner was not present while the document was being transcribed, is difficult to know.

A case that suggests the problems in making a clear generalization in this matter is that of Anna Moody of Farmington, who applied in March 1744 for a divorce on the grounds that her husband was missing and presumed lost at sea. This petition has what appears to be her signature, but it is in the same hand as the text. One result of her case was that Ebenezer Moody's estate was inventoried and distributed to his heirs. The probate court records include Anna Moody's bond to execute her husband's estate; as administratrix, she signed with her mark. Contradictory evidence abounds. In 1768, Elisabeth Gillet of Windsor applied for a divorce from her husband, Benjamin; she submitted two different petitions, each by a different clerk, and each with what purported to be her signature, but in the hand of the clerk who drafted the document. When she came to write her will, in 1805, she signed her mark.[9]

Petitions from the Hartford District for the decade between 1766 and 1775 reflect growing literacy throughout the colony, specifically among women. Only two people signed with marks (both women), but the

9. Divorce petition of Anna Moody, Mar. 1744, Conn. Sup. Ct. File Papers, Hartford Dist., Conn. State Lib.; Divorce petition of Elisabeth Gillet, Aug. 10, 1768, *ibid.*

number of petitions apparently signed by the copyist is substantially decreased. Only twelve, or about a third, of the signatures are questionable; thirteen women, or nearly half the female petitioners in that decade, signed their petitions themselves. (All of the eight men were able to sign.) In general, a higher proportion of the applicants were able to sign their names. Moreover, fewer of the people who applied to the Superior Court for redress of marital grievances were involved with transients. This evidence might, of course, be taken to testify to an increase in educational levels and economic prosperity. But nothing we know about colonial society suggests that the numbers of poor and transient people were diminishing on the eve of the Revolution; in fact, the opposite seems true according to county court records noting increased construction of jails

Divorce petition of Elisabeth Gillet, August 10, 1768.
Courtesy Connecticut State Library, Hartford. Photograph by Gus Johnson.

and poorhouses.[10] It is probable that the class of people who felt it possible to petition the court was shifting, and the most desperate, who were always least inclined to approach the dignified and distinguished members of the bench, were even less inclined to go there as time went on.

Because the easiest way to prove adultery if the accused parties would not admit to it was to have a witness, divorce testimony provides some evidence of the small degree of physical privacy in the colonial household. Especially before the war it was not unusual for plaintiffs to provide corroborative evidence from someone present in the bedroom, and sometimes even in the bed, where the illicit sexual behavior took place. For example, when Sarah Fuller appeared before the Connecticut Superior Court in 1744 to "be Discharged from her marriage Bonds," the crucial testimony was provided by John Neland, who had gone with Fuller's husband, John, and Peninah Toole to Dutchess County, New York, where this couple attempted to persuade a local justice of the peace to marry them. The magistrate also took in lodgers; he hesitated to marry the two, but was unwilling to lose the profit of a night's bed and board and promised to "consider of it—till morning."

> Germond [the justice of the peace] sd they had but one bed and sd
> fuller and sd Peninah and the Deponent must Lodge together. . . .
> The Deponent then took a child—sd Peninah had whilst sd Fuller
> and sd Peninah undrest to go to bed. sd Fuller put of his cloathes
> to his shirt and breeches and sd Peninah pulled off her cloaths to
> her shift and very short petticoat near or quite to her knees then
> they both went to bed together and the Deponent Lay at sd Fuller
> back after some time sd fuller unbutoned his breeches the Deponent
> asked . . . why he did so he sd to scratch his belly. . . . the Deponent
> turning his had felt sd fuller's Buttocks naked. . . . sd fuller had
> Carnal knowledge of sd peninah by the beds quivering and other
> sensible signs.

The next morning, John Fuller and Peninah Toole presented themselves

---

10. See especially Kenneth Lockridge, "Land, Population and the Evolution of New England Society, 1630–1790; and an Afterthought," in Stanley N. Katz, ed., *Colonial America: Essays in Politics and Social Development* (Boston, 1971), 466–491; Gary B. Nash, "The Transformation of Urban Politics: 1700–1765," *Journal of American History*, LX (1973), 605–632; and Gary B. Nash, "Up From the Bottom in Franklin's Philadelphia," *Past and Present*, No. 77 (1977), 57–83.

before witnesses, but not the justice of the peace, and said marriage oaths to each other. Then presumably all four—Fuller, his new wife, her child, and Neland—went back to Sharon, Connecticut, to face the wrath of Sarah Fuller.[11]

The people who described their marriages to divorce courts left little doubt that marriage was, among other things, an economic relationship. Women were undeniably important to the family economy, and on rare occasions when they refused their services, their husbands were shocked and distressed. David Frisbie, begging for a divorce from his wife in 1783, asserted that he had "never . . . received from her any kind of aid or assistance in Supporting the Family of Children which he had by her."[12] Ezra Belding, petitioning for a divorce in 1788, complained that his wife had "wholly neglected all care of domestic affairs, and by every method in her Power endeavoured to waste & embezzle his Estate."[13]

Women often had a clear sense of the economic value they had brought to their marriages. When Elisabeth Gillet petitioned for a divorce in 1768, claiming desertion, neglect, and nonsupport, she added that "as she brot Considerable estate to the sd Benjn in marriage & she has had great fateague & has done much to pay the Debts and Save the Estate— [she pleads] that she may hold & be entituled to her thirds in the sd Benjamins Estate during her life sd divorce notwithstanding." But her divorce was not granted until she reapplied in 1772, when she said only that her husband had set out for North Carolina and had not been heard from since 1765. She then asked for liberty to marry again, saying nothing about property claims. This version of divorce in effect pronounced Benjamin Gillet dead and gave the petitioner a claim to a third of his estate as his widow.[14] Sarah Whitney announced that she would be only too happy to let her husband have the divorce he wished for—if she could be guar-

11. Divorce petition of Sarah Fuller, Aug. 27, 1744, Conn. Sup. Ct. File Papers, Hartford Dist.

12. Divorce petition of David Frisbie, Jan. 30, 1783, *ibid.* The Frisbie divorce was bitterly contested, resulting in a great deal of testimony by friends of both parties. David Frisbie's friends emphasized that his wife, Mary, had ignored, mistreated, neglected, and abused their youngest child, behavior that they obviously found unacceptable. Their testimony implied their strong expectation that a good marriage was an affectionate one. Deborah Morris of Branford, who had been their neighbor, testified that Mary "did Wickedly Neglect to take care of a young Sick Child of theirs," and that she had said she "wished she had her sd Husbands heart between two Stones, and She would pound it to pieces" (Deposition of Deborah Morris, Feb. 27, 1783, *ibid.*). Eight other people filed depositions.

13. Divorce petition of Ezra Belding of Wethersfield, Feb. 20, 1788, *ibid.*

14. Divorce petitions of Elisabeth Gillet, Aug. 10, 1768, Mar. 9, 1772, *ibid.*, and Mar. 6, 1770, Sept. 1772, Conn. Sup. Ct. Recs., Hartford Dist., Rec. Bk. 17, Conn. State Lib.; Will

anteed the property she had generated during the years of their marriage. Her husband, Asa, was a poor man when he married, but Sarah

> hath when in hea[l]th been always the Mistress of his house without assistance through a Course of large Business which he hath Carried on Employing many Workmen for the Whole Time since our Marriage untill he had Acquired an Estate of about 400.0.0 Lw [lawful] Money During which Time the said Sarah Lived a Laborious Life of Toyl & Business in the Interest of Said Asa with the greatest Chearfulness in hopes of Enjoying the Benefit of her Labour. . . . The said Asa hath Given and Secured to said Sarah forty Pound L^{ll} [lawful] Money for no other Purpose but to hire her not to appear before Your Honours in Defence of her Character that his Malicious story might be told without Contradiction which however was no Inducement to her to neglect the Defence of her honor and Chastity The True Inducement being only a Desire to be Released from a Cruel Yoke-Fellow who had her assistance in acquiring his Whole Estate and hath now stripped her of the Whole and Turned her out from his House Estate and Family to Suffer and Want. She . . . Relieth upon the Candour and Justice of this Honorable Court that when a Bill of Divorce is Granted to said Asa a Third Part at Least of his Estate will by your Honors be ordered and allotted to her for her Support During Life as by Law your Honors Can do not only as a Just Reward of her Labour in Acquiring the Same but as a Security that the Publick Should not be burthened with her Maintainence when there is a Sufficient Estate in the Hands of said Asa to which she is now Legally & Justly Intituled as being the fruits of her Labour.[15]

A husband's failure to support his wife economically—rarely mentioned in the prewar cases—was introduced into petitions filed during and after the war. This neglect was not statutory grounds for divorce, of course, but it was, apparently, persuasive evidence of effective desertion and may have added verisimilitude to the claim that an adulterer was ignoring his wife. Thus Huldah Archer, who accused her husband of

---

of Elisabeth Gillet, 1802, probated 1805, Granby, Conn., Probate Court Records, Conn. State Lib., Hartford.

15. Both Asa and Sarah Whitney petitioned for divorce in Mar. 1774; neither petition was granted. In Mar. 1775 Asa was granted a divorce on the grounds of adultery when his wife failed to appear (Conn. Sup. Ct. Recs., New London Dist., Rec. Bk. 18, and Conn. Sup. Ct. File Papers, New London Dist., Record Group 3, Conn. State Lib.).

spending his nights in the company of "lewd women," took care first to testify that Joseph Archer had "totally Abandoned the Petitioner and Deprived her of Considerable part of her Cloathing and all her Household Furniture, and has also totally Neglected to Support & Maintain the Petitioner." She wanted not only a divorce, but a declaration that her wearing apparel and household furniture "be restored to her" and that "such further proportion of the sd Josephs Personal Property be vested in the Petitioner as to your honours shall appear just and Reasonable as your honours by Law are Enabled to do."[16]

Temperance Northern was deserted by her husband after twenty-two years of marriage in 1770; twelve years later she finally petitioned for divorce, complaining that Timothy had spent all of their estate "in drinking and debauchery." Elizabeth Foster provided testimony that her husband had been heard to refuse her maintenance; Hepzibah Bragg provided testimony from the people with whom she lodged that she had received no financial assistance from her husband. Susannah Whiting's husband had left her and their children "in a suffering condition" for more than three years: "She hath ever since, by every possible exertion, just found means, with the assistance of her Charitable Friends, to prevent any public charge."[17] And Aehsah Evans, who could barely sign her name, was pathetically frank about her financial expectations. She had married Elijah Evans

> who, although destitute of property at the time of marriage gave Such evidence of his ability, and Spirit of industry, as aforded a reasonable prospect of acquiring a comfortable Support for a family. Notwithstanding which the sd. Elijah Soon after our marriage commenced a strolling manner of Life, and instead of applying himself to agriculture with which he was acquainted, went into the business of Pedling about the Country, articles of but small advantage to the Public, and the profits of which (if any) were intirely inadequate to the Support of a family, in consequence of which Your Petitioner,

16. Petition of Huldah Archer of Farmington, Jan. 10, 1782, Conn. Sup. Ct. File Papers, Hartford Dist. The petition is marked "Granted," but it is not clear whether property arrangements were made to her satisfaction.

17. Divorce petition of Temperance Northern, Aug. 16, 1782, *ibid.*; Divorce petition of Elizabeth Foster, Feb. 10, 1783, *ibid.*; Divorce petition of Hepzibah Bragg, Sept. 1, 1784, *ibid.*; Divorce petition of Susannah Whiting of Hartford, Feb. 14, 1792, *ibid.*, and Feb. 1792, Conn. Sup. Ct. Recs., Hartford Dist., Rec. Bk. 25. See also the petition of Paulina Preston, Mar. 30, 1792, Conn. Sup. Ct. File Papers, Hartford Dist., and Sept. 1792, Conn. Sup. Ct. Recs., Hartford Dist., Rec. Bk. 25.

(who previous to her connection with the said Evans, was happy under the care of an indulgent father, and in a House furnished with the comforts of Life) was herself with two Children which she had by said Evans, for the Course of Eight or nine Years Subjected to a Series of want and distress.

When her husband finally deserted her, in 1785, the petitioner was "cast, with her Children upon her friends for support, [and] . . . reduced to the alternative of remaining a burden to her friends, or of seeking relief from your Honors." For Aehsah Evans, divorce was the beginning of poor relief. She wanted either financial assistance from the court or a divorce so that she would be free to marry again "or [do] otherwise as may appear best for the Support of your Petitioner."[18]

Economic complaints, which in many petitions are simply general statements designed to increase the authenticity of "totall neglect of duty," also took the form of specific demands for property settlement in the postwar years. The implication of the Connecticut divorce statute was that if the wife was the innocent party, she retained her dower right to the husband's estate. In cases in which a desertion proceeding was an effort to get an absent husband declared missing and presumed dead, the probate court proceeded readily to the distribution of the husband's estate, and the wife apparently had little difficulty in getting her dower right. But it is not at all clear that divorced women in other situations had so easy a time securing their share of an estate; virtually none of the deserting husbands in the eighteenth century appear to have left wills.

Not until the 1790s did women ask with any frequency for property settlements as an integral part of their divorces. Such requests had been rare before the war; five years after the war only about one-tenth of all divorce petitions in the Hartford District included a property settlement. All twelve requests came from women. In no case did a man have to demand restoration of property he had given his wife. The implications of property law were that family property was the husband's unless specifically reserved to the wife; it was the women who had to make special efforts to preserve their property.

Neither mental nor physical cruelty was statutory grounds for dissolution of marriage. The only way to claim divorce for cruelty was by direct petition to the legislature. Cruelty was, however, often implied and

18. Petition of Aehsah Evans of Granby, Aug. 26, 1788, Conn. Sup. Ct. File Papers, Hartford Dist.

Divorce petition of Aehsah Evans, August 26, 1788.
Courtesy Connecticut State Library, Hartford. Photograph by Gus Johnson.

occasionally described in petitions presented to the Superior Court. With the passage of time, people were increasingly likely to voice their expectations of marital affection and their disappointment when they received instead hostility and abuse.

In 1739 Ann Catton of Simsbury submitted "her Petition for divorce for the hardness of heart." Mehitable Griswold unsuccessfully submitted documentation of an increasingly unpleasant nineteen-year marriage: for the last ten years her husband had "behaved very unkindly to her"; for the last six he "entirely Neglected the Marriage Bed"; for the last three he had "not provided for her and threatens her life if she comes to live with him." Two women testified that Mehitable had appeared at their house "one night some years ago without a Cote in her shift and stays and apron and . . . with both her hands tyd together and her arms bludy." Ephraim Griswold was reported to have told a friend that "he did not love his wife no better than a squaw and that he would sell her to turks or Spannards if he had the opportunity."[19]

Unhappiness might be cited, but it could not be pressed very far, for it was the shakiest of grounds for divorce. When the only available options for ending a bad marriage are adultery, fraudulent contract, and desertion, the easiest way to be free may well be to walk away. This expedient action could be directly proven, and a court that had earned the reputation of routinely granting a divorce if the claim fit the statute requirement—as the Connecticut Superior Court surely had—was certainly presented with many tailor-made desertion cases. However, the complex causes that often led to desertion—cruel treatment, financial disappointment, frustrated ambition, friction with in-laws—could seldom be kept out of highly contested proceedings. When a couple's private problems were exposed in the course of desertion, public quarreling, or litigation, the community and the courts were drawn beyond the limits of the law and into the fray.

The divorce suit of William Thrall of Windsor, which remained in court for over five years, reveals a severely troubled marriage full of cruelty and desperation. The grounds for Thrall's case were clear: in the summer of 1732 Hannah Thrall took her young daughter, Charity, and fled from their home. William Thrall immediately charged his wife with desertion. But the voluminous and convoluted testimony in the

19. Divorce petition of Ann Catton, Sept. 3, 1739, Conn. Sup. Ct. File Papers, Hartford Dist., and Sept. 4, 1739, Conn. Sup. Ct. Recs., Hartford Dist., Rec. Bk. 7. Mehitable Griswold's divorce papers of Mar. 1746 are in the Conn. Sup. Ct. File Papers, Hartford Dist. Her petition was ultimately withdrawn.

lawsuit describes not only a physical, but also an emotional, separation between husband and wife and the community's perception of that rift.

The testimony of George Bradley, who was present at the final argument, suggests two reasons for Hannah Thrall's action. First, she could not stand living with her mother-in-law. "She would not live with him Except sd William Thrall would gett his Mother out of the House or goe and Live in another House. . . . she said she could live well Enough . . . as any Person need to live with her Husband, but she could not or would not live in the House with his Mother." Second, Hannah Thrall believed that she could support herself financially outside the home, despite her husband's objections. "She said she had Provided a Place to be at or Board att and designed to Work at her Trade and would have her Husband lend her some Money by her Work or Trade; her Husband told her if she could Work abroad he thought she might at Home, and he . . . would have her finish the Waste Coat she began some years ago." William Thrall was also openly cruel in his reaction to his wife's absence. Apparently he alternately locked her out and then demanded she return home.

This domestic scandal could not be contained within a simple divorce procedure. Because the community as a whole had an interest in ending the dispute, four ministers of the North Association of the County of Hartford were asked by the church at Windsor to mediate, a practice not uncommon in dealings with prominent families. They ruled that "if a man by his hard usage and cruel treatment drive his wife away from him or neglect her necessary departure and use not the proper Means to recover her he is to be esteemed the Desertor."

This ruling, which showed compassion for the victimized wife, illustrates the community's need to identify a single guilty party in a marriage dispute. The function of divorce was emphatically not to make both individuals happy, but to eliminate sources of social disorder. Mere unhappiness was not enough; equal fault seemed to justify continued misery. And nothing was more likely to vitiate a petition than for both parties to join in pleading for dissolution of their marriage. Asa Whitney of Preston petitioned for divorce on the grounds that his wife, Sarah, had become "visibly cold & very Indifferent"; she replied that she would like nothing better, and that was enough to get his petition denied.[20]

20. Depositions and testimony in divorce suit of William and Hannah Thrall, 1734–1735, Conn. Sup. Ct. File Papers, Hartford Dist., and Mar. 1737, Conn. Sup. Ct. Recs., Hartford Dist., Rec. Bk. 7; Petitions of Asa and Sarah Whitney, Conn. Sup. Ct. Recs., New London Dist., Rec. Bk. 18, and Conn. Sup. Ct. File Papers, New London Dist., Record Group 3.

How much hidden collusion there was in eighteenth-century desertion petitions is impossible to estimate. But if desertion may have occasionally been the result of collusion, it must also have created desperation. Through the stilted formulae of the women's petitions rings the authentic note of suffering: the woman left with no one to support her though she is "Bigg with Child," the woman left with the "large family left in Low Circumstances," the woman left "destitute of the Necessary Supports of Life." It is the rare petition, even at the end of the eighteenth century, that makes any mention of a property settlement; it was even rarer for the parties to a divorce to have left a will. One concludes that there was probably very little property left to fight over. Divorce in the Revolutionary era was not the mark of liberation: it was the gambit of the desperate. And the sadness to which the Connecticut petitions overwhelmingly testify suggests why the passage of statutory divorce laws would become, in other states in the nineteenth century, a "woman's issue."

The immediate impact of the Revolution on marriages is not obvious. Only a very few divorce petitions filed during the war or in its aftermath directly mention wartime circumstances. There was, however, the plaintiff Seth Arnold, who reported that in 1781, "viewing his Bleeding Country beset with her Enimies which loudly Calld for her Sons to Step forth in her defence, Animated with Zeal in the defence of his Country he Listed Soldier in the Continental Army . . . notwithstanding all the Tender ties of his Wife and Children." He returned home a year later only to be "shoked and Greatly Surprised and Mortefyed" to discover that his wife had given birth to an illegitimate child the day before. Deborah Robinson married a British soldier who promptly deserted her; Ezra Belding's wife apparently slept with the hired man while her husband was serving with the Continental army. But these examples are exceptional.[21]

The war's effect on marital stability can be measured only indirectly. There was a decline in divorce proceedings, a direct result of the failure of courts to remain in session. The disruptions of the war meant that the Superior Court sat irregularly and infrequently; when it was in session it heard fewer cases, shifting attention from private debts and divorces to accusations of trading with the enemy, smuggling, or expressing sympathy for the crown. The Superior Court records for 1776 and 1777 are appar-

21. Divorce petition of Seth Arnold of Farmington, Aug. 19, 1782, divorce petition of Deborah Robinson of Simsbury, Mar. 8, 1784, and divorce petition of Ezra Belding of Wethersfield, Feb. 20, 1788, all in Conn. Sup. Ct. File Papers, Hartford Dist.

ently complete, and they reveal only five divorce cases in two years, a sharp drop from prewar levels. But there was an increase in divorce proceedings in the postwar years.

Although reference to affectionate relationships did not make divorce proceedings more persuasive to the court, wartime and postwar petitions mentioned the absence of love and affection more often than had earlier ones. The frequency of allusions to the emotional satisfactions expected of marriage also increased. Though unhappiness did not constitute a formal ground for divorce, this complaint apparently came to seem acceptable as evidence that a marriage was not a normal one.

The men who petitioned for divorce in the 1770s included Daniel Osgood, who had lived "in Love and Concord" with his wife until she became "uneasy and discontented" and eloped; Elijah Metcalf, whose wife's "affections . . . were fixed on every lude person that she could allure"; and William Walbridge, who complained that his wife, Ester, had left him ten years before "without Cause or Prevocation . . . leaving the Petitioner with a family of Children disconsolate." When Nathaniel Fenton applied for a divorce in 1776 on the grounds of adultery, claiming that his wife was pregnant by another man, Sarah Fenton filed a dignified confession: "This may Certify you (or any whome it may Concern) that the Child that I am now like to have I was Pregnant with before I married . . . with my Husband Nathanel Fenton and that the Child is non of his, Under which Circumstances I think it Just that he should have a Bill of Divorce and shall not Oppose him in Trying for the same, as I have no Inclination of ever Cohabiting with him any more, which even to offer, would be doing Injustice to Mr. Fenton."[22]

Samuel Gridley complained that soon after he had married Catharine Thompson, "he soon found to his great grief and surprize, she became alienated in affection towards the melmst [memorialist]," and that with time, she had only become "more averse and implacable." He testified that she had absented herself from him for three years and that "her heart was set upon another man." Having satisfied the terms of desertion, Gridley's petition was granted, but only over the protest of Catharine, whose petition was equally emotional: "During the first seven months of

22. Divorce petition of Daniel Osgood, Aug. 16, 1770, *ibid.*; Divorce petition of Elijah Metcalf, Aug. 14, 1771, *ibid.*, and Dec. 1771, Conn. Sup. Ct. Recs., Hartford Dist., Rec. Bk. 17; Divorce petition of William Walbridge of Stafford, Aug. 18, 1777, Conn. Sup. Ct. File Papers, Hartford Dist., and Sept. 1777, Conn. Sup. Ct. Recs., Hartford Dist., Rec. Bk. 18; Divorce petition of Nathaniel Fenton, Feb. 14, 1776, and deposition from Sarah Fenton, Apr. 12, 1776, Conn. Sup. Ct. File Papers, Hartford Dist.

marriage, he was destitute of proper Affection to her, which he manifested by a Disposition to find Fault with her and her Children [by a previous marriage] in the most indifferent Matters, notwithstanding her utmost Endeavors to please him, and being determined to remove every possible Ground of Uneasiness, she consented that her Children should be put out to Strangers, altho, on sundry Accounts, very inconvenient." She maintained that he had deserted her, and on the rare occasions that he was at home, he was "soured by Disaffection" and made her "most uncomfortable." He offered her little for her economic support: "Being thus reduced to Want, and encompassed with Difficulties, she was obliged to work for others in the most servile Employments to procure the Necessaries of Life." When Gridley finally returned, he "threatened her, assaulted her Person, slandered her Reputation and at Length plundered her of her Goods, wearing Apparel, her Bed from under her, Turned her out of Doors, let out the House to a Stranger, posted her, neglected her in Sickness."[23]

Anna Kibbee complained that her husband, Amariah,

> soon after their intermarriage began to manifest an aversion to the person company & conversation of your unfortunate Petitioner notwithstanding her most dutiful behavior towards him & utmost endeavours to render his Life comfortable & happy—which aversion continued to encrease until he in a great measure diserted her. . . . tis no pleasure to the unhappy Petitioner to enlarge on the ingratitude & cruelty of the man on whom she had once fondly fixed her heart & hopes for Life—She weeps in Silence forsaken & unpitied by the Author of her ruin—

Her petition was supported by the testimony of several neighbors, among them Samuel Hall and Thomas Wood, who reported that they had "often heard Amariah Kibbe . . . say that he would Never take his wife Anna home to Live with him . . . saying he had not Love for her sufficient to move him to take care of her." Amariah himself acknowledged the facts in his wife's petition, "tho' melancholly are the Truth," and stated that he had "no objection to the Prayer of said Petitioner being granted." This agreement between husband and wife would in the past have sealed the

23. Divorce petition of Samuel Gridley, Aug. 10, 1778, Conn. Sup. Ct. File Papers, Hartford Dist.; Petition of Catharine Gridley, Aug. 18, 1778, *ibid.*

fate of Anna's petition; in 1777 it apparently only delayed the procedure a few months, and the divorce was granted.[24]

The most emotional of these petitions was submitted by the unhappy Abigail Dayton of Southington in 1783. It suggests her expectations— and disappointments—in marriage. Twelve years before, she had married Israel Dayton "and entered into the connubial Relation with him with the most sanguine Expectations of enjoying the Happiness that usually attends the Marriage States, trusting with the most entire Confidence in his Fortitude to protect, his Wisdom to counsel, his Love to cherish, and his Diligence to support her." But she soon found that despite her "uncorrupted Fidelity to the Man of her Heart, that her Expectations were vain, and that her Portion would be to drag out a miserable Existance. . . . he was soon infatuated [with] the most unmanly and groundless Jealousies of her Fidelity. . . . the Love of his Espousals was converted, by Degrees, into the most rankerous Hate, and instead of a Bosum Friend, is become an inveterate Enemy." As she saw it, he had "dissolved the Marriage Covenant between us. . . . every valuable Purpose, for which the marriage Relation was originally intended, is under present Circumstances, defeated." But Abigail Dayton was required to continue to live with the man who had become "instead of a Bosum Friend . . . an inveterate Enemy." It was not until 1791 that the Superior Court accepted a joint petition, from Bela and Fanny Backuss, who accused each other of adultery and begged to be separated.[25]

The General Assembly of Connecticut continued to receive divorce petitions after the war and considered seventy-four of these pleas between 1789 and 1818. Fifty-five of these petitions mentioned cruel or abusive treatment; seven of the complainants were men. They included James

24. Petition of Anna Kibbee, Jan. 1777, Aug. 20, 1777, Conn. Sup. Ct. Recs., Hartford Dist., Rec. Bk. 18, and Mar. 1777, Sept. 1777, Conn. Sup. Ct. File Papers, Hartford Dist.; Certificate of Amariah Kibbee, Jan. 14, 1777, *ibid.*, and Conn. Sup. Ct. Recs., Hartford Dist., Rec. Bk. 18.

25. Divorce petition of Abigail Dayton of Southington, Mar. 9, 1783, Conn. Sup. Ct. File Papers, Hartford Dist.; Memorandum granting divorce to Bela Backuss and Fanny Backuss of Windham, Mar. 1791, Conn. Sup. Ct. Recs., Hartford Dist., Rec. Bk. 25. Had the Backusses presented their joint request for divorce in North Carolina, as John and Elizabeth Nelson did in 1786, they would have had no chance. "Unhappily for them," the Nelsons wrote to the North Carolina Assembly, "your Petitioners have been Married upwards of eight years, and find after many attempts and tryals that having lost all manner of Affection for each other it is not possible they can ever live together." Their petition was summarily rejected (Petition of John Nelson and Elizabeth Nelson of Craven County, N.C., Oct. 25, 1786, Legislative Papers, Box 66, State Dept. Archives and Hist., Raleigh, N.C.).

Bacon, whose wife had threatened to kill him, and forty-eight-year-old Araunah Williams, whose eighteen-year-old wife had treated Williams's aged father with such "great cruelty and violence . . . that his father had been forced to flee to friends for protection and soon became insane." Women dominated the ranks of petitioners to the legislature as they had to the courts; in the ten years between 1789 and 1798, the assembly received thirty-three requests, twenty-six from women. Cruelty was not always a successful plea, especially if documentation was limited or lacked detail. Ruth Shelton's request for a divorce on the grounds that her husband had "refused to provide her with a physician or proper attendance or medicine during illness," for example, was denied.[26]

Divorce does seem to have been more comfortably accepted in postwar Connecticut. It may have been the growing ease of divorce, and the increased willingness to make it a part of the social order, that led the Congregational ministers of New Haven to raise the issue as a matter of public policy for the new nation.

The occasion began innocuously enough. The Consociation of New Haven was asked to mediate in a dispute between a wife who believed herself deserted and a husband who claimed that he had fled the area "to escape the disgrace and hardships of imprisonment for debt." Eventually he returned to find that she had regarded herself as fully abandoned and was in love with another man.

The New Haven ministers castigated the wife (whom they did not name) for denying the husband access to her bed. "*The wife,*" Benjamin Trumbull wrote in a 1788 pamphlet summarizing their views, "*hath not the power of her own body, but the husband.*"[27] In the same year, the ministers petitioned the legislature for a revision of the divorce statute.[28]

Some of their arguments were technical; they complained, for example, that divorce cases had become so routinized that virtually no effort was usually made to find the accused partner, and that bills of divorce were often granted "entirely on the representations of the party suing for a divorce."[29] The right of every man to be heard in his own defense was ignored. Trumbull contrasted the sloppiness of divorce procedure with

26. Connecticut Archives, 2d Ser., Conn. State Lib., Hartford.

27. Benjamin Trumbull, *An Appeal to the Public, Especially to the Learned, with respect to the Unlawfulness of Divorces, in all Cases, Excepting those of Incontinency* (New Haven, Conn., 1788), 36.

28. Petition of the General Association, Sept. 9, 1788, "Lotteries and Divorces," Conn. Archives, 1st Ser., I, Item 322a.

29. Trumbull, *Appeal to the Public*, 40.

the care taken in attaching the property of absconding debtors (who were, after all, as difficult to find as absconding husbands).

But for the most part, Trumbull and the ministers rested on a narrow and scriptural doctrine of divorce, insisting that the English legal practice was the only proper one. "Jealousy is the rage of a man," Trumbull wrote. "Nothing . . . so totally alienates affection. . . . It creates the utmost confusion in families, and with respect to inheritances . . . exposeing him to make heirs of the issue of his wanton neighbors. It is, beyond all other instances of misconduct, a total inversion of the institution and principal ends of marriage." Nothing but adultery, the ministers argued, was proper grounds for divorce.[30]

Had their argument been accepted by the assembly (it was not), Connecticut would have returned to the conditions that prevailed in most other states. And Aehsah Evans, Sarah Whitney, David Frisbie (whose wife had neglected their frail son), and the women who were abandoned by wandering men, all would have been locked into miserable marriages. But Trumbull did not pause. He believed that what was at stake was nothing less than the morals and the virtue of the Republic. He estimated with rough accuracy that approximately thirty cases came before the Superior Court each year and that the numbers were growing; and he leaped to the conclusion that this trend paralleled not the pursuit of happiness, but the decline of the Republic. He quoted Seneca on the frequency of divorce before the fall of Rome: "There will be few or no marriages without divorce." The pamphlet took on the traditional tone of the jeremiad. "The great facility" with which divorces were obtained caused "vice to walk with a bare face and a stretched out neck." And Trumbull concluded with this wistful observation: "No man, perhaps, was ever more engaged in obtaining a divorce, or more loudly complained . . . than the famous JOHN MILTON; yet as the laws of his country would admit of no divorce, he became reconciled to his wife, and lived happily with her ever afterwards."[31]

Trumbull and his colleagues lost their campaign to tighten the divorce laws. They did achieve a limited success with a 1797 statute increasing the responsibility of the court to summon the defendant in a divorce case,

30. *Ibid.*, 8–11. Because the ministers doubted that their proposals would be effected, they stressed their general wish "that proper punishments be appointed and inflicted on the faulty party, in every case of divorce, by which, divorce may occur, with respect to the faulty party, [to] be a source of shame, of pain & disability" (Petition, Sept. 9, 1788, "Lotteries and Divorces," Conn. Archives, 1st Ser., I, Item 322a).

31. Trumbull, *Appeal to the Public*, 49, 41n.

thereby requiring a lawsuit rather than a simple petition for the proceeding. The formalities involved in dissolving a marriage grew; so did the expenses. In the early nineteenth century it was increasingly likely that each party would have an attorney and that a real effort would be made to integrate a property settlement into a divorce settlement. These added complications and costs were surely a deterrent. Even when divorce had been cheap and relatively easy, it had been inhibited by the forbidding mechanics of dealing with the Superior Court. One suspects that by the nineteenth century, when procedural expenses had been increased, divorce seemed an even more distant remedy for the most desperate.[32]

Milton had argued that "domestic liberty" was a necessary ingredient in a free society. But even Connecticut, the state that had enjoyed for the longest period the most liberal divorce law, was highly ambivalent on the extent to which "domestic liberty" ought to prevail within its definition of the "family state."[33] It was not unfair to ask whether the pursuit of happiness did not imply the right to be free of an unhappy marriage. One disenchanted husband, John Christian Smith, presented his case to the South Carolina legislature in rhetoric that echoed the Declaration of Independence:

> Since Marriage was instituted for the purpose of promoting the happiness of individuals and the good of society and since the attainment of those objects depends entirely on the Domestic harmony of the parties connected and their living together in a perfect union of inclinations interests and affections when it becomes impossible for them to remain longer united when mutual wretchedness must be the consequence of continuing their connection or the purposes for which marriage was instituted then entirely faile it produces effects directly contrary to those which were expected from its influence and the good of Society no less than the well-being of individuals requires that it should be disolved and that the parties should be left free to form such other domestic connections as may contribute to their felicity.[34]

32. "An Act in addition to the act relating to bills of divorce," giving instructions for procedure in bringing in a petition of divorce, May 1797, "Lotteries and Divorces," Conn. Archives, 2d Ser., II, Item 129.

33. "Explanation of Bill on Divorce," n.d., *ibid.*, Item 130.

34. Petition of John Christian Smith, 1791, Petition 54, General Assembly Petitions, 1791, S.C. Dept. Archives and Hist. For a pamphlet defending divorce and permission for remarriage that quotes Milton and draws an analogy between the unhappy marriage and slavery, see *An Essay on Marriage; or, The Lawfulness of Divorce* (Philadelphia, 1788).

Smith got no sympathy from the legislature, though other modern revolutionary governments gave high priority to the liberalization of divorce. The French divorce law of 1792, which made divorce available nationally on the simple condition of mutual consent as well as for a long list of infringements of the marriage bond like adultery and condemnation to an "infamous punishment," had been an important and explicit part of the Jacobin program. This system of civil divorce was restricted by the Code Napoleon in 1804, but was not eliminated until the Bourbon Restoration.

In America civil divorce became available only haltingly, and only in Pennsylvania was it adopted as part of the republican renovation. As noted earlier, Pennsylvania had attempted to pass a divorce law before the Revolution, but it was promptly disallowed by the Privy Council. Not long after the war ended, the Pennsylvania Assembly took advantage of its independence to assert the right to regulate marriage and to invent a mode of divorce that could be handled through the courts rather than the legislature. The preamble to the 1785 act treated divorce as an element of a well-regulated social order, implicitly responding to charges like Trumbull's that divorce was an emblem of social disorder: "Whereas it is the design of marriage, and the wish of parties entering into that state that it should continue during their joint lives, yet where the one party is under natural or legal incapacities of faithfully discharging the matrimonial vow, or is guilty of acts and deeds inconsistent with the nature thereof, the laws of every well-regulated society ought to give relief to the innocent and injured person."[35]

Other than in New England and Pennsylvania, divorce remained possible, when at all, primarily by way of a private bill passed in the legislature, a device that required some political sophistication for success. Nor was it always effective. The sad experience of Nancy Shippen Livingston, which is unusually well documented, suggests both the extent to which women's life choices were dominated by their menfolk and the consequences of living in a social order in which divorce was rare.

Nancy Shippen was born into a rich Philadelphia family. Her mother was a Lee of Virginia; her father was William Shippen, who briefly headed the Continental army's hospital department. She lived in Philadelphia after the patriots took possession of the city, an eligible debutante, falling in love with Louis Guillaume Otto, a young member of the French

35. See Thomas R. Meehan, " 'Not Made Out of Levity': Evolution of Divorce in Early Pennsylvania," *PMHB*, XCII (1968), 441–464.

Nancy Shippen Livingston, attributed to Benjamin Trott.
Printed in Ethel Armes, ed., *Nancy Shippen: Her Journal Book* (Philadelphia, 1935).

legation. French observers like François-Alexandre-Frédéric, duc de la Rochefoucauld-Liancourt would comment on the freedoms that young American women apparently enjoyed, but Nancy Shippen's father coldly and briskly married her off to Henry Beekman Livingston, who was thirty-one years old and had a reputation as a rake. William Shippen explained the match frankly: "Nancy is much puzzled between Otto & Livingston. She loves the first and only esteems the last. . . . L— has 12 or 15,000 hard. O— has nothing now, but honorable expectations hereafter. A Bird in hand is worth 2 in a bush." Louis Otto was left to complain that he could not see "for what reason in this *free* Country a Lady of Sixteen years who is handsome enough to find many admirers and who had all the advantages of a good education must be married in a hurry and given up to a man she dislikes."[36]

Henry Beekman Livingston proved as bad as his reputation. When a daughter was born shortly after the marriage, the Livingstons forced Nancy to turn the baby over to them to be brought up; she was limited to scattered visits to the child. Henry did all he could to smear her reputation. By 1789 when she was ready to divorce him, she discovered that Revolutionary freedom did not clearly extend to the right to be free of an unhappy marriage. A New York divorce still required a private bill passed by the legislature, and it was widely understood that the passage of such a bill required that it be shepherded through the assembly by an astute politician committed to its success. Nancy Shippen's uncle Arthur Lee thought her foolish to attempt the proceedings, but suggested that she try to hire Aaron Burr, who had, after all, been clever enough to marry a rich old woman. When Henry Livingston tried to abscond with his child, the best that even the experienced Lee could suggest was that Nancy "try to interest the Ladies—particularly Mrs McKean & Mrs. Judge Shippen." Nancy Shippen was caught in a cruel, but common, predicament: if she were formally divorced, her husband would have full custody of their daughter and might take the child from her sight forever. The only way to keep her child nearby was to remain married to Livingston, though quietly and unofficially living separately. Eventually it would be Henry Beekman Livingston who arranged a divorce—as it happened, in Connecticut.[37]

A divorce remained nearly as difficult to obtain in the new republic as

36. Ethel Armes, ed., *Nancy Shippen: Her Journal Book* (Philadelphia, 1935), 101, 108.
37. *Ibid.*, 273, 291–292.

it had been in the colonies. The rhetoric of revolution, which emphasized the right to separate from dictatorial masters, implicitly offered an ideological validation for divorce, though few in power recognized it. In the quiet and private world in which women like Nancy Shippen lived, Revolutionary ideology had made only one relevant promise, but that promise was never given high priority and was not fulfilled.

Chapter 7

"WHY SHOULD GIRLS BE LEARND OR WISE?": EDUCATION AND INTELLECT IN THE EARLY REPUBLIC

And why should girls be learnd or wise,
Books only serve to spoil their eyes.
The studious eye but faintly twinkles
And reading paves the way to wrinkles.

—John Trumbull

Needlework picture of a Harvard College building (*ca.* 1750–1775). The woman who made this picture used needlework, a typically female medium, to depict an institution that excluded her. See Samuel Eliot Morison's effervescent essay

"Needlework Picture Representing a Colonial College Building," *Old Time New England*, XXIV (1933), 67–72.
Courtesy Massachusetts Historical Society, Boston. Photograph by George M. Cushing.

"I EXPECT TO SEE our young women forming a new era in female history," wrote Judith Sargent Murray in 1798.[1] Her optimism was part of a general sense that in the post-Revolutionary world all possibilities were open; as Benjamin Rush put it, the first act of the republican drama had only begun. The experience of war had given words like *independence* and *self-reliance* personal as well as political overtones. Ordinary folk had learned that the world could, as the song played at Yorktown had it, turn upside down: the rich could quickly become poor, wives might suddenly have to manage the family economy. Women might even, as the famous Deborah Gannett had done, shoulder a gun. Revolutionary experience taught that it was useful to be prepared for a wide range of unusual possibilities; political theory taught that republics rested on the virtue and intelligence of their citizens. The stability and competence on which republican government relied required a highly literate and politically sophisticated constituency. Maintaining the Republic was an educational challenge as well as a political one.

The years immediately after the Revolution witnessed a great expansion of educational opportunity, an expansion sustained by the belief that the success of the republican experiment demanded a well-educated citizenry. Listing reading, writing, measurement and arithmetic, geography, and history as the subjects that ought to be taught in primary schools, Thomas Jefferson said the purpose of these institutions was to "instruct the mass of our citizens in these their rights, interests and duties, as men and citizens."[2] Interest in formal education was also encouraged by industrial developments that put a premium on certain basic intellectual skills. The self-sufficient farmer might manage without literacy, but any boy expecting to run a small artisan's shop or to work in a business enterprise of some sort would need to be able to read, to write orders, and to keep accounts. Schemes for educating the "rising generation" proliferated. The need for literate workers would translate into heightened economic, as well as intellectual, opportunity for teachers, who found their skills in demand. "The Spirit for Academy making is vigorous," Ezra Stiles wrote joyfully in 1786. In Connecticut alone, Stiles counted twelve private academies, established by the subscriptions of philanthropic citizens in the previous five years.[3]

1. Judith Sargent Murray, *The Gleaner* (Boston, 1798), III, 189.
2. Quoted in Fred M. and Grace Hechinger, *Growing Up in America* (New York, 1975), 41.
3. Nov. 17, 1786, Dexter, ed., *Literary Diary of Ezra Stiles*, III, 247–248. For an exten-

Institutions for boys' education seemed to flourish in the early Republic. But what of institutions for girls? "Schools and academies there are, intended for training up boys, and young gentlemen, in sundry branches of useful learning," mused Samuel Magaw in 1787, "but female instruction hath been left, as it were, to chance. . . . As if of trivial moment; no great deal hath been said about it, and still less accomplished."[4]

The reasons for this disparity reached far back into the history of Western thought. Deeply rooted in each of the colonists' native cultures was the assumption that women's energies were properly fully devoted to the service of their families. If learning was intended to prepare young men for active roles in the public sector and for service to the state, the shelter of coverture seemed to make sophisticated learning of little use to a woman. The first European academic institutions had been church related, intended to prepare men for the clerical life; the colleges at Oxford, Cambridge, Paris, and Bologna, which developed and fixed the definition of classical education, were male preserves. In schools that prepared boys for college, as Walter J. Ong has suggested, the teaching of Latin functioned as a "puberty rite" by which young men were introduced into an exclusively male world of scholarly learning. By contrast, the cultural world that women inhabited was practical, technical, and vernacular. A woman could not enter the academy, because it offered not disembodied knowledge but a classical curriculum designed to prepare young men for survival in a political world, a curriculum in which the requisite skills ranged from polemics and oratory to the making of war.[5] Academic study, a meritorious male pursuit, seemed self-indulgent when found among women. Americans inherited the image of the learned

sive treatment of chartered private boys' academies, see James McLachlan, *American Boarding Schools: A Historical Study* (New York, 1970).

4. Samuel Magaw, "An Address delivered in the Young Ladies Academy, at Philadelphia, on February 8th, 1787, at the close of a Public Examination," *Am. Museum*, III (1788), 25–28.

5. Walter J. Ong, *The Presence of the Word: Some Prolegomena for Cultural and Religious History* (New Haven, Conn., 1967), 245–255. Ong suggests that "romanticism gave the final blow to polemic Latin-sustained oralism" (*ibid.*, 252). The change is symbolized by a shift in the definition of artistic inspiration from the muses ("strongly feminine figures . . . obviously the projections of the male psyche") to romantic creativity, which produces "something out of nothing, like God's act of creation," and (though Ong does not say so) like women's act of childbearing. The romantic version makes the sources of creativity available to women also, who flourished as romantic writers. Ong maintains that the art of oratory was inaccessible to women because "without artificial amplification, the normal woman's voice simply cannot reach the thousands who found themselves enthralled by the

woman as an unenviable anomaly and kept alive the notion that the woman who developed her mind did so at her own risk.

Educational options for girls were far more limited than they were for boys. "How many female minds, rich with native genius and noble sentiment, have been lost to the world, and all their mental treasures buried in oblivion?" asked the *Royal American Magazine* shortly before the war. "I regret the trifling narrow contracted Education of the Females of my own country," Abigail Adams wrote to her husband in 1778. "You need not be told how much female Education is neglected, nor how fashionable it has been to ridicule Female learning."[6]

That some well-known couples, like John and Abigail Adams, were equally facile with words has perhaps camouflaged the extent to which they were exceptional in their generation. There was more likely to be severe disparity in the verbal fluency of husband and wife, brother and sister. Other pairs may be more representative than the Adamses: Benjamin Franklin is an instructive contrast to his nearly illiterate—though nonetheless intelligent and shrewd—wife, Deborah. Elbridge Gerry courted a young woman who was, though the daughter of a state legislator, so illiterate she could not read his love letters.[7] Even Eliza Lucas Pinckney, who raised her daughter Harriott to read Latin and French, was sensitive to the gap in verbal fluency between the sexes; what could not be excused in a man was pardonable in a woman, because less was expected from her. Scolding her grandson Daniel Horry about his deficiencies in "orthography," Eliza Pinckney compared standards of learning for men and women: "To be greatly deficient in this matter is almost inexcusable in one of our Sex, who have had an Education above that of

bellowing of the old-line male orator" (*ibid.*, 249–250). However, voice projection is an acquired, not a natural, skill; great actresses of the premechanized theater, from Susannah Cibber to Katharine Hepburn, have shown that women can become excellent orators.

6. Clio [pseud.], "Thoughts on Female Education," *Royal American Magazine* (Jan. 1774), 9–10; Abigail Adams to John Adams, June 30, 1778, *Adams Family Correspondence*, III, 52.

7. Compare also the prose of Philip Van Cortlandt with that of his sister Cornelia Van Cortlandt Beekman as it appears in Jacob Judd, ed., *Correspondence of the Van Cortlandt Family of Cortlandt Manor, 1748–1800*, II (Tarrytown, N.Y., 1976), 27–29. Elbridge Gerry courted, but did not marry, a young woman who was not taught to read and write because her grandfather had insisted that all girls needed to learn was to "make a shirt and a pudding." See Abigail Adams to John Adams, Aug. 14, 1776, *Adams Family Correspondence*, II, 94–95, 95n. Anne Firor Scott has written a subtle interpretation of Jane Franklin Mecom's life in "Self-Portraits: Three Women," in Richard Bushman *et al.*, eds., *Uprooted Americans: Essays to Honor Oscar Handlin* (Boston, 1979), 46–55.

a chamber maid, unpardonable then it must be in a scholar, as it must proceed entirely from Idleness and inattention."[8]

Even in bookish families the literacy gap was marked. Isaiah Thomas, the well-known printer and editor of the *Worcester Spy*, was one of the greatest book collectors of his generation. His catalog of his splendid library, which became the foundation of the American Antiquarian Society, fills 217 closely written pages. His wife, Mary, also kept her own list of books. Hers is an exceptionally long list for a woman of her generation—but it covers only seven pages.[9] Differences in education might reinforce the sense of distinct male and female worlds. When Ezra Stiles commissioned paintings of himself and his wife in 1771, he took enormous pains to prescribe the composition of the background of his portrait. The artist was instructed to include "part of a Library—two Shelves of Books—a Folio shelf with *Eusebij Hist. Ecc.*, Livy, Du Halde's Hist^y of China, and one inscribed Talmud B. . . . On the other Shelf are Newton's Principia, Plato, Watts, Doddridge." Stiles's catalog of items continued for four paragraphs. He knew precisely why he wanted all these things cluttering up the background: "These Emblems are more descriptive of my Mind, than the Effigies of my Face." It is symptomatic of the domestic dynamics of the Stiles family that Elizabeth Stiles appears against a plain drapery.[10]

These disparities in literacy—from the basic ability to sign one's name and to read simple prose to the sophisticated ability to read difficult or theoretical prose, foreign languages, and the classics—have enormous implications for the history of the relations between the sexes. One of the most important measures of modernization in a society may well be the degree to which print replaces oral communication. To the extent that female culture had relied on the spoken word, it was premodern at a time when male culture was increasing its dependence on written communication.[11] Literacy, after all, is more than a technical skill. It makes possible certain kinds of competencies. It makes practical the maintenance of a

8. Eliza Lucas Pinckney to Daniel Horry, n.d., Pinckney Papers, Folder 7, South Carolina Historical Society, Charleston.

9. Mary Thomas's Book Catalogue, Isaiah Thomas Papers, American Antiquarian Society, Worcester, Mass.

10. Aug. 1–19, 1771, Dexter, ed., *Literary Diary of Ezra Stiles*, I, 131–144.

11. Harry Stout has suggested, for example, that the religious revivals of the early 19th century may represent the temporary revitalization of an older form of transmitting information, challenging the modern reliance on print ("Culture, Structure, and the 'New' History: A Critique and an Agenda," *Computers and the Humanities*, IX [1975], 213–230, esp. 223–224).

communication network wider than one's own locality. It may promote skepticism about local opinions by promoting access to other viewpoints. Increased dependence on writing rather than on oral communication would ultimately help to bridge the gap between male and female experience, since the spoken word—depending as it does on the physical presence of the speaker—conveys the speaker's gender in a way that the written word cannot.[12]

The closing of the literacy gap between American men and women cannot yet be precisely dated. It occurred sometime between 1780— the year Kenneth Lockridge estimates that New England women's sign literacy was half that of men's—and 1850, when the first federal census that measured basic literacy reported little difference between the numbers of northeastern men and women who could read and write. Since the old people, who had been educated before and during the Revolution, accounted for most of the illiterates in 1850, we can assume that major improvements in female education took place between 1790 and 1830 or so. The literacy gap between men and women persisted longer in the South than in the North, and it persisted in technical competencies long after it had been bridged for simple reading and writing.[13] No social change in the early Republic affected women more emphatically than the improvement of schooling, which opened the way into the modern world.

Those who wished to improve educational opportunity for women

12. See Jack Goody and Ian Watt, "The Consequences of Literacy," *Comparative Studies in Society and History*, V (1962), 334: "The mere size of the literate repertoire means that the proportion of the whole which any one individual knows must be infinitesimal in comparison with what obtains in oral culture. Literate society, merely by having no system of elimination, no 'structural amnesia,' prevents the individual from participating fully in the total cultural tradition to anything like the extent possible in non-literate society." Margaret Mead remarked that "primitive education was a process by which continuity was maintained between parents and children. . . . Modern education includes a heavy emphasis upon the function of education to create discontinuities" ("Our Educational Emphases in Primitive Perspective," *American Journal of Sociology*, XLVIII [1943], 637).

13. Kenneth Lockridge, *Literacy in Colonial New England: An Enquiry into the Social Context of Literacy in the Early Modern West* (New York, 1974), 38–44 and *passim*; Daniel Calhoun, *The Intelligence of a People* (Princeton, N.J., 1973), 76 and *passim*. In 1929 Thomas Woody commented on the substantial disparity in literacy between colonial men and women; his call for additional study in this area has only begun to be answered (*A History of Women's Education in the United States*, I [New York, 1929], 159). Woody's book remains the basic survey history, but it is diffuse and often anecdotal at the expense of analysis. A new appraisal remains to be written. For a recent case study, see Linda Auwers, "The Social Meaning of Female Literacy: Windsor, Connecticut, 1660–1775," Newberry Library Papers in Family and Community History, No. 77–4A, Newberry Library, Chicago. Even in 1980, it is generally agreed that women are less likely than men to be well educated in mathematics and science.

Samuel King, *Ezra Stiles* (1771).
Courtesy Yale University Art Gallery; bequest of Dr. Charles Jenkins. Photograph by
Joseph Szaszfai.

Samuel King, *Elizabeth Hubbard Stiles* (1771).
Courtesy Yale University Art Gallery; bequest of Dr. Charles C. Foote.

had to work against a pervasive skepticism. Abigail Adams had been right to note that female education was ridiculed when it was not neglected. "Deluded maid! thy claim forego," began a poem "To a Lady, Who Expressed a Desire of Seeing An University Established for Women."[14] It was not only Latin, but all serious learning, that was an exclusively male puberty rite. Those who would add scholarly indoctrination to female adolescent experiences were inventing a ritual and an institution that threatened the woman's traditional life pattern of unremitting physical toil and unremitting social subservience. "Tell me," the Philadelphian Gertrude Meredith wrote angrily, "do you imagine, from your knowledge of the young men in this city, that ladies are valued according to their mental acquirements? I can assure you that they are not, and I am very confident that they never will be, while men indulge themselves in expressions of contempt for one because she has a *bare elbow*, for another because she . . . never made a *good pun, nor smart repartee. . . .* [Would they] not titter . . . at her expense, if a woman made a Latin quotation, or spoke with enthusiasm of Classical learning?" When Gertrude Meredith visited Baltimore, she found that her mildly satirical essays for the *Port Folio* had been enough to transform her into a formidable figure. "Mrs. Cole says she should not have been more distressed at visiting Mrs. Macaulay the authoress than myself as she had heard *I was so sensible*, but she was very glad to find I was so free and easy. You must allow that this compliment was elegantly turned," she concluded dryly.[15]

A similar complaint about the widespread contempt for female intelligence was made by an essayist known only as "Sophia."

> A woman who is conscious of possessing, more intellectual power than is requisite in superintending the pantry, and in adjusting the ceremonials of a feast, and who believes she is conforming to the will of the giver, in improving the gift, is by the wits of the other sex

14. *Am. Museum*, XI (1792), Pt. i, app. 1, 3. See also *Burlington Advertiser* (Burlington, N.J.), Dec. 6, 1791.

15. Letter signed M. G., "American Lounger," *Port Folio* (Apr. 7, 1804), 106; Gertrude Meredith to David Meredith, May 3, 1804, Meredith Papers, Hist. Soc. Pa., Philadelphia. The educated woman's resentment of those denigrating her learning appears frequently in the letters of Eliza Southgate and Eliza Wilkinson. See especially *A Girl's Life Eighty Years Ago: Selections from the Letters of Eliza Southgate Bowne* (New York, 1887), 35–40, 58–61, 99–104. Eliza Wilkinson complained that a man habitually conversed with a woman only in terms of "unmeaning flattery" and then "the moment she quits him, or he her, he laughs at the poor credulous fool . . . who is to blame?—no sooner are we entered in our teens, but we hear nothing else but Encomiums on our beauty" (Letters of Eliza Wilkinson, n.d., typescript, Wilkinson Papers, 8–9, S. Caroliniana Lib., Univ. S.C., Columbia).

Thomas Sully, *Gertrude Gouverneur Ogden Meredith* (1808).
Courtesy Historical Society of Pennsylvania, Philadelphia.

denominated a learned lady. She is represented as disgustingly slovenly in her person, indecent in her habits, imperious to her husband, and negligent of her children. And the odious scare-crow is employed, exactly as the farmer employs his unsightly bundle of rags and straw, to terrify the simple birds, from picking up the precious grain, which he wishes to monopolize. After all this, what man in his sober senses can be astonished, to find the majority of women as they really are, frivolous and volatile; incapable of estimating their own dignity, and indifferent to the best interests of society?

The "Female Advocate" of New Haven was moved to write her angry pamphlet when she heard "it observed . . . that our sex arrived at its zenith of improvement, at the age of twenty-one. . . . is it possible said I to myself? have I never improved, since that age, which is the period of admiration by the gay, the volatile and unprincipled. If so, what a pitiable misfortune. . . . I who have been looking forward with such flattering hopes . . . that I should be advancing in grace, and augmenting in knowledge, with views penetrating to a future world, and expanding with eternity."[16]

These women were not creating their own paranoid images of discouragement. The very newspapers for which they wrote often printed articles insisting that intellectual accomplishment was inappropriate in a woman, that the intellectual woman was not only an invader of a male province, but also somehow a masculine being. "Women of masculine minds," wrote the Boston minister John Sylvester John Gardiner, "have generally masculine manners, and a robustness of person ill calculated to inspire the tender passion." Noah Webster's *American Magazine*, which in its prospectus had made special appeal to women writers and readers, published this unsigned comment: "If we picture to ourselves a woman . . . firm in resolve, unshaken in conduct, unmoved by the delicacies of situation, by the fashions of the times, . . . we immediately change the idea of the sex, and . . . we see under the form of a woman the virtues and qualities of a man." Even the *Lady's Magazine*, dedicated to demonstrating that "the F E M A L E S of Philadelphia are by no means deficient in *those*

16. "Sophia," *Evening Fireside* (Philadelphia), Apr. 6, 1805; *The Female Advocate* (New Haven, Conn., 1801), 3. "One would think," remarked "Aspasia" writing for the *American Museum*, that men like these "were throwing sarcasms on their own sex, when they draw the following conclusions—that the more a woman's understanding is improved, the more apt she will be to despise her husband—that the strengthening of her reason will weaken her affection" (*Am. Museum* [1789], 149).

talents, which have immortalized the names of a *Montague*, a *Craven*, a *More*, and a *Seward*, in their inimitable writings," issued a cautionary tale, whose moral was that although "learning in men was the road to preferment . . . consequences very opposite were the result of the same quality in women." After Amelia, a clergyman's only daughter, is taught Latin and Greek, she becomes "negligent of her dress" and filled with "pride and pedantry" that "grew up with learning in her breast." Eventually both sexes avoid her, the emblem of the fabled "white-washed jackdaw (who, aiming at a station from which nature had placed him at a distance, found himself deserted by his own species and driven out of every society)." The author concluded with an explicit moral: "This story was intended (at a time when the press overflows with the productions of female pens) . . . to admonish them, that . . . because a few have gained applause by studying the dead languages, all womankind should [not] assume their Dictionaries and Lexicons; else . . . (as the Ladies made rapid advances towards *manhood*) we might in a few years behold a sweepstakes rode by women, or a second battle at Odiham, fought with superior skill, by Mesdames Humphries and Mendoza."[17]

Improvements in women's education, although impeded by criticisms like these, did come. Between 1790 and 1830 facilities for girls' education expanded and improved, especially in the North, making possible the closing of the literacy gap. The reasons for this are related both to the political revolution and to the industrial revolution. The political revolution had been an act of faith. Believing as they did that republics rested on the virtue of their citizens, Revolutionary leaders had to believe not only that Americans of their own generation displayed that virtue, but that Americans of subsequent generations would continue to display the moral character that a republic required. The role of guarantor of civic virtue, however, could not be assigned to a formal branch of government.

17. *Mercury and New-England Palladium* (Boston), Sept. 18, 1801; *American Magazine* (Feb. 1788), 134; *Lady's Magazine* (Jan. 1793), 68–72. (The "battle at Odiham" refers to a famous bareknuckle prizefight fought in 1788 by Daniel Mendoza and Richard Humphries in Hampshire, England.) Other attacks on female pedantry that express the fear that intellectual women will be masculine, are found in *Am. Mag.* (Mar. 1788), 244–256 ("To be lovely you must be content to be women . . . and leave the masculine virtues, and the profound researches of study to the province of the other sex"); *Mercury and N.-E. Palladium*, Sept. 4, 18, 1801, Dec. 4, 1801, Mar. 5, 9, 1802; Benjamin Silliman, *Letters of Shahcoolen, a Hindu Philosopher, Residing in Philadelphia; to His Friend, El Hassan, an Inhabitant of Delhi* (Boston, 1802), 23–24, 62; *Am. Museum* (Dec. 1788), 491; and *Boston Weekly Magazine* (Mar. 24, 1804), 86 ("Warlike women, learned women, and women who are politicians, equally abandon the circle which nature and institutions have traced round their sex; they convert themselves into men").

Instead it was hoped that other agencies—churches, schools, families—would fulfill that function.[18] And within families, the crucial role was thought to be the mother's: the mother who trained her children, taught them their early lessons, shaped their moral choices. To determine to what extent this role was assigned to women or to what extent they claimed it themselves requires a calculus too precise for the historian. But it is clear that women integrated these expectations into their own understanding of what a mother ought to do. Motherhood was discussed almost as if it were a fourth branch of government, a device that ensured social control in the gentlest possible way. If the Republic indeed rested on responsible motherhood, prospective mothers needed to be well informed and decently educated. The industrial revolution, occurring at the same time, reinforced the need for improved education. As the postwar world became more print-oriented, and as it became harder to function in it as an illiterate, interest in the improvement of girls' schooling increased.[19]

An important shift in public expectation was marked by the change in wording of the Massachusetts school law of 1789. As Kathryn Kish Sklar has pointed out, this law for the first time spoke of schoolmistresses as well as of schoolmasters. It probably validated an increasingly frequent practice, rather than initiated a new one.[20]

There was an enormous amount of variation in the educational oppor-

18. See Linda K. Kerber, *Federalists in Dissent: Imagery and Ideology in Jeffersonian America* (Ithaca, N.Y., 1970), 206–212.

19. These developments are discussed in detail in Cott, *Bonds of Womanhood*, esp. chap. 3. Cott correctly links changes in education to changes in the domestic economy. Her book provides the most subtle analysis yet of the intrusion of the industrial revolution into household production. Daughters, for example, had contributed to the family economy by carding, spinning, dyeing, and weaving. In between their tasks, they had also taught younger siblings and neighbor children the rudiments of reading, writing, and household skills. In the course of a generation their roles were usurped by steam-powered factories. Daughters were left without their traditional work, but with a continuing obligation to contribute to the family economy. Many followed their work to the mills; others extended their informal teaching to work as paid teachers in new schools. In Cott's analysis, these changes do not connect with politics until a later generation of young women—Grimkes and Stanton—develop an explicitly feminist ideology in the 1830s.

20. In 1778, for example, Groton had begun to count girls in its school census: "Voted, That the children be numbered through the town; males unmarried from four years old to twenty-one; females unmarried from four years old to eighteen" (Caleb Butler, *History of the Town of Groton* . . . [Boston, 1848], 221). See also Mary Eastman, "The Education of Woman in the Eastern States," in Annie Nathan Meyer, ed., *Woman's Work in America* (New York, 1891), 3–53; Cott, *Bonds of Womanhood*, 30, 102–103, 112–114; and Kathryn Kish Sklar, "Growing Up Female in Eighteenth-Century Massachusetts" (paper delivered at the University of Michigan, 1977).

tunities open to girls in the late eighteenth century. Quakers and Moravians had early established coeducational schools or pairs of schools (one for boys and a matching one for girls). In New England, girls and younger children of both sexes began to attend schools in special summer sessions, when boys were working in the fields. (Girls' major contributions to the family economy were likely to be indoor winter activities: spinning, dyeing, sewing, preserving foods.) Education costs were low during these months, for schoolhouses did not need to be heated, and teachers were young women paid substantially less than their male counterparts. The marginality of many of these schools is exemplified in the account kept by Elizabeth Bancroft of her experiences teaching a summer school in Maine from 1793 to 1795. She frequently interrupted her sessions "because of company"; in 1794 she dismissed her school for two weeks so that she could take a trip to Salem with her mother. When school was out she welcomed the end of her "tiresome tasks," and when she closed it for good she announced that she could "once more enjoy the sweets of liberty."[21]

As public monies were allocated to pay female teachers' salaries, the functions of these summer schools were gradually integrated into the year-round public grammar school. Middle-class girls began to attend schools for lengthened periods of time. Town academies began to include "female departments," and private schools for boys, like Timothy Dwight's at Greenfield Hill, Connecticut, were enlarged "to comprehend the Ladies."[22] Women opened schools for girls; it was, as one founder put it, a "poor but not ungenteel way" to earn a living. The insecurity of these schools is implied in the hesitant wording of their public announcements, which invariably express an assurance of the proprietor's "respectability."[23] An early historian of female education has called them

21. Elizabeth Bancroft Diary, 1793–1795, Am. Antq. Soc., Worcester, Mass. Ruth Henshaw was a contemporary who kept a considerably more substantial school, but even she seems to have felt it was permissible to interrupt it (Ruth Henshaw Bascom Diary, June–July 1801, Am. Antq. Soc., Worcester, Mass.). My impression is that women thought their church had the strongest claim on their attention and regular attendance; it is a long time before school appearance commands equal loyalty. See Diary of Eliza Ann Hull [Staples], 1818–1819, Conn. State Lib., Hartford.

22. The Newark Academy began as a boys' school in 1795; in 1802 a female boarding school was added, but only a single set of classes was apparently held until 1809, when boys and girls were firmly separated: "They enter the academy on different streets, and all intercourse is precluded" (Key to the Quarterly catalogues of the names of the young ladies, at the Newark Academy, under the instruction of Rev. Timothy Alden, with a historical sketch of the Academy [Newark, N.J., 1810], 8–11).

23. Anne Hart to Oliver Hart, May 14, 1781, Hart Papers, S. Caroliniana Lib., Univ.

"adventure" schools; certainly they were often marginal commercial enterprises and varied greatly in their merits. But they were one of the few publicly approved ways by which a respectable woman could build an institution, and several schools that later achieved fame began in this way. Sarah Pierce of Litchfield, Connecticut, gathered several girls around her dining room table in 1792; her academy grew to become one of the most formidable schools in the Northeast, attracting students from as far away as the British West Indies.[24]

The records of one small Maryland school suggest some of the problems these ambitious spirits faced. Attendance fluctuated wildly. In 1783, Sarah Callister taught nine girls who came for two quarters, ten for all three. Twelve girls stayed only a month. In 1788 Mrs. Callister heard that a teacher had left Annapolis and contemplated moving there to fill the gap: "I would undertake to teach reading, & the several needleworks that Mrs. Smith did (& writing, if required) I would also take Boarders." Her new school seems never to have materialized. "I have done every thing my small abilities would allow for a livelihood," she mourned, "& O painfull! Affliction, caprice, has rendered my endeavours vain!"[25] Sarah Callister discovered that although keeping a private school might appear at the outset as a simple extension of domesticity, it was also a business enterprise, requiring a high degree of assertiveness and skill if it were to succeed.

Esther Slocum turned a marginal school near Greenwich, Connecticut, into a prosperous enterprise by force of will and administrative skill. She actively recruited students. "As, many of the scholars that attended my

S.C., Columbia. Anne Hart's husband was a revival minister associated with Gilbert Tennent; he had left her in Charleston while he spread the gospel in Philadelphia. For "respectability," see school advertisements in the *Aurora* (Philadelphia), Mar. 24, 26, 1796, and in Woody, *History of Women's Education*, I, 217–227. An impoverished female relative wrote to Jedidiah Morse, the geographer, in 1796: "I am not doing much business at present but hope to open the store in the spring if I can get the store open and a few young ladies to board and instruct. . . . I think I shall be quite happy" (Mrs. M. Morse to Jedidiah Morse, Dec. 1796, Jedidiah Morse Papers, Box 1, Manuscripts and Archives Division, The New York Public Library, Astor, Lenox and Tilden Foundations, New York City). Sarah Osborn's diary reveals the motives of a woman who built her home school into a substantial enterprise. See Samuel Hopkins, ed., *Memoirs of the Life of Mrs. Sarah Osborn . . .* (Worcester, Mass., 1799), and Mary Beth Norton, ed., "'My Resting Reaping Times,' Sarah Osborn's Defense of Her 'Unfeminine' Activities, 1767," *Signs*, II (1976), 515–529.

24. Emily Noyes Vanderpoel, *Chronicles of a Pioneer School from 1792 to 1833: Being the History of Miss Sarah Pierce and Her Litchfield School* (Cambridge, Mass., 1903).

25. Sarah Callister to Robert Couder, Aug. 1788, Sarah Callister to Mr. Crookshanks, Aug. 27, 1788, Henry Callister Papers, Maryland Diocesan Archives of the Protestant Episcopal Church, Maryland Historical Society, Baltimore.

School that Summer, had, previous to my arrival, been taken up by the *'native'* schools, my only resort was, to go to those who had been among my greatest opposers, & who had never been known to send their children to teachers from other states. But not believing that they would do *more* than deny me, I ventured to go, & strange to tell, was in no instance denied but *one*, & that was occasioned alone by poverty." Slocum recruited five older girls who were "resting contented with their attainments," though they had never learned to write and could only read with difficulty, and elicited from them "a determination to 'labour for learning.'" In less than a year after her arrival in Connecticut, she had recruited thirty-six students for her daily school, and more for her Sunday school, and cheerfully reported that she found each season more interesting than the last.[26]

These schools were often defended on the grounds that they would serve a new purpose. The education of young women had traditionally been an education for marriage—if at all possible, an upwardly mobile marriage. Girls were said to need a new kind of education because their traditional training had been superficial and their resulting behavior shallow. How, it was asked, can women's minds be free if they are taught that their sphere is limited to fashion, music, and needlework? Fashion became an emblem of superficiality and dependence. It was distasteful in a wife, inappropriate in a republic. The Philadelphia *Lady's Magazine* criticized a father who prepared his daughters for the marriage market: "You boast of having given your daughters an education which will enable them 'to shine in the first circles.' . . . They sing indifferently; they play the harpsichord indifferently; they are mistresses of every common game at cards . . . ; they . . . have just as much knowledge of dress as to deform their persons by an awkward imitation of every new fashion which appears. . . . Placed in a situation of difficulty, they have neither a head to dictate, nor a hand to help in any domestic concern."[27] Teaching young girls to dress well was part of the larger message that their primary lifetime goal must be marriage; fashion was a feature of sexual politics. "I have sometimes been led," remarked Benjamin Rush, "to ascribe the invention of ridiculous and expensive fashions in female dress entirely to the gentlemen in order to divert the ladies from improving their minds

26. Esther Slocum to Christopher Slocum, June 21, 1825, Slocum Family Papers, Manuscripts and Archives Div., N. Y. Pub. Lib., Astor, Lenox and Tilden Foundations, New York City.

27. *Lady's Mag.* (Aug. 1792), 121–123.

and thereby to secure a more arbitrary and unlimited authority over them."[28]

In the marriage market, beauty, flirtatiousness, and charm were at a premium; intelligence, good judgment, and competence (in short, the republican virtues) were at a discount. Because it seemed appropriate for women in a republic to have greater control over their own lives, "the *dependence* for which women are uniformly educated" was deplored. The Republic did not need fashion plates; it needed citizens—women as well as men—of self-discipline and of strong mind. The contradiction between the counsel given to young women and their own self-interest, as well as the best interests of the Republic, seemed obvious. In theory the marriage market undercut the Republic.[29]

The idea that political independence should be the catalyst for a new female self-reliance that would free women from the constraints of the marriage market and prepare them to be economically independent appears in its most developed form in the work of Judith Sargent Murray. In 1784 she published a prescient argument calling for the strengthening of what she called "Self-Complacency in Female Bosoms." Lacking a strong and positive sense of their own identity, she complained, young women had no personal resources with which to resist the marriage market, and so they rushed into marriages to establish their social status.[30] Eight years later, widowed and remarried to the Universalist minister John Murray, she developed this theme at great length in a series of essays, which were published in the *Massachusetts Magazine* between

28. Benjamin Rush, "Thoughts upon Female Education, Accommodated to the Present State of Society, Manners and Government in the United States of America" (Philadelphia, 1787), in Frederick Rudolph, ed., *Essays on Education in the Early Republic* (Cambridge, Mass., 1965), 39.

29. "The greater proportion of young women are trained up by thoughtless parents, in ease and luxury, with no other dependence for their future support than the precarious chance of establishing themselves by marriage: for this purpose (the men best know why) elaborate attention is paid to external attractions and accomplishments, to the neglect of the more useful and solid acquirements. . . . [Marriage is the] *sole* method of procuring for themselves an establishment" (*New York Magazine* [Aug. 1797], 406). For comment on the marriage market, see letter signed "A Matrimonial Republican," *Lady's Mag.* (July 1792), 64–67, and "Legal Prostitution, Or Modern Marriage," *Independent Chronicle* (Boston), Oct. 28, 1793. For criticism of fashion, see *Am. Mag.* (Dec. 1787), 39; *ibid.* (July 1788), 594; *Am. Museum* (Aug. 1788), 119; and *Massachusetts Mercury* (Boston), Aug. 16, 1793, Jan. 16, 1795.

30. "Desultory Thoughts Upon the Utility of Encouraging a Degree of Self-Complacency, Especially in FEMALE BOSOMS," *Gentlemen and Ladies Town and Country Magazine* (Oct. 1784), 251–252.

1792 and 1794 and collected under the title of *The Gleaner* in 1798. In these essays, Murray insisted that instruction in a manual trade was especially appropriate in a republic, and she decried the antiegalitarian habit of assuming that a genteel and impractical education was superior to a vocational one. She was critical of fathers who permitted their sons to grow up without a useful skill and was even more critical of parents who "pointed their daughters" toward marriage and dependence. This direction made girls' education contingent on a single event. It offered young women a single vision of the future. "Our girls, in general, are bred up with one particular view, with one monopolizing consideration, which seems to absorb every other plan that reason might point out as worthy [of] their attention: An establishment by marriage; this is the goal to which they are constantly pointed, the great ultimatum of every arrangement: *An old maid*, they are from infancy taught, at least indirectly, to consider as a contemptible being; and they have no other means of advancing themselves but in the matrimonial line."

Murray's own prescription was rather different. "I would give my daughters every accomplishment which I thought proper," she wrote, "and, to crown all, I would early accustom them to habits of industry and order. They should be taught with precision the art economical; they should be enabled to procure for themselves the necessaries of life; independence should be placed within their grasp."[31] The more competent the woman, the less vulnerable she would be to the pressures of the marriage market. "THE SEX should be taught to depend on their own efforts, for the procurement of an establishment in life. The chance of a matrimonial coadjutor, is no more than a probable contingency; and if they were early accustomed to regard this *uncertain* event with suitable *indifference*, they would make elections with that deliberation, which would be calculated to give a more rational prospect of tranquillity." She drew on her own experience to observe that even the happily married might find themselves widowed and would be grateful for their own competence. "The term, *helpless widow*, might be rendered as unfrequent and inapplicable as that of *helpless widower*; and although we should undoubtedly continue to mourn . . . yet we should derive consolation from the knowledge . . . that a mother could *assist* as well as *weep* over her offspring."[32] She scattered throughout the *Gleaner* essays fictional versions of self-respecting women in the characters of Margaretta, Mrs. Virgilius, and

31. Murray, *The Gleaner*, I, No. 17, 167, 168.
32. *Ibid.*, III, No. 91, 219.

Penelope Airy. Repeatedly she counseled that a woman should be encouraged to develop competence: "She *should reverence herself.*"[33]

To illustrate her point, Murray wrote a story about two sisters, Helen and Penelope. Helen is skilled only in embroidery and music. She has "many sighing swains"; she spends her time in reading novels and her inheritance on new clothes. Penelope, on the other hand, takes seriously the advice of their Aunt Dorothy, who "wishes not to see us dependant upon any one; she is anxious to inspire our bosoms with the *noble ardour of independence.*" Penelope takes independence to be her "ardent pursuit": she wakes at sunrise and spends her day studying music, drawing, and geography because these skills "polish my mind." She eschews fashionable clothes and does needlework for pay, observing that "it is really surprising, how much *order* and *industry* will accomplish." Penelope shares with Helen a delight in dancing, cards, and even theater, but these pastimes are not the main purpose of her life. Nor is she in a hurry to marry; "respectability, usefulness, tranquillity, independence, social enjoyments and holy friendship, are to be found in a single life." Murray was surely optimistic in her estimate of the extent to which financial independence could be earned by seamstresses in the 1790s, but she showed that because of this independence, Penelope could resist inappropriate suitors. Eventually Penelope is properly appreciated and marries "an amiable man" with a "moderate fortune." Helen's dissipated manners have frightened off suitors, and, as the tale ends, she is living in spinsterhood and economic dependence on her sister.[34]

The model republican woman was competent and confident. She could resist the vagaries of fashion; she was rational, benevolent, independent, self-reliant. Nearly every writer who described this paragon prepared a list of role models, echoing the pantheon of heroines admired by the fundraising women of Philadelphia in 1780. There were women of the ancient world, like Cornelia, the mother of the Gracchi; rulers like Elizabeth of England and the Empress Catherine the Great of Russia; a handful of Frenchwomen: Mme de Genlis, Mme de Maintenon, and Mme Dacier; and a long list of British intellectuals: Lady Mary Wortley Montagu, Hannah More, Elizabeth Carter, Mrs. Knowles (the Quaker who had bested Dr. Samuel Johnson in debate), Mary Wollstonecraft, and Catharine Macaulay.[35] Such women were rumored to exist in America; they

33. *Ibid.*, I, No. 20, 193. See also *ibid.*, I, 168: "I would teach them '*to reverence themselves*'" (Murray's italics).

34. *Ibid.*, I, No. 18, 172–173, 176–181.

35. For examples of such lists, see *ibid.*, III, 200–219; John Blair Linn, *The Powers of*

were given fictional form by Murray and Charles Brockden Brown. Those who believed in these republican models demanded that their presence be recognized and endorsed and that a new generation of young women be urged to find in them patterns for their own behavior.

The creation of such women in America became a major educational challenge. Writers were fond of attributing the inadequacies of American women to early upbringing and environmental influences, a point also raised by English critics like Mary Wollstonecraft. Images of confinement, of involuntary domestication, recur frequently in the language of these critics. Must women remain, Wollstonecraft asked, "immured in their families groping in the dark?" An American pamphlet writer complained that a boy was usually permitted to stay in school longer than his sister, who was arbitrarily "removed from every mean[s] of literary improvement, and . . . immured in a house. . . . If she be not sent to a nunnery, she is at least confined to domestic labor, and utterly secluded from all public concerns."[36] "Will it be said that the judgment of a male of two years old, is more sage than that of a female's of the same age?" asked Judith Sargent Murray. "But . . . As their years increase, the sister must be wholly domesticated, while the brother is led by the hand through all the flowery paths of science." The *Universal Asylum* published a long and thoughtful essay by "A Lady" who argued that "in the nursery, strength is equal in the male and female." When a boy went to school, he immediately met both intellectual and physical challenge. His teachers instructed him in science and language; his friends dared him to fight, to run after a hoop, to jump a rope. Girls, on the other hand, were "committed to illiterate teachers, . . . cooped up in a room, confined to needle work, deprived of exercise." Thomas Cooper feared a trend. "We

---

Genius, a Poem in Three Parts, 2d ed. (Philadelphia, 1802); *Weekly Magazine* (Philadelphia), Aug. 4, 11, 1798; *Port Folio*, Feb. 12, 1803, Sept. 27, 1806; and J. A. Neale, "An Essay on the Genius and Education of the Fair Sex," *Philadelphia Minerva*, Mar. 14, 1795. For the admiration expressed by Abigail Adams and Mercy Otis Warren for Catharine Macaulay, see Abigail Adams to Isaac Smith, Jr., Apr. 20, 1771; Abigail Adams to Catharine Sawbridge Macaulay, n.d., 1774; and Mercy Otis Warren to Abigail Adams, Jan. 28, 1775, all in *Adams Family Correspondence*, I, 76–77, 177–179, 181–183. Theodosia Prevost Burr found charming irony in Catherine the Great's designs on Turkey in 1791: "It is a diverting thought, that the mighty Emperor of the Turks should be subdued by a woman. How enviable that she alone should be the avenger of her sex's wrongs for so many ages past" (Theodosia Prevost Burr to Aaron Burr, July 27, 1791, Matthew L. Davis, ed., *Memoirs of Aaron Burr. With Miscellaneous Selections from His Correspondence*, I [New York, 1836], 301).

36. Mary Wollstonecraft, *A Vindication of the Rights of Woman*, ed. Miriam Brody Kramnick (Harmondsworth, England, 1975), 87; *Female Advocate*, 27–28.

first keep their minds and then their persons in subjection," he wrote. "We educate women from infancy to marriage, in such a way as to debilitate both their corporeal and their mental powers. All the accomplishments we teach them are directed, not to *their* future benefit in life, but to the amusement of the male sex; and having for a series of years, with much assiduity, and sometimes at much expense, incapacitated them for any serious occupation, we say they are not fit to govern themselves."[37]

This ideology of self-reliance, it should be said, paid little direct attention to those for whom the marriage market promised upward mobility, and who therefore considered matchmaking a useful aspect of republican opportunity. More sophisticated education might be championed as a means of avoiding the marriage market, but many families who seemed to accept the reform in fact redefined it as a means of strengthening their daughters' position within the marriage market. They were responsive to the arguments that an educated girl would have more marital choices.

A character in a school graduation play performed in Greenfield, Massachusetts, in 1800 remarks: "Uncle Tristam says he hates to have girls go to school, it makes them so darn'd uppish & so dread[?] proud that they wont work. . . . But why do you need so much larning; you study religion, d'ye mean to preach? No, I see the trick, you mean to marry parsons, & make us poor farmers girls call you madams. . . . Brother George says Philosophers used to wear long beards—he makes fun of you, and calls you the smooth skin'd philosophers." Gradually Nelly is persuaded to admit that educated men speak to educated women with respect. She comes to see schooling as a way to make herself appealing to men more refined than "humdrum" farmers. She goes to a dance with the students and finds that she is treated like a lady. "They did not say: come along Nell & here it goes Nell—but shall I have the pleasure to dance with you Miss Nelly. . . . they treated me so well that it really made me feel *purely*." At last she reflects, "If I really thought I could get a nice

37. *Massachusetts Magazine*, II (Mar. 1790), 133; *Universal Asylum and Columbian Magazine* (July 1791), 9–10; Thomas Cooper, "Propositions Respecting the Foundation of Civil Government," *Political Arithmetic* (Philadelphia?, 1798), 27–28. See also *Boston Wkly. Mag.* (May 21, 1803), 121–122; *Am. Museum* (Jan. 1787), 59; and *Lady's Mag.* (June 1792). The "Female Advocate" offered an explicit answer to the question of where female genius might be found: "Let the . . . women be viewed as intitled to a share with the men, in literary concerns, and we should find, not once in an age only, but every year, there would arise female geniuses unsurpassed by all the boasted superiority of the present assumers of universal merit" (*Female Advocate*, 25). Aaron Burr permitted himself to wonder out loud about the distinctions between male and female education; see Aaron Burr to Theodosia Prevost Burr, Feb. 15, 1793, Davis, ed., *Memoirs of Burr*, I, 362.

husband I don't know but I should try to larn." This goal inspires her final decision: "I'll go to school with all my heart. . . . Well now this beat all, that you should by Arithmetic [increase] the likelihood of being married—I'll learn arithmetic, I will, I will."[38]

In Greenfield as elsewhere in the early Republic, female learning was thus explicitly put to the service of upward social mobility. Sarah Pierce took great pride in her students' intellectual accomplishments—but she also was conscious that one of the best advertisements for her school was the highly "suitable" marriages some of her girls made with students from Tapping Reeve's nearby Litchfield Law School. If there was a disjunction between the expressed ideology of a girls' school and the semiconscious motives of its adherents, it was a contradiction from which other institutions—churches, benevolent societies—also suffered.

Even were it granted that girls ought to be educated for the Republic, what ought that education to comprise? Ought it to be the same as boys' schooling? Ought the goal of the Republic to be a generation of learned ladies? Was the "Lady" who wrote a long imitation of Alexander Pope for the *American Museum* correct in her claim that women might even share that distinctly masculine passion, ambition?

> In either sex the appetite's the same,
> For love of pow'r is still the love of fame.
> .   .   .   .
> In education all the diff'rence lies;
> Women, if taught, wou'd be as learn'd and wise
> As haughty man, improv'd by arts and rules . . .[39]

As these verses suggest, opinions on women's education were inextricably tangled with opinions about the capacity of women's minds; educational policy was dependent on assumptions about the female intellect. At one end of the spectrum of reforming opinion was the "Female Advocate," who indulged in a proposal—only half in jest—that the tables be turned. "What would be the consequence," she asked, "if the doors of our seminaries were as effectually shut against the gentlemen, as they now are against the other sex; and colleges and superior schools of scientific improvement, were appropriately thrown open to the benefit of the female

---

38. Journal of Sally Ripley, Am. Antq. Soc., Worcester, Mass.

39. "On Pope's Characters of Women," By A Lady, *Am. Museum*, XI (1792), app. 1, 13–15.

world . . . ?" At the other end was Samuel Harrison Smith, who began the essay that won the American Philosophical Society's 1797 prize for the best plan for a national system of education by proposing "that every male child, without exception, be educated." He said nothing about female children.[40]

The founders of the new girls' schools were striking out on new terrain. Since women were not being prepared for the traditional professions— law, medicine, the clergy—teachers could not easily assume that girls ought to have the same studies as did boys. Indeed teachers were forced to confront the question, For what profession were girls being prepared? With near unanimity they answered that girls were being prepared to be wiser wives and better mothers. Domesticity was treated as a vocation, motherhood a profession.[41] Devising a curriculum for girls was an exercise in answering the question, What does a woman need to know?

Judith Sargent Murray recommended a course of study that could be taught at home by mothers. A woman, she thought, should be able to write and converse elegantly and correctly, pronounce French, read history, comprehend some simple geography and astronomy. All these a mother would teach to her children.[42] Perhaps the best-known proposal for a new female curriculum was prepared by Benjamin Rush, who prescribed reading, grammar, penmanship, "figures and bookkeeping," and geography. He added "the first principles of natural philosophy," vocal music to soothe cares and exercise the lungs (but not instrumental music, which seemed to him a waste of valuable time for all but the most talented), and history as an antidote to novel reading.

Rush offered his model curriculum in a speech to the Board of Visitors of the Young Ladies' Academy of Philadelphia, later published and widely reprinted under the title "Thoughts Upon Female Education, Accommo-

40. *Female Advocate*, 29; Samuel Harrison Smith, "Remarks on Education: Illustrating the Close Connection between Virtue and Wisdom" (Philadelphia, 1798), in Rudolph, ed., *Essays on Education*, 211. Smith did acknowledge that female instruction was important, but concepts of its makeup seemed so varied that he feared to make any proposals and despaired of including women in his scheme. "It is sufficient, perhaps, for the present, that the improvement of women is marked by a rapid progress and that a prospect opens equal to their most ambitious desires" (*ibid.*, 217). The other prizewinner, Samuel Knox, proposed to admit girls to the primary schools, but not to the academies or colleges. Knox's "An Essay on the Best System of Liberal Education" is reprinted in Rudolph, ed., *Essays on Education*, 271–372. See also Charles E. Cunningham, *Timothy Dwight, 1752–1817: A Biography* (New York, 1942), 154–163, and Nov. 17, 1786, Dexter, ed., *Literary Diary of Ezra Stiles*, III, 247–248.

41. Cott, *Bonds of Womanhood*, chap. 2, esp. 70–74.

42. Murray, *The Gleaner*, I, No. 7, 68–71.

dated to the Present State of Society, Manners and Government in the United States of America." The academy claimed to be the first female academy chartered in the United States. When Rush spoke on July 28, 1787, he was offering practical advice to a new school, which he linked to the greater cause of demonstrating the possibilities of women's minds. Those who were skeptical of education for women, Rush declared, were the same who opposed "the general diffusion of knowledge among the citizens of our republics." Rush argued that "female education should be accommodated to the state of society, manners, and government of the country in which it is conducted." An appropriate education for American women would be condensed, because they married earlier than their European counterparts. It would include bookkeeping, because American women could expect to be "the stewards and guardians of their husbands' property" and executrices of their husbands' wills. It would qualify them for "a general intercourse with the world" by an acquaintance with geography and chronology. If education is preparation for life, then American women required a newly tailored educational program.[43]

The curriculum of the Young Ladies' Academy (which one of the school's Board of Visitors called "abundantly sufficient to complete the female mind") included reading, writing, arithmetic, English grammar, composition, rhetoric, and geography. It did not include the natural philosophy Rush hoped for (although Rush did deliver a dozen vaguely scientific lectures), advanced mathematics, or the classics. Most significantly, needlework was not a part of the curriculum.

The Young Ladies' Academy was a private school, appealing to parents who wanted their daughters to emerge from home tutoring into a more public form of education without having to board away from home. Although incorporated by charter, the academy did not receive public funds. Within a year after its opening it enrolled nearly a hundred girls. The teachers were male. Students wrote their exercises in copybooks with covers carrying a series of maxims that offer insight into the school's ideology. The first cover slogan was a general call to learning: "HEAR, ye

43. Rush, "Thoughts Upon Female Education," in Rudolph, ed., *Essays on Education*, 25–40. Rush seems to have partially overstated his assertion that American conditions demanded more mathematical and economic sophistication of women than did European. According to Daniel Scott Smith, "Inheritance and the Position and Orientation of Colonial Women" (paper delivered at Berkshire Conference of Women Historians, 1974, Schlesinger Library, Radcliffe College, Cambridge, Mass.), Rush's female contemporaries seem to have been *less* likely to be named executrices than their ancestors; when they were, a male heir was more likely to be named as a partner. It is not yet established to what extent the exclusion of women was an aspect of the modernization of finance and the economy.

children. . . . Wisdom is the principal thing; therefore get wisdom, and with all thy getting get understanding." Those that followed were an explicit rationale for female education: "That learning belongs not to the female character, and that the female mind is incapable of a degree of improvement equal to that of the other sex, are narrow and unphilo-sophical prejudice. The present times exhibit most honorable instances of female learning and genius. The superior advantages of boys' education are, perhaps the sole reason of their subsequent superiority. Learning is equally attainable, and I think equally valuable, for the satisfaction aris-ing from it, to a woman as a man."[44]

The academy's ideology and pride permeated all its public statements. The school even published a collection of early graduation addresses with the telling title *The Rise and Progress of the Young Ladies' Academy of Philadelphia*. These speeches commonly indulged in hyperbole. "Now daily experience and common observation teach us," said Ann Loxley, the 1790 valedictorian, "that no age, sex or denomination are deprived of the means whereby an ample and sufficient knowledge of the different branches of the arts and sciences may be acquired." Dr. Benjamin Say told the 1789 graduates that they had "all the advantages. . . . the different branches of science, which are taught in the Young Ladies' Academy . . . are abundantly sufficient to unfold the latent buds of your minds, and expand their variegated beauties." As testimony to their seriousness of purpose, members of the board of trustees came regularly as visitors to hear and validate examinations. The seal of the school showed seven books surrounded by the motto, "The Path of Science."[45]

Still, we must be cautious about taking the school's slogans literally. There was something of a discrepancy between promise and practice; the options opened to young women were considerably narrower than those opened to their brothers. The pride women expressed in their new learn-ing was balanced by the promise that traditional values would be upheld and maintained. Eliza Laskey devoted much of her 1793 valedictory oration, for example, to the subject of "*Modesty*, this cardinal female accomplishment." She promised "deference and respect to our superiors," "subjection and obedience to our parents," "decorum and obedience to our parents," "decorum and decency." She did cling to the "liberty to speak on any subject which is suitable," and she did distinguish modesty

44. For comments on the size of the school and the appeal of a nonboarding environ-ment, see *The Rise and Progress of the Young Ladies' Academy of Philadelphia* (Philadel-phia, 1794), 16–17, 7–8. Copybook in Rush Papers, Hist. Soc. Pa., Philadelphia.
45. *Rise and Progress of the Young Ladies' Academy*, 39–40, 30–31.

from "dull and rigid silence," warning against taking "silence . . . for virtue, ignorance . . . for religion, and affectation for politeness."[46] Even Benjamin Rush placed a narrower construction on his educational prescriptions for women than he did on those he made for men.

Rush tended to link women's need for knowledge to their duty as wives and mothers, and in the process he drifted inexorably (and perhaps unconsciously) from technical to vocational guidance. He delivered lectures on natural philosophy to the young men at the College of Philadelphia, but these talks were substantially revised when presented to the Young Ladies' Academy under the ambivalent title of "Lectures, Containing the Application of the Principles of Natural Philosophy, and Chemistry, to Domestic and Culinary Purposes." He understood, he said, "how much duty and necessity conspire to confine a lady to her house." In these lectures he dispensed information that might be found useful in homes, from the chemical qualities of asbestos to a felicitously phrased warning about the dangers of insect transmission of disease: "*Insects* doubtless were designed by Providence to answer some useful purposes certain it is that they are standing monuments of the *fall* of man: they tell us that we have forfeited our right to the earth; and that, while we are in this world, we are in an enemy's country." The culmination of Rush's lectures suggests the ultimate purpose for women's scientific studies— better management of households, and more specifically, kitchens. The image of the kitchen he had in mind was definitely an upper-class kitchen, one inhabited not only by insects and germs, but also by servants, a class of people he clearly associated with "vice, or ill manners."

> There is one, and but one, method of preventing the disorders of a kitchen—and that is by the presence of a mistress. The tongue, eyes and ears of a mistress in her kitchen are an effectual remedy for all disorders; It is inconceivable what good effects would be produced by a lady visiting her kitchen two or three times a day. It would promote economy, and by that means give a wife a complete influence over her husband; for certain it is, that a man will love that woman most, whose affection for himself he feels, every time he sits down for a meal, or puts his hand in his pocket. *see Solomon's character of a virtuous woman—Prov XXXI 10.[47]

46. *Ibid.*, 92–97.
47. These lectures seem not to have been prepared for publication. Rush's manuscript notes are in his supplemental notebooks in the Rush Papers, Hist. Soc. Pa.

The curriculum of the Young Ladies' Academy could also be found, with moderate variations, at female branches of town academies and at female boarding schools, where needlework, music, and dancing were often additional subjects. It became common practice for schools to require each student to keep a journal of the day's lessons and sermons; these journals show the extensive reliance on rote learning and on working one's way slowly, lesson-by-lesson, chapter-by-chapter, through a text—a technique common in boys' schools as well. The informal comments added to the journal entries make them a window into the girls' schools, a rich source of insight into the quality of daily life there.

Nevertheless, these journals must not be read as private diaries (though they often masquerade as such). They originated as school exercises and were regularly reviewed by teachers. At the Newark Academy in New Jersey, keeping a journal was an explicit part of the curriculum, "a happy expedient for giving" the students "a facility of expression," according to Principal Timothy Alden. Sarah Pierce set a formal quota for her girls: "sixty lines of good writing every week." Some years later, a perceptive girl in Margaret Fuller's Providence, Rhode Island, school described the dynamics of the assignment accurately. "It appears to me," she remarked, "that these Journals must be very nice keys—by which, the teachers, can unlock the hearts, the characters, and as it were read the very thoughts of their scholars."[48]

The new women's seminaries of the post-Revolutionary era, with their grammar books, their translations from the classics, their "Ladies' Libraries," can be seen as efforts to absorb women into a modern culture that increasingly relied on print. The common practice of requiring a school journal was in part a device for monitoring a pupil's studies, but it also may have been a mode of forcing her to give a written, rather than an oral, account of her experiences. The journal writer must transfer her private feelings into written words for public scrutiny; through her entries the adult can monitor the development of the self-conscious use of the public medium.

Less inhibited by traditional assumptions about what had "always

48. *Quarterly Catalogue of the names of the young ladies, who belong to the Newark academy, under the instruction of Rev. Timothy Alden* (Newark, N.J., 1811), 38; Journal of Mary C. Camp [at Sarah Pierce's School], July 1818, Conn. State Lib., Hartford; Journal of Anna D. Gale [at Margaret Fuller's School], Feb. 15, 1838, Gale Family Papers, Am. Antq. Soc., Worcester, Mass. See also Mary Chester to Edwin Chester, May 29, 1819, Vanderpoel, *Chronicles of a Pioneer School,* 191: "My time is wholly taken up. I have to keep a journal and write compositions which with other studies occupy all the time of a moderate genius."

been done," the curriculum of the new girls' schools could be imaginative, even adventurous. This feature of the schools is not often recognized. Because the usual textbooks were "so dry & devoid of interest that children" were "disgusted by them," the founders of girls' academies were often driven to prepare their own collections or to write their own teaching materials. Finding "from long experience . . . that children and youth imbibe ideas most easily, when placed in the form of question and answer," Sarah Pierce wrote a world history in dialogue form for her students.[49] Some of the first American history and geography textbooks were written by Emma Willard, who objected to the usual practice of beginning the study of history with the ancient world. She believed that young women needed to know the history of their own country more than they needed to know about Greece and Rome, and when she found no texts that suited her, she wrote some good ones herself. Indeed, Willard's teaching methods, as Anne Firor Scott has shown, encouraged active, not passive, learning and anticipated the approach of John Dewey and other progressive educators of the twentieth century. "Each individual is to himself the centre of his own world," Willard observed, "and the more intimately he connects his knowledge with himself, the better will it be remembered." In her geography classes, the first assignment was to draw a map of one's hometown.[50] Acting was introduced; instead of pompous graduation orations, girls read poetry or presented dramatic skits.[51]

Perhaps the most far-reaching reform was the wholesale elimination of the classics from the curriculum. Classics were already coming to be regarded as a decorative accomplishment for men. They had never been part of the education of lower-class boys and were on their way to becoming a vestigial part of the training of all except prospective lawyers and doctors at the close of the eighteenth century. A very few individuals did try to bridge the intellectual gap between men and women by introducing women to the classics, but most who did so tutored their daughters at home and risked the label of eccentricity. Aaron Burr, for example, made certain that his daughter, Theodosia, learned Latin and Greek. He insisted that her tutor demand much of her and scribbled for her a mock

---

49. Vanderpoel, *Chronicles of a Pioneer School*, 82, 81.

50. Emma Willard, *History of the United States, or Republic of America* (New York, 1828–1849), v–vi; Anne Firor Scott, "What, Then, is the American: This New Woman?" *JAH*, LXV (1978), 689–691.

51. Several examples are published in Vanderpoel, *Chronicles of a Pioneer School*, 84–145. Sally Ripley's diary includes the full texts of two one-act plays.

Needlework picture by Mary M. Franklin (1808). Silk, ink, and watercolor. Teachers at girls' academies frequently translated formal learning into familiar media. In Pleasant Valley, New York, a schoolgirl embroidered a map of the

world. Did the effort improve her knowledge of geography?
Courtesy The Henry Francis du Pont Winterthur Museum.

journal entry that suggests his high expectations: "Learnt 230 lines which finished Horace. heigh ho. for Terence & the Greek Grammar Tomorrow. . . . Began Gibbon this evening—I find he requires as much study as Horace."[52] But in his educational standards, as in so much else, Burr is a poor guide to things of which his contemporaries approved.

Benjamin Rush is a better guide. Rush thought of the classics as remnants of aristocratic education unsuited to a republican nation and an industrial economy. He had no patience at all with the Latin quotations that dotted the oratory and philosophical writings of his day. "Do not men use Latin and Greek as scuttlefish emit their ink," he bitterly asked John Adams, "on purpose to conceal themselves from an intercourse with the common people?"[53]

Rush was convinced that the stronger the emphasis on the classics in American schools, the greater would be the gap between men and women (as well as between rich and poor). Decrying "the present immense disparity which subsists between the sexes, in the degrees of their education and knowledge," he predicted that abandoning the classical languages would contribute greatly to diminishing that disparity. "One cause of the misery of many families, as well as communities, may be sought for in the *mediocrity* of knowledge of the women. They should know more . . . in order to be happy themselves, and to communicate happiness to others. By ceasing to make Latin and Greek a necessary part of a liberal education, we open the doors for every species of improvement to the female part of society."[54]

Rush promised to write an essay about Latin and Greek addressed specifically to American women, but never got around to it.[55] He did, however, keep the issue alive in the scientific lectures he delivered to female audiences. "It was for many ages unfortunately the practice to wrap

52. Aaron Burr to Theodosia Burr, Dec. 16, 1793, Burr Papers, Microfilm, Reel 3, 430, N.-Y. Hist. Soc., New York City; Aaron Burr to Theodosia Burr, Feb. 13, 1794, Davis, ed., *Memoirs of Burr*, I, 376. See other letters on the subject in Davis, ed., *Memoirs of Burr*, I, 364, 369–370, 373, 376, 378, 380–387, 392–393, and Herbert S. Parmet and Marie B. Hecht, *Aaron Burr: Portrait of an Ambitious Man* (New York, 1967), 89–90. See also Harriott Pinckney to Mrs. Favell, Mar. 1763, Pinckney Papers.

53. Benjamin Rush to John Adams, July 21, 1789, Butterfield, ed., *Letters of Rush*, I, 524.

54. "Observations Upon the Study of Latin and Greek Languages," in Benjamin Rush, *Essays, Literary, Moral and Philosophical* (Philadelphia, 1798), 44. For Latin as a path to male upward social mobility, see Richard Cranch to Billy Cranch, June 13, 1783, Cranch Papers, Lib. Cong.

55. Benjamin Rush to John Adams, July 21, 1789, Butterfield, ed., *Letters of Rush*, I, 524.

Charles Févret de Saint-Mémin, *Theodosia Burr* (1796).
Courtesy National Portrait Gallery, Washington, D.C.

up the sciences in the dead languages," he told schoolgirls in 1801, "by which means the knowledge of them was confined exclusively to the members of the learned professions. After the revival of letters by means of the reformation and the art of printing, the sciences were emancipated from the dead languages, but they were so much envelopped in obscure and technical terms as to be intelligible only to gentlemen. Of late years pains have been taken to render them intelligible to ladies."[56] Rush thought of himself as an important vehicle for this transmission of knowledge; as we have seen, he gave several series of scientific lectures at the Young Ladies' Academy, he urged his son James to deliver a Princeton commencement lecture on "the influence of female education . . . upon the prosperity of our country" (even offered to write it), and he continued in an informal way to air his thoughts on the subject to his friends. In 1810 John Adams transmitted a message from his wife that reflected Rush's sentiments rather than John Adams's own energetic defense of the classics: "Mrs. Adams says she is willing you should discredit Greek and Latin because it will destroy the foundation of all the pretensions of the gentlemen to superiority over the ladies and restore liberty, equality and fraternity between the sexes."[57]

In the long run, American curricula developed as Rush wished. But in the short run, which extended well past Rush's own lifetime, boys' schools continued to be classically oriented. Nancy Cott has argued forcefully that the more women's schools stressed the special suitability of their curricula for women, the more "the predominant philosophy of

56. Apr. 16, 1801, Supplemental Notebook of Benjamin Rush, Rush Papers, Hist. Soc. Pa.

57. Benjamin Rush to James Rush, June 4, 1805, Butterfield, ed., *Letters of Rush*, I, 895; John Adams to Benjamin Rush, Oct. 13, 1810, John A. Schutz, ed., *The Spur of Fame: Dialogues of John Adams and Benjamin Rush, 1805–1813* (San Marino, Calif., 1966), 170. Women seem to have understood that they were denied the classics because of their sex. See, for example, Susannah Rowson's preface to her play *Slaves in Algiers*: "I am fully sensible of the many disadvantages under which I consequently labor from a confined education; nor do I expect my style will be thought equal in elegance or energy, to the productions of those who, fortunately, from their sex, or situation in life, have been instructed in the classics, and have reaped both pleasure and improvement by studying the Ancients in their original purity" (*Slaves in Algiers* [Philadelphia, 1794], ii). Maria Edgeworth complained that boys' education was badly skewed by attention to dead languages and that the effort of learning elegant Latin hampered development in English: "Girls usually write much better than boys; they think and express their thoughts clearly at an age when young men can scarcely write an easy letter upon any common occasion. . . . If they [women] do not acquire a classic taste, neither do they acquire classic prejudices: nor are they early disgusted with literature, by pedagogues, lexicons, grammars, and all the melancholy apparatus of learning" (*Letters for Literary Ladies* . . . [Georgetown, D.C., 1810], 30–31).

female education encouraged women to understand gender as the essential determinant of their lives."[58] The elimination of the classics was an important contribution to this development, little though Rush may have intended it.

"Really now what do you think of these times? Everybody is going to school, do you think they gets any good by it?" asks a character in Sally Ripley's Greenfield graduation play. More formally, and with pardonable overstatement, Judith Sargent Murray reported in 1798, "Female academies are every where establishing." Murray regarded these schools as a logical expression of a progressive desire for "the establishment of the female intellect." The implication of her remark is not that the schools were intended to prove that females had intellects but that women needed institutional frameworks or "establishments" in which to exercise their minds. An early supporter of the Philadelphia Young Ladies' Academy openly stated that the lack of "institutions of learning" had suppressed genius in embryo. "We must (if open to conviction,) be convinced that *females* are fully capable of sounding the most profound depths and of attaining to the most sublime excellence in every part of science," wrote J. A. Neale. Some years later Emma Willard, the brilliant founder of the most innovative boarding school of her generation, suggested that the headship of a school presented an opportunity for "master spirits," whom "Domestic life cannot hold." She warned that a desire for "pre-eminence" could turn sour in marginal institutions devoted to the proprietor's profit and urged the creation of large, state-supported female academies in part as a way of establishing a healthy outlet for female ambition.[59]

Some of the early students expressed an impatience with the limitations of the standard curriculum. These young women, like the founders themselves, wanted more. Molly Wallace spoke of "the domestic situation to which, by nature and custom we *seem* destined." She was aware that even her graduation address itself, delivered to an adult audience of both sexes, might be regarded as a radical innovation in 1792, and she took pains to defend oratory as a skill appropriate to women. "Why is a boy diligently and carefully taught the Latin, the Greek, or the Hebrew lan-

58. Cott, *Bonds of Womanhood*, 123.
59. Journal of Sally Ripley; Murray, *The Gleaner*, III, No. 88, 188, No. 89, 198; J. A. Neale, *Philadelphia Minerva*, Mar. 21, 1795; Emma Willard, *An Address to the Public . . . Proposing A Plan for Improving Female Education* (Middlebury, Vt., 1819), 8–10, 34. Emma Willard's career is discussed in detail in Scott, "This New Woman?" *JAH*, LXV (1978), 679–703.

guage, in which he will seldom have occasion, either to write or converse? Why is he taught to demonstrate the propositions of Euclid, when during his whole life, he will not perhaps make use of one of them? . . . These things are commonly studied, more on account of the habits, which the learning of them establishes, than on account of any important advantages which the mere knowledge of them can afford. So a young lady, from the exercise of speaking before a properly selected audience, may acquire some valuable habits." When she gave the graduation address in 1793, Priscilla Mason was proudly aware that it was unusual for a woman to address "a promiscuous assembly" and vigorously defended the propriety of women becoming accomplished orators; she included the resentful comment that "our high and mighty Lords . . . have denied us the means of knowledge, and then reproached us for the want of it. . . . They doom'd the sex to servile or frivolous employments, on purpose to degrade their minds, that they themselves might hold unrivall'd, the power and pre-eminence they had usurped." It was becoming possible, through academies like her own, for women to increase their knowledge, but the forums in which they might use that competence were still unavailable: "The Church, the Bar, and the Senate are shut against us."[60]

More than two generations passed before women began to press at the boundaries of "the Church, the Bar, and the Senate," a delay understandable only in the context of the nearly united hostility that greeted those who encouraged women to learn the skills needed for public life. The prediction that intellectual accomplishment would unsex women was regularly coupled with the warning that educated women would abandon their proper sphere, that the female pedant and the housekeeper were never found in the same person. The most usable target for the opposition seems to have been Mary Wollstonecraft, whose life and work linked criticism of women's traditional status with free love and political radicalism.

Mary Wollstonecraft's *Vindication of the Rights of Woman* was her generation's most coherent statement of what women deserved and what they might become. The influence of any book is difficult to trace, and although her book was printed in Philadelphia shortly after its original publication in 1792, it would be inaccurate to credit Wollstonecraft with the responsibility for raising in America questions relating to the status of women. It seems far more likely that she expressed what a larger public

60. Molly Wallace, "Oration," June 12, 1792, *Rise and Progress of the Young Ladies' Academy*, 73–79 (my italics); Priscilla Mason, "Oration," May 15, 1793, *ibid.*, 90–95.

Frontispiece from *Lady's Magazine*, I (1792). "The Genius of the Ladies
Magazine, accompanied by the Genius of Emulation, who carries in her hand a
laurel crown, approaches Liberty, and kneeling, presents her with a copy of the
Rights of Woman." This print served as the frontispiece of a journal addressed to
"the *fair daughters* of Columbia," which reprinted extensive extracts from *A
Vindication of the Rights of Woman* shortly after its original publication in
London. A note in the magazine's first issue complained: "The men have leisure
enough to read, and every access to books at college, &c. but our sex are kept at
very short allowance by our parents, who are afraid to give us improper books,
and do not know what are or are not proper."
Courtesy The Library Company of Philadelphia.

was already experiencing or was willing to hear. Wollstonecraft's castigations of fashionable women and coquettes, of fiction reading and excessive romanticism, of sporadic and eccentric systems of female education, all found resonant echoes in America. "In very many of her sentiments," remarked the Philadelphia Quaker Elizabeth Drinker, "she, as some of our friends say, *speaks my mind*."[61]

Wollstonecraft's primary target was Rousseau, whose definition of a woman's sphere was, as noted earlier, a severely limited one. "The empire of women," Rousseau had written, "is the empire of softness, of address, of complacency; her commands are caresses; her menaces are tears." Wollstonecraft perceived that to define women this way was to condemn them to "a state of perpetual childhood"; she deplored the "false system of education" that made women "only anxious to inspire love, when they ought to cherish a nobler ambition, and by their abilities and virtues exact respect." Women's duties were different from those of men, but they similarly demanded the exercise of virtue and reason. Women would be better wives and mothers if they were taught that they could not depend on frivolity and ignorance. Wollstonecraft ventured the suggestion that women might study medicine, politics, and business, but whatever they did, they should not be denied civil and political rights, they should not have to rely on marriage for assurance of economic support, and they should not "remain immured in their families groping in the dark."[62]

Aaron Burr immediately recognized the *Vindication* as "a work of genius" and recommended it to his wife with the promise to read it aloud to her. "I had heard it spoken of with a coldness little calculated to excite attention; but as I read with avidity and prepossession every thing written by a lady, I made haste to procure it, and spent the last night, almost the whole of it, in reading it." But he knew himself to be unusual: "Is it owing to ignorance or prejudice that I have not yet met a single person who had discovered or would allow the merit of this work?"[63] If Burr could greet Wollstonecraft's work as the common sense of the matter, others met it with hostility. The *Vindication* was a popular subject of

61. Elizabeth Drinker, diary entry for Apr. 22, 1796, in Henry D. Biddle, ed., *Extracts from the Journal of Elizabeth Drinker, from 1759 to 1807, A.D.* (Philadelphia, 1889), 285.

62. Rousseau, *Emilius*, III, 10; Wollstonecraft, *Vindication*, ed. Kramnick, 79, 87. Most of Rousseau's critics, male and female, were more troubled by the passionate behavior he endorsed in *La Nouvelle Héloïse* than they were by *Emile*.

63. Aaron Burr to Theodosia Prevost Burr, Feb. 16, 1793, Davis, ed., *Memoirs of Burr*, I, 363.

satire, especially after the author's death in childbirth in 1797, when her husband, William Godwin, published a memoir revealing that she had lived with another man, and with Godwin himself, before her pregnancy and marriage. Critics were then freed to discount her call for reform as the self-serving demand of a woman of easy virtue, as Benjamin Silliman did throughout his *Letters of Shahcoolen*. Timothy Dwight, who had himself offered young women a more advanced education than had almost any other schoolmaster of his day, shuddered at Wollstonecraft and held "the female philosopher" up to ridicule in "Morpheus," a political satire that ran for eight installments in the *Mercury and New-England Palladium*. Dwight calls Wollstonecraft "an unchaste woman," "a sentimental lover," "a strumpet." As Silliman had done, he linked her radical politics to free love. "Away with all monopolies," Dwight has Wollstonecraft say in fictional dialogue. "I hate these exclusive rights; these privileged orders. I am for having everything free, and open to all; like the air which we breathe." "Love, particularly, I suppose, Madam[?]" asks Dwight's protagonist. "Yes, brute, love, if you please; and everything else," Wollstonecraft replies.[64]

Even Charles Brockden Brown's feminist tract *Alcuin* concluded with a long gloss on the same theme: to permit any change in women's status was to imply the acceptance of free love. Alcuin, who has been playing the conservative skeptic, concludes that once it is established that marriage "has no other criterion than custom," it becomes simply a "mode of sexual intercourse." His friend Mrs. Carter protests energetically that free love is not at all what she wanted: "When I demand an equality of conditions among beings that equally partake of the same divine reason, would you rashly infer that I was an enemy to the institution of marriage itself?" Brown lets her have the last word, but he does not make Alcuin change his mind.[65]

Dwight had one final charge to make against Wollstonecraft; he attacked her plea that women emerge from the confines of their families. "Who will make our puddings, Madam?" his protagonist asks. When she responds, "Make them yourself," he presses harder: "Who shall nurse us when we are sick?" and, finally, "Who shall nurse our children?" The last question reduces the fictional Mary to blushes and silence.[66]

64. *Mercury and N.-E. Palladium*, Nov. 24, 27, 1801, Dec. 8, 11, 15, 1801, Mar. 2, 5, 9, 1802. Identification of Dwight as author is made by Robert Edson Lee, "Timothy Dwight and the Boston *Palladium*," *NEQ*, XXXV (1962), 229–239.

65. Brown, *Alcuin*, 87–88.

66. *Mercury and N.-E. Palladium*, Mar. 9, 1802.

A similar, but real, conversation is reported by Eliza Wilkinson of Stono, South Carolina. During the Revolution she bravely maintained her parents' plantation and stood up to intrusive British soldiers. Late in the war she heard a conversation with visiting patriot officers, who expressed their political principles strongly. She was tempted to join the conversation. But

> the men say we have no business with political matters. . . . it's not in our sphere! and Homer . . . gives us two or three broad hints to mind our domestic concerns—*spinning* weaving, &&—and leave affairs of higher nature to the Men: But I must beg his pardon—I won't have it thought that because we are the weaker Sex (as to bodily strength my dear) we are Capable of nothing more, than minding the Dairy—visiting the Poultry house, and all such domestic concerns. . . . we can form conceptions of things of higher Nature: and have as just a sense of honor, glory and great actions as those "Lords of the Creation"—what contemptible Earth Worms those Authors make us! they won't even allow us the liberty of thought! . . . surely we may have sense enough to give our Opinions . . . without being reminded of our Spinning and household affairs, as the only matters we are capable of thinking, or speaking of, with justness or propriety.[67]

In practice, however, it was virtually impossible for women to "give. . . Opinions . . . without being reminded of . . . Spinning." The intellectual world of republican America was a milieu in which female learning was easily equated with pedantry and masculinity. To resist these assumptions was to undertake a great deal. The familiar litany of notable women was one attempt to create an alternate vision, but most of these women were long since dead. What American women needed—not least for rhetorical purposes—was an example of a woman of substantive intellectual accomplishment who had not rejected the domestic world when she moved into the public one. After 1797, Mary Wollstonecraft was no longer available for that role. Once Catharine Macaulay had married William Graham, a man much younger than herself, she was also vulnerable to

---

67. Eliza Wilkinson to Miss M ——— P ——— , n.d., Caroline Gilman, ed., *Letters of Eliza Wilkinson During the Invasion and Possession of Charleston . . .* (New York, 1839), 61. This is only one of the many emphatically phrased comments that Wilkinson made about the way men encouraged female frivolity.

snide remarks about her unusual domestic arrangements.[68] Hannah Adams was an eccentric spinster and so could be used in support of the anti-intellectual argument that intellect in woman unfitted her for domesticity.[69] Little seems to have been made of the model of Mercy Otis Warren, perhaps because of the long gap in her public career as a writer. Warren was virtually the only prominent American example who could be trotted out against the complaint that intellect necessarily meant rejection of domesticity and of domestic work. "What a pity," mourned Sarah Vaughan, accepting the stereotype, "that superior understanding & superior cultivation in our sex should so often root out those amiable domestic, and useful qualities that ever will be most praise worthy in us."[70] The integration of intellect and domesticity shimmered, miragelike, in the distance.

In the face of this ridicule, American intellectuals who sought to find a vehicle by which women might demonstrate their intellectual competence had to move cautiously. Improved education needed utilitarian justification. The girls who attended the new schools, and the parents who sent them there, had no intention of abandoning female domestic roles. The new education would have to be offered in terms acceptable to families in which women's lives were already uncertain, jarred by war and by new industrial patterns that changed the demand for household crafts. Women did not come to the new schools to be made even more insecure.

In response to their needs, Judith Sargent Murray, Susannah Rowson, and Benjamin Rush developed an ideology for women's education in a

68. Sarah Vaughan, for example, told Catharine Livingston that she had refused to accompany her parents when they called on Macaulay in Philadelphia in 1785. But when Macaulay returned the visit, Sarah Vaughan had to be polite, despite her scorn for a woman who "carried with her a living monument of her want of common understanding and delicacy. . . . I heard in company that her teeth are false, has plumpers in her cheeks to hide the hollowness, toothlessness gives, and that she paints" (Sarah Vaughan to Catharine Livingston, May 20–26, 1785, Ridley Papers, Box 3, Mass. Hist. Soc.).

69. Timothy Alden, the master of the girls' school at the Newark Academy in New Jersey, did encourage his pupils to admire Hannah Adams; in 1812 he dedicated the school's Quarterly Catalogue to her: "In her researches after useful and important knowledge, she has long been a model of patience and perseverance worthy the imitation of the young ladies of America" (Dedication, Quarterly Catalogue of Newark Academy).

70. Sarah Vaughan to Catharine Livingston, May 20–26, 1785, Ridley Papers, Box 3. For a continuing insistence on the courtesies due her sex, see Mercy Otis Warren to John Adams, Aug. 15, 1807, "Correspondence between Adams and Mercy Warren," Mass. Hist. Soc., Colls., 5th Ser., IV, 455. In the midst of a vituperative exchange, Warren moaned, "As you seem to have almost run out the threat of self-eulogism, you may, perhaps, for want of other matter, continue to reproach and affront a writer whose sex alone ought to have protected her from the grossness of your invectives" (ibid.).

republic, defending improvement in education without repudiating the relationship of women to their households. These reformers avoided challenging directly the old anti-intellectualism that could be counted on to be voiced whenever claims were made for women's intellectual prowess. Instead they contented themselves with deploring the "dependence for which women are uniformly educated"; they argued that political independence in the nation should be matched by self-reliance on the part of women. The model republican woman was to be self-reliant (within limits), literate, untempted by the frivolities of fashion. She had a responsibility to the political scene, though was not active in it. As one fictional woman put it, "If the community flourish and enjoy health and freedom, shall we not share in the happy effect? If it be oppressed and disturbed, shall we not endure our proportion of evil? Why then should the love of our country be a masculine passion only?"[71] A woman's competence was not assumed to extend to the making of political decisions. Her political task was accomplished within the confines of her family. The model republican woman was a mother.

The Republican Mother was an educated woman who could be spared the criticism normally addressed to the Learned Lady because she placed her learning at her family's service. Benjamin Rush addressed the issue directly in his lectures on natural philosophy and chemistry for the Young Ladies' Academy: "Among the various illiberal reasons which have hitherto been given for neglecting the education of ladies, one has been —That a liberal education renders ladies inattentive to domestic duties— How praise worthy then would it be in such ladies to shew, by their conduct, that this remark is not only illiberal, but also ill founded." Rush urged an explicitly instrumental definition of the uses of education: families would be improved if women were educated. Education, he claimed, would provide "subject for rational and improving conversation. . . . it will cause your society to be sought for, and courted, by sensible men. . . . it will afford you pleasure in solitude."[72]

Anticipating the critics, the Young Ladies' Academy promised "not wholly to engross the mind" of each pupil, "but to allow her to prepare for the duties in life to which she may be destined." Miss P. W. Jackson, graduating from Mrs. Rowson's Academy, explained what she had learned of

71. [Hannah Webster Foster], *The Coquette* . . . (Charlestown, Mass., 1802), 63.

72. Benjamin Rush, "Lectures, Containing the Application of the Principles of Natural Philosophy, and Chemistry, to Domestic and Culinary Purposes," Rush Papers, Hist. Soc. Pa.

the goals of the educated woman: "A woman who is skilled in every useful art, who practices every domestic virtue . . . may, by her precept and example, inspire her brothers, her husband, or her sons, with such a love of virtue, such just ideas of the true value of civil liberty . . . that future heroes and statesmen, when arrived at the summit of military or political fame, shall exaltingly declare, it is to my mother I owe this elevation." By their household management, by their refusal to countenance vice, crime, or lack of benevolence in their suitors and husbands, women had the power to direct the moral development of the male citizens of the Republic. The influence women had on children, especially sons, gave them ultimate responsibility for the future of the new nation.[73]

Rarely, in the literature of the early Republic, do we find any objection to the notion that women belong in the home; we can, however, find the argument that the Revolution had enlarged the significance of what women did in the home. Benjamin Rush's phrasing of this point is instructive. When he defined the goals of republican women, he was careful not to include a claim of political power: "The equal share that every citizen has in the liberty and the possible share he may have in the government of our country make it necessary that our ladies should be qualified to a certain degree, by a peculiar and suitable education, *to concur in instructing their sons in the principles of liberty and government*."[74]

The Republican Mother's life was dedicated to the service of civic virtue: she educated her sons for it, she condemned and corrected her husband's lapses from it. If, according to Montesquieu's commonly accepted claim, the stability of the nation rested on the persistence of virtue among its citizens, then the creation of virtuous citizens was dependent on the presence of wives and mothers who were well informed, "properly methodical," and free of "invidious and rancorous passions." It was perhaps more than mere coincidence that *virtù* was derived from the Latin word for *man*, with its connotations of virility. Political action seemed somehow inherently masculine. Virtue in a woman seemed to require another theater for its display. To that end the theorists created a mother who had a political purpose and argued that her domestic behavior had a direct political function in the Republic.

This constellation of ideas, and the republican rhetoric that made it

73. *Rise and Progress of the Young Ladies' Academy*, 74, 94; James Milnor, "On Female Education," *Port Folio*, 3d Ser. (May 1809), 388; *Boston Wkly. Mag.* (Oct. 29, 1803).

74. My italics. Rush, "Thoughts Upon Female Education," in Rudolph, ed., *Essays on Education*, 28.

convincing, appear at great length in the Columbia College commencement oration of 1795 entitled "Female Influence." Behind the flowery rhetoric lurks a social and political message.

> Let us then figure to ourselves the accomplished woman, surrounded by a sprightly band, from the babe that imbibes the nutritive fluid, to the generous youth just ripening into manhood, and the lovely virgin. . . . Let us contemplate the mother distributing the mental nourishment to the fond smiling circle, by means proportionate to their different powers of reception, watching the gradual openings of their minds, and studying their various turns of temper. . . . Religion, fairest offspring of the skies, smiles auspicious on her endeavours; the Genius of Liberty hovers triumphant over the glorious scene. . . . Yes, ye fair, the reformation of a world is in your power. . . . Reflect on the result of your efforts. Contemplate the rising glory of confederated America. Consider that your exertions can best secure, increase, and perpetuate it. The solidity and stability of the liberties of your country rest with you; since Liberty is never sure, 'till Virtue reigns triumphant. . . . Already may we see the lovely daughters of Columbia asserting the importance and the honour of their sex. It rests with you to make this retreat [from the corruptions of Europe] doubly peaceful, doubly happy, by banishing from it those crimes and corruptions, which have never yet failed of giving rise to tyranny, or anarchy. While you thus keep our country virtuous, you maintain its independence.[75]

Defined this way, the educated woman ceased to threaten the sanctity of marriage; the bluestocking need not be masculine. In this awkward and, in the 1790s, still only vaguely expressed fashion, the traditional womanly virtues were endowed with a political purpose. "Let the ladies of a country be educated properly," Rush said, "and they will not only make and administer its laws, but form its manners and character."[76]

Americans who admired bluestockings and those who feared them could agree on one point: in a world where moral influences were fast dissipating, women as a group seemed to represent moral stability. Few

75. N.Y. Mag. (May 1795), 301–305.
76. Rush, "Thoughts Upon Female Education," in Rudolph, ed., Essays on Education, 36. This was a compromise with which even the "Female Advocate" could be comfortable. "May I not ask," she had written, "is not a woman of a capacious and well stored mind, a

in the early Republic demanded, in a sustained way, substantial revisions in women's political or legal status, and few spoke to the nascent class of unskilled women workers. In refuting charges that free love and masculinization would follow from increased sophistication and improved learning, defenders of female education found themselves developing a strident prediction of continuing domesticity. The domestic function of the preindustrial woman had needed little ideological justification; it was implicit in the biological and political economy of her world. Someone had to keep the spinning wheel turning and the open-hearth fire constantly tended, and the nursing mother who could not leave her infant was the obvious candidate. In the domesticity of the preindustrial woman there was no sharp disjunction between ideology and practice. But the Revolution was a watershed. It created a public ideology of individual responsibility and virtue just before industrial machinery began to free middle-class women from some of their unremitting toil and to propel lower-class women more fully into the public economy. The terms of domesticity were changed, and pundits could not bring back the past. The best they could do was to assert that properly educated republican women would stay in their homes and, from that vantage point, shape the characters of their sons and husbands in the direction of benevolence, self-restraint, and responsible independence. The prescription rang shrill. So long as the literature of domesticity persisted, it would always embody an anti-intellectual connotation, a skepticism about the capacities of women's minds.

---

better wife, a better widow, a better mother, and a better neighbor; and shall I add, a better friend in every respect?" (*Female Advocate*, 33–34.) See also Ruth H. Bloch, "American Feminine Ideals in Transition: The Rise of the Moral Mother, 1785–1815," *Feminist Studies*, IV (1978), 101–126.

Chapter 8

"WE OWN THAT

LADIES SOMETIMES READ":

WOMEN'S READING IN

THE EARLY REPUBLIC

After my Funeral Charges and just Debts are
paid, I recommend, give & Bequeath to my
Beloved Daughter Idea Strong, my Bibles and
inferior, orthodox Treatises on Religion and
Morality, or relative or appertaining to vital
Piety or practical Godliness, & all other Books,
Pamphlets or Manuscripts, except Romances
(if any left extant) which I have long since
(though not early enough) intentionally consigned or destinated to deserved Oblivion in
native Shades of Chaos.

> —Will of Jedidiah Strong,
> Litchfield, Connecticut,
> March 31, 1801

Frontispiece from *Columbian Magazine, or Monthly Miscellany* (1787).
Columbia presents two children to the goddess of wisdom, who leans on a
pedestal inscribed, "Independence the reward of Wisdom, Fortitude and
Perseverance."
Courtesy The Library of Congress, Washington, D.C.

THE VISION OF the Republican Mother owed a debt to the Enlightenment and to the Revolution. To the mother's traditional responsibility for maintenance of the household economy, and to the expectation that she be a person of religious faith, were added the obligation that she also be an informed and virtuous citizen. She was to observe the political world with a rational eye, and she was to guide her husband and children in making their way through it. She was to be a teacher as well as a mother.

All agreed that this Republican Mother should be alert and reasonably well acquainted with public affairs. But advice to women on what they should read was accompanied by insistent warnings—of which Jedidiah Strong's is the most extreme—of what not to read.[1] The literary culture of republican America was bifurcated. Men were said to read newspapers and history; women were thought to exercise their weaker intellects on the less demanding fare of fiction and devotional literature. A vigorous proscriptive literature warned of dangers women risked if they persisted in what was said to be their taste for frivolous and romantic fiction. Occasionally we even come upon condemnation of reading itself, on the grounds that the new generation of women was being diverted from their proper household tasks. Women made their own responses to this campaign—quietly persisting in their choice of fiction and religious biography, writing romantic fiction that counseled against the loss of self-control, and revising their understanding of housekeeping to make room for their own participation in the world of the imagination.

"Sent the amiable Woodbridge his shirt and with it a letter—What the Consequence will be I know not," confided Polly Rogers to her diary.

> Read in a *sweet novel* the D——r brought me. It affected me so,
> I could *hardly* read it, and was often obliged to drop the Book to
> suppress my grief! Went to bed, Lay, and *thot* of the Lovely
> Woodbridge—shed a *torrent* of tears, at the *Recollection* of past
> interviews with him! . . . he (Woodbridge) press'd me to his *Bosom*
> with a *fondness* I thought expressive of approbation *never never*
> P——y hesitate a *moment* to Let me know if 'tis in my power to make
> you happy! would you would you no Sir! said I, at the same time

---

1. Jedidiah Strong's will is on file in the Conn. State Lib., Hartford. Strong was famous for his headstrong temper and his irascibility. His divorce case, which took much of the time of the Connecticut legislature, appears in *Conn. State Recs.*, VII, 206, 282.

kissing his Hand with *trembling* Lips! . . . I flew to my Chamber,
& with the *avidity* of a *Lover opened* the Seal and read! sheding
tears as I *read*.

By May, "the amiable Woodbridge" had apparently transferred his affections to someone else, and Polly wrote, "O had I *less* sensibility I should not *feel* so much, nor so *severely* my present situation."[2]

As this diary of a young woman in a small western Massachusetts town suggests, reading fiction could play a very important part in a woman's private life and imagination. In the eighteenth century the novel first came into its own as a genre, and the best fiction—*Tom Jones, Clarissa, La Nouvelle Héloïse*—won a large audience. In their substitution of individualized, realistic plots for the traditional plots taken from history and mythology, novels were different from earlier prose fiction. Their abandonment of traditional structure, accompanied by widespread and easy use of quasi-autobiographical detail, resulted, as Ian Watt has put it, in a genre marked by its "defiant . . . assertion of the primacy of individual experience." It was this assertiveness that made the new fiction startling and appealing. The classical unities of place and time were broken by time sequences imitative of human experience. Characters became real people with real names who led lives much like those of their readers.[3]

But women did not always confine their reading to fiction. Surviving lists from booksellers, lending libraries, and diarists indicate clearly that it is impossible to make absolute gender distinctions about the reading audience of any book. Women read *Cato's Letters* and Paley's *Natural Theology*; men read fiction.[4]

Lists alone, however, cannot suggest much about what might be called the psychodynamics of reading. What did novels *mean* to the people who

2. Journal of Polly Rogers, Jan. 10–11, May 14, 1785, Am. Antq. Soc., Worcester, Mass.
3. Ian B. Watt, *The Rise of the Novel: Studies in Defoe, Richardson and Fielding* (Berkeley, Calif., 1957), 15. This paragraph relies heavily on chap. 2. See also Joseph J. Ellis's shrewd observations in *After the Revolution: Profiles of Early American Culture* (New York, 1979), 94–97.
4. See, for example, Mary Thomas's Book Catalogue, Isaiah Thomas Papers, Am. Antq. Soc., and the inventory of Mary Ann Woodrow Archbald's library, Archbald Papers, Sophia Smith Collection, Smith College Library, Northampton, Mass. Library loan lists appear in Chester T. Hallenbeck, "A Colonial Reading List from the Union Library of Hatboro, Pennsylvania," *PMHB*, LVI (1932), 289–340; the Salem (Mass.) Social Library, Tapley, *Salem Imprints*, 247; the Brentwood (New Hampshire) social library, 1823, Am. Antq. Soc., Worcester, Mass.; Thomas Bradford's bookstore and library, 1772, Hist. Soc. Pa.

bought or borrowed them? What role did reading play in their imaginative lives? Books were cheaper, and more widely available, for the post-Revolutionary generation than they had been for their parents (although not nearly as easily available as they would be after the invention of better methods of type founding in the 1830s).[5]

For an understanding of the role of reading in one woman's life, we can turn to the revealing diary of Elizabeth Drinker. "It looks as if I spent most of my time reading, which is by no means the case," she wrote in 1795. "A book is soon run over. . . . I believe I may say, without vanity, that I was never an indolent person, or remarkably Bookish, the more so for 5 or 6 years past, than at any other period since I was married, having more leisure [now as a grandmother]—when my Children were young, I seldom read a volume."[6]

Elizabeth Drinker's memory was accurate. Her diary entries are very scanty in the years before the Revolution, and she rarely mentioned a book. During the excitement of the war years, especially during the time her husband was exiled, she kept a careful account of events in which she participated or which she observed, but once Henry Drinker returned she drifted out of the habit of regular entries. When she reached her fifties, the yellow fever epidemic of 1793 sent her back to her diary as a chronicler of the course of the disease, and thereafter book titles appear with great regularity in her journal.

Although she never failed to feel guilty about it, she did read fiction. "Read a romance or novel, which I have not done for a long time before," she remarked on March 30, 1795. "It was a business I followed in my younger days, not so much as many others, 'tho more than some others." Even Royall Tyler's *The Contrast*, widely honored as the first native American play, made her uncomfortable. She called it "a small ridiculous novel" (meaning, one supposes, that it was fiction) and felt it necessary to account for her weakness in reading it: "S. Kidd's brother brings them to her, he lives, I believe at a book shop tho I have read some

5. Women could be very conscious of the increased availability of books in their own lifetime. In 1836, Margaret Browne wrote to her friend Eliza Quincy, wife of the president of Harvard, that she thought the "increase and circulation of new books" a mixed blessing. "Do you think that either you or I, if we were fourteen years of age, would now become as conversant as we then were with the English classics and poets, which are now reposing in sullen dignity on her bookshelves, while every table is littered with annuals and monthly and weekly journals?" (Eliza Susan Quincy, *Memoir of the Life of Eliza S. M. Quincy* [Boston, 1861], 299).

6. Diary of Elizabeth Drinker, May 22, 1795, Hist. Soc. Pa.

of them myself, I have been talking to her against the practice."[7] She thought Ann Radcliffe's *The Italian* "trash" and could justify Radcliffe's *The Mysteries of Udolpho* only because she did needlework while her married daughter read the book aloud: "Molly has been for some days past, at times reading while we work'd, three romantic vol. intitled The Misteries of Udolphia—a tremendous tale—but not quite like the old fashion Gothick stories that I was fond of when young. 'tis seldom I listen to a romance, nor would I encourage my Children doing much of that business."[8] But Mrs. Drinker found it hard to stay away. When she finished reading "a foolish Romance entitled The Haunted priory," she made a point of reporting that she had also "finished knitting a pair large cotton stockings, bound a petticoat and made a batch of Gingerbread— this I mention to shew that I have not spent the day reading."[9]

"I read a little of most things." Because she was a serious and committed Quaker, a member of an old and prominent Quaker family, instructive Quaker tracts and histories appear and reappear in her diary entries. Although her politics were unambivalently conservative and Federalist, her reading was catholic. She read Thomas Paine as well as attacks on him; she read criticisms of "Peter Porcupine" as well as "Porcupine's" attacks on the Federalists. She even perused the *Confessions* of Jean Jacques Rousseau, remarking, "I like him not, or his ideas."[10] She ordered "Bolinbroke on the study and use of History" from the library, but was dismayed to conclude "that it set at nought the Holy Scriptures." She was even embarrassed that it was signed out in her name and "sent it back unread."[11]

The sheer volume of Elizabeth Drinker's reading is impressive. In 1796, the year she read Mary Wollstonecraft's *Vindication* and made her well-known elliptical remark about it, Elizabeth Drinker read a collection of fifty Cheap Repository tracts and at least twenty-eight pamphlets on religious and political subjects. She read both sides of the pamphlet war for and against William Cobbett (three years later she followed the published transcript of the Rush-Cobbett trial). In 1796 she read at least sixteen books in addition to Wollstonecraft's, some in several volumes. Among her selections were Dante's *Inferno*, Erasmus Darwin's *The Botanic Gar-*

---

7. *Ibid.*, Mar. 30, 1795, July 26, 1797.
8. *Ibid.*, July 11, 1797, June 20, 1795.
9. *Ibid.*, Feb. 29, 1796.
10. *Ibid.*, end of 1800; Reading list of Elizabeth Drinker, May 6, 1800.
11. Diary of Elizabeth Drinker, July 24, 1800.

den (which she liked very much), and Madame de Genlis's *Adelaide and Theodore*. Though she was no Jacobin, she read six volumes of Wollstonecraft's friend Helen Maria Williams, and several books of poetry, including the sentimental verse of the Della Cruscans. Despite all her embarrassment, Elizabeth Drinker read at least eight novels, including William Godwin's *Caleb Williams*, a book she felt free to like since she as yet knew nothing of the author's politics.

Reading was an integral part of Elizabeth Drinker's daily life, but it was an element about which she always felt self-conscious. She needed to reassure herself and the descendant whom she imagined to be the ultimate reader of her diary that she had not been irresponsible in the amount of time she devoted to reading. She retained from her younger years the sense that there was something inappropriate, even immodest, about fiction. "It may appear strange to some," she wrote, "that an infirm old Woman should begin the year reading romances—'tis a practice I by no means highly approve, yet I trust I have not sined."[12]

Drinker's self-consciousness suggests the impact of the enormous proscriptive literature that counseled everyone, but especially women, against reading novels. Young women were thought to be most vulnerable to the attractions of irresponsibility and passion as depicted in novels, and few observers credited women with a catholicity of tastes and interest approaching Drinker's. "Novels are the favourite, and most dangerous kind of reading, now adopted by the generality of young ladies," thundered Hannah Webster Foster in 1798. "I say dangerous . . . [because they] fill the imagination with ideas which lead to impure desires . . . and a fondness for show and dissipation. . . . They often pervert the judgment, mislead the affections, and blind the understanding." *The American Lady's Preceptor*, a collection of "essays and poetical effusions, designed to direct the female mind," which was widely used in schools, warned that reading novels would encourage self-indulgent "sensibility."[13]

It was assumed that romantic fiction could affect its readers' actual behavior—and for the worse. "Never let my poor Child Read a Novel or Romance," cried the unhappy Elizabeth Gouverneur, divorced by her husband for bearing a child that was not his. "These I am sure helped to [shape] Ideas in my head which perhaps I never should have had, and the

---

12. *Ibid.*, Jan. 7, 1796. She had just read *The Victim of Magical Illusions*. See also Scott, "Self-Portraits," in Bushman *et al.*, eds., *Uprooted Americans*, 46–55.

13. Hannah Foster, *The Boarding School; Or, Lessons of a Preceptress to Her Pupils* . . . (Boston, 1798), 18; *The American Lady's Preceptor* (Baltimore, 1810), 14–17.

person who brought them to me took care to pick out such as would Suit his Purpose."[14] The young William Gaston, lonely in boarding school, wrote to warn his younger sister against romantic novels: "Under those stories, which are thought entertaining, lies a venomous poison. . . . setting aside religion, they never fail to inspire those who read them, with romantic ideas, to give them a disgust for all serious employments." Even Mercy Otis Warren, who wrote her own fiction in the form of plays, warned a niece about to marry that novel reading made for inefficient housewifery: "Throw away no part of your time, in the perusal of . . . the puerile study of romance." John Trumbull versified the fears and dangers.

> We own that Ladies sometimes read,
> And grieve *that* reading is confined
> To books that poison all the mind
> The bluster of romance, that fills
> The head brimfull of purling rills
> And swells the mind with haughty fancies
> . . . .
>   For while she reads romance, the Fair one
> Fails not to think herself the Heroine
> . . . .
> Thus *Harriet* reads, and reading really
> Believes herself a young *Pamela*,
> The high-wrought whim, the tender strain
> Elate her mind and turn her brain . . .[15]

Fiction itself warned against fiction. The first step in the seduction of the title character of *Laura* is taken when her suitor, Belfield, provides her with Pope's "Letter of Eloise to Abelard" and copies of romantic novels. Alicia Sheridan LeFanu's *Lucy Osmond* was written "to exemplify the danger attending the early study of works of mere imagination," and the young heroine is early cautioned against novels. *Emily Hamilton* was offered by "A Young Lady of Massachusetts" as "a Novel founded

14. *Isaac Gouverneur Jr. v. Elizabeth Gouverneur,* Chancery No. 41, Mar. 31, 1787, Historical Documents Collection, Queens College, City University of New York. I am indebted to Leo Hershkowitz for this reference.

15. William Gaston to Mrs. Gaston, Jan. 4, 1792, William Gaston Papers, Southern Historical Collection, University of North Carolina, Chapel Hill, N.C.; Mercy Otis Warren to Rebecca Otis, n.d., 1776, Mercy Otis Warren Letterbook, Warren Papers, Mass. Hist. Soc.; John Trumbull, "The Progress of Dulness," in Edwin T. Bowden, ed., *The Satiric Poems of John Trumbull* (Austin, Tex., 1962), 88.

on incidents in real life," and therefore more wholesome than the usual novel, which was frequently "in the highest degree prejudicial to young minds, by giving them wrong ideas of the world, and setting their tastes so high as to occasion a disrelish for those scenes in which they are necessitated to take a part."[16] The famous Irish novelist Maria Edgeworth wrote an epistolary novel, reprinted in America, in which one sister, Julia, indulges her taste for romances and acquires "the eager genius, the exquisite sensibility of enthusiasm" rather than her sister Caroline's "stoical serenity of philosophy." Julia's preference for romance leads her directly to the choice of a flashy but unreliable husband, causing her disappointment in marriage, her separation from her beloved children, and her premature death.[17] It was warnings like these that Elizabeth Drinker took to heart, and that are reflected in her diary entries begrudging the time spent on fiction.

When some twenty young women organized the Boston Gleaning Circle in 1805, they defined it as a self-improvement society. They met every week to read and discuss "any book favourable to the improvement of the mind"—by which they meant "Divinity, History, Geography, Astronomy, Travels Poetry &c but Novels and Romances are absolutely excluded." The danger of reading novels, these young women told each other, was that young people "will expect to meet in life the romantic incidents portrayed by the pen of the Novelist. . . . [In life,] the roses and thorns are intermixed, but in Novels the thorns come first, and the roses afterwards." They thought even virtue was too neatly rewarded in fiction, as it often was not on earth, and so a misleading impression of the instrumentality of good behavior might be given.[18]

These attacks on fiction, it is clear, were in large part attacks on emotion, on passion, and on sexuality. Even cautionary fiction, like *Charlotte Temple*, could be dangerous because it offered details of seduction in the very act of warning young women to be on their guard against rakes. The worst books were those that seemed to endorse the passionate way of life as a course to be emulated. The very worst example, the one fulminated against most vehemently, was Julie, Rousseau's *Nouvelle Héloïse*. Had *La Nou-*

---

16. [Mrs. Leonara Sansay or Rebecca Rush?], *Laura, By a Lady of Philadelphia* . . . (Philadelphia, 1809), 40–44; Alicia Sheridan LeFanu, *Lucy Osmond* (New York, 1804); [Sukey Watson], *Emily Hamilton* (Worcester, Mass., 1803), iii–iv.

17. "Letters of Julia and Caroline," reprinted in Edgeworth, *Letters For Literary Ladies*, 5–6. Similar plot outlines were used by Judith Sargent Murray in *The Gleaner* and Charles Brockden Brown in *Ormond*.

18. Boston Gleaning Circle, Record Book, Regulation #5, Boston Pub. Lib.; Boston Gleaning Circle, Minute Book, 25, Boston Pub. Lib.

velle Héloïse been a typical Sturm und Drang novel, Judith Shklar has observed, "the heroine would have defied her parents, run off with her lover, given birth to an illegitimate child, killed the child out of shame, and then died alone and in misery. The hero would, after similar disasters, have killed himself, or gone mad." But Julie invites her lover to visit while her own husband is home, she maintains throughout her love and affection for both men, and all major characters find a measure of happiness by the novel's close. This ending made Rousseau seem the more dangerous. For the English educator Hannah More, "novel" was a shorthand way of referring to Rousseau, and when she said Rousseau, she was thinking of *La Nouvelle Héloïse*. "Novels . . . are continually shifting their ground, and enlarging their sphere, and are daily becoming vehicles of wider mischief," she complained in *Strictures on the Modern System of Female Education*, published in London in 1799 and in Connecticut in 1801. "Rousseau . . . annihilates the value of chastity, and with pernicious subtlety attempts to make the heroine appear almost more amiable without it."[19]

Julie—her name is sometimes mistranslated as Eloisa—appears and reappears in American fiction as a leitmotif, warning against the pleasures of passion. Martha Read's heroine Monima, browsing in her father's library, comes upon Rousseau's Eloisa, but she is forbidden to read it.[20] In 1802 a Washington, D.C., publisher reprinted an English cautionary novel in which an adulteress reflects: "In the impassioned letters of Heloise, I found sentiments so congenial to my own, that, regardless of the danger of perusing them in my present situation, I could read nothing else: and I was soon so fascinated with the beauties of the style, and the originality of the thoughts, that I considered every doctrine they contained as infallible. . . . like Heloise, [I] persuaded myself that there were moments of happiness for which life and honor would not be too great a sacrifice."[21] As late as 1823, *La Nouvelle Héloïse* was still considered dangerous. From Augusta, Georgia, Henry H. Cumming wrote to his fiancée that he suspected from her last letter that she was secretly reading "the enthusiastic (but unfortunately, *crack-brained*) Rousseau." Al-

19. Judith N. Shklar, *After Utopia: The Decline of Political Faith* (Princeton, N.J., 1957), 29–30; Hannah More, *Strictures on the Modern System of Female Education* (Hartford, Conn., 1801), 25.

20. Martha Read, *Monima; or, The Beggar Girl* (New York, 1802), 367–369.

21. *The Adulteress, or Memoirs of Characters Now Living In The Fashionable World* (Washington, D.C., 1802), 16, 42–48. Another extensive attempt to use a fictional vehicle to condemn Rousseau is *Lucy Osmond*, a British novel republished in New York in 1804.

though he admired some of Rousseau's work and promised to study it with her in French, he warned that "Julia or the modern Elisa probably contains as many glowing expressions of both sentimental & voluptuous love, and as much immorality as any book in any language."[22]

Historians of American ideas have generally concluded that Rousseau seems to have had relatively little appeal to Americans of his own generation. He was not quoted, for example, in the debates at the Constitutional Convention; major political theorists like Madison, Jefferson, and Adams made little use of his work. *The Social Contract* was not widely available in American libraries until well into the nineteenth century, and when influential Americans encountered it, they seem to have found it either perplexing or frightening.[23] But what has been missed in this analysis is the widespread popularity of Rousseau's less theoretical works in America, particularly of *Emile* and *Héloïse*. Each of these books had significant, even revolutionary, things to say about women and their role in society. As we have seen, *Emile*'s Sophie provided the terms for much debate on the appropriate education for women, and she figured in Wollstonecraft's searing attack on Rousseau. *Héloïse*'s celebration of women's passion and instinct prompted an equally intense debate on the nature of women's emotions and the extent to which they could be trusted. There was thus a gender-distinction to be made on the ways Americans used the major works of the European Enlightenment. If *The Social Contract* or *The Spirit of the Laws* were "men's books," *Emile* and *Héloïse* were in some sense women's books. The throngs of second-rate heroines with names like Julia or Eloisa evince the extraordinary appeal of Rousseau's passionate women. The continued attack on romantic fiction for suggesting to young women that they might give free rein to their passions was in some measure a response to Rousseau.

Fiction that taught women to trust their passions was criticized in the picaresque *Female Quixotism*, published in Boston in 1801 and specifically addressed to "all Columbian Young Ladies, who read Novels and Romances."[24] It took as its subject a romantic girl whose head had been

22. Henry H. Cumming to Julia A. Bryan, May 17, 1823, Hammond-Bryan-Cumming Papers, S. Caroliniana Lib., Univ. S.C., Columbia.

23. David Lundberg and Henry F. May, "The Enlightened Reader in America," *American Quarterly*, XXVIII (1976), 285; Paul Merrill Spurlin, *Rousseau in America: 1760–1809* (University, Ala., 1969).

24. [Tabitha Gilman Tenney], *Female Quixotism: Exhibited in the Romantic Opinions and Extravagant Adventures of Dorcasina Sheldon*, I (Boston, 1801), iii. The book is an extended parody of Charlotte Lennox's *The Female Quixote; or the Adventures of Arabella* (London, 1752), which in turn is an extended parody of romantic heroines.

turned by the "unrestrained perusal" of fiction. Its author, writing under the possible pseudonym Tabitha Tenney, linked her attack on passion to the need to build virtuous republican citizens.

The heroine, Dorcas Sheldon, has no mother to protect her from reading the novels in her father's large collection of history and fiction. Dorcas's father does not realize that novels that may be harmless when read by men may have a "dangerous tendency to a young inexperienced female mind." Because novels have taught that love is a "violent emotion," Dorcas distrusts her own quiet affection for her first suitor. When his letter of proposal does not come up to the epistolary standard of her favorite novels, she rejects him.[25]

The departure of this young man leaves a series of increasingly unpalatable options. Dorcas's suitors include anti-intellectual men, who disapprove of all reading: "enemies to female improvement, thought a woman had no business with any book but the bible, or perhaps the art of cookery; believing that everything beyond these served only to disqualify her for the duties of domestic life." There finally appears a dashing adventurer, to whose obvious faults she is blinded by her appetite for mystery and romance. She explains away her father's demurrers by reflecting that her favorite heroines had often had cruel and unsympathetic parents. She changes her name to the more poetic "Dorcasina." She hides notes in hollow trees. She does not resist an abduction because she had "frequently read of ladies being forcibly carried off by resolute lovers." In short, she makes a fool of herself. "Oh! those poisonous, those fatal novels!" exclaims her father. "How have they warped your judgment. . . . Would to heaven people could find some better employment, than thus turning the heads of inexperienced females!"[26]

But Dorcas's novels have misled her. The false realism of the picaresque novel encouraged the unsophisticated girl to conclude that fiction reported life as it might be lived. Although she first came to her novels for entertainment, Dorcas soon finds herself using them as guides to her conduct, and from them she learns hopelessly inappropriate and artificial forms of behavior. Sure that the only certain guide is emotion and passion, she learns to distrust her own reason in the belief that people have no rational control over their relationships.

In a mode more subtle than the didactic essays of Hannah More and Judith Sargent Murray, the tale of Dorcasina suggests what contempo-

25. [Tenney], *Female Quixotism*, I, 7, 15.
26. *Ibid.*, 17, 129, 171.

raries found to criticize in the new fiction. Novels celebrated passion; they suggested that women were well guided by their own emotions. They encouraged people to break out of socially accepted roles, roles thought to be guided by reason. These novels may be understood as examples of the new sensibility that would be labeled romanticism, with which Americans would eventually make their peace. Dorcasina's experiences of romantic love were set against the requirements of the republican enlightenment: rationality and self-control. As Murray argued, the Republic had defined an ideal filled with political implications for woman: she was to be clearheaded and in control of her own emotions so that she could in turn control her husband and her children and thereby guarantee the virtuous behavior on which the security of the Republic depended. The Republic did not need emotional women who could easily be manipulated by men for their own gratification or who would lure men away from the path of virtue. Novels seemed to offer approbation for precisely the sort of behavior that political and didactic literature had labeled a danger to the Republic.

Thus the extensive didactic literature critical of women's interest in fiction served an implicit political purpose. It began with a political ideal of what women *ought* to be and attempted to persuade women to emulate one social type—the Roman—at the expense of another—the romantic. It sought to substitute civic virtue for passion. The continued popularity of the criticized fiction, however, suggests that the didactic literature fell on deaf ears. Even so conservative a woman as Elizabeth Drinker read the forbidden genre, though not without embarrassment.

Some demographers have shown that there was a sharp rise in the incidence of premarital pregnancy in the late eighteenth and early nineteenth centuries. This increase in what can easily be called "passionate behavior" accompanied the proscriptive literature against novel reading; in that context, the attacks on romantic fiction may be seen as a response to a perceived rise in deviant sexual behavior. It is not completely clear how this apparent rise in premarital pregnancy ought to be interpreted. It is, however, safe to suggest that it almost certainly is not a mark of increased options and freedom for women; it may well have signified the reverse. At least one historian has suggested that pregnancy may have been a tactic by which young couples pressured parents into allocating property earlier than they otherwise might have, and so may be seen as an emblem of declining prosperity. But the proscriptive moralizers blamed the alleged decline in morality not on economic pressures, but on women who indulged their passions because fictional models had made the previously unthinkable seem possible. Though the demographic record suggests that most of these seduced women ultimately married, the didactic purpose of the cautionary novelists dictated that fictional heroines who were seduced must ultimately also be abandoned.[27]

If women were not to read fiction, what ought they to read? Admonitions against novel reading were characteristically accompanied by the recommendation that women read history instead. Mercy Otis Warren's "rational system" left no time to be "thrown away in the perusal of books that have not a tendency to instill lessons of virtue and science." She thought women ought to read "authentic history, which is now written in a style equally elegant to the many volumes of romance, which in the present age croud upon the public." As Warren's endorsement suggests, there was a double rationale for encouraging the study of history. The entire literate culture agreed that knowledge of history helped develop a sense of social perspective. The classic statement is David Hume's brief essay "Of the Study of History," published in 1741. Hume limits his analysis to a very specific recommendation "to my female readers" of historical study "as an occupation, of all others, the best suited both to their sex and education." Hume contrasted histories with novels, which he believed offered "false representations of mankind." Novels encouraged, he thought, an expectation of human perfection and a belief that love is the primary "passion which governs the male world," rather than the "avarice, ambition, vanity, and a thousand other passions" that in fact regularly overcame love. Women read fiction self-indulgently. Hume urged them to satisfy their passion for intrigue with real plots instead of fictional ones: with Cato's sister and Brutus, rather than Fulvia and Philander. At the same time that history satisfied the taste for excitement and for magnificent spectacles, it was also "a most improving part of knowledge." Much of "what we commonly call erudition ... is nothing but an acquaintance with historical facts." History, he thought, was an easy way to achieve a reputation as an intellectual, for it "opens the door ... to most of the sciences" and "extends our experience to all past ages, and to the most distant nations." Nearly a

27. Daniel Scott Smith and Michael S. Hindus, "Premarital Pregnancy in America, 1640–1971: An Overview and Interpretation," *Journal of Interdisciplinary History*, V (1975), 537–570. Nancy Cott has linked the skepticism of passion to the role of evangelical religion and to women's desire to demonstrate their strength in overcoming sexual temptation, a strength that could then be used in support of a claim to increased independence and political autonomy ("Passionlessness: An Interpretation," *Signs*, IV [1979], 219–236).

century later, the young women of the Boston Gleaning Circle echoed Hume. "The mind enlarges, its local prejudices subside," they wrote, urging each other to read history. The struggles of the people of the past suggested solutions to private problems and to public dilemmas. The uses made of historical precedent in the political debates of the early Republic are ample evidence of the pervasiveness of this assumption. Counseling women to read history was in part to encourage them to become more involved in the intellectual life of the Republic.[28]

In the endorsement of historical study there was also an appreciation of the narrative value of good history and a lurking hope that a taste for narrative could be more wholesomely satisfied by true tales of life and manners, of kings and queens, of battles and leaders, than by fictional accounts of the emotional struggles of ordinary young women. History seemed "safe" in a way that the sciences, the classics, and philosophy were not.[29] It promised learning, but not too much learning. The essayist who believed that "history and natural philosophy are alone sufficient to furnish women with an agreeable kind of study" also recommended that women "avoid all abstract learning, all difficult researches, which may . . . change the delicacy in which they excel into pedantic coarseness." Serious mental exercise was thought to be literally dangerous to women. The *Port Folio*, for example, published the widely reprinted memoir of Elizabeth Graeme Ferguson, a Philadelphia bluestocking who had translated *Télémaque* in order "to relieve and divert her mind" from a broken engagement. "But this, instead of saving," had the result of "impairing her health." Historical narrative seemed to promise to improve the mind without exciting the passions. Women were urged to read history, but not

28. Mercy Otis Warren to Mary Warren, Nov. 1791, Mercy Otis Warren Letterbook, Warren Papers, 486; David Hume, "Of the Study of History," in *Phil. Works of Hume*, IV, 528–533; Boston Gleaning Circle, Minute Book, 101. For other advice to women to read history, see Noah Webster, "Importance of Female Education," *Am. Mag.* (May 1788), 369; *Wkly. Mag.*, Apr. 7, 1798, Aug. 4, 11, 1798; and Milnor, "On Female Education," *Port Folio*, 3d Ser. (May 1809), 392.

29. Hume felt confident that historians' minds, constrained by reality, were protected against poetic or philosophical flights of fancy; good historians would inevitably be defenders of virtue. He claimed that even the amoral Machiavelli did not deny the reality of "moral distinctions" when he acted primarily as a historian rather than as a philosopher. Historical study had for Hume, as for so many others who wrote on this subject, the added advantage that a woman so prepared would be more attractive to men: "A woman may behave herself with good manners, and have even some vivacity in her turn of wit; but where her mind is so unfurnished, it is impossible her conversation can afford any entertainment to men of sense and reflection" (Hume, "Of History," in *Phil. Works of Hume*, IV, 531).

to study it intensely; they might read *The History of England*, but they were not to think of themselves as Catharine Macaulays. History was the anti-intellectual's compromise with higher learning.[30]

The line between the novel and the history, however, was not so clear. Samuel Richardson's implicit promise that he would report human experience in accurate detail seems to have had a historical dimension, and the immense care novelists took to render a setting accurately suggests an interest historians would share. It is no accident that the subtitle of *Clarissa* is *The History of a Young Lady*. The novel that purported to be "founded on fact" sought to straddle the ground between fiction and history. The novel that masqueraded as "true history" sought to claim the respectability of history and the appeal of romantic fiction: it could criticize fiction at the same time that it capitalized on the taste for romance.

One of the most popular of these masquerades was *The Coquette*, an epistolary novel set in Massachusetts that claimed to be a true narration of the lives of real people. It was written by Hannah Webster Foster, who had also compiled *The Boarding School*, a popular textbook of belles lettres for women. *The Coquette* is the history of Eliza Wharton, a young woman who scorns a virtuous minister because he seems too serious. She throws herself at a young gentleman of uncertain background who is as rakish as it is possible to be in a small New England town. In the end the minister finds another virtuous woman and settles into a happy marriage, while the fallen coquette, who has maintained her romanticism against the advice of mother and friends, is seduced and abandoned. Left to bear her illegitimate child alone in the bedroom of a distant tavern, she dies soon after of exposure and malnutrition.

The twentieth-century reader cannot help noting an uncanny resemblance between the pattern of the fictional Eliza Wharton's life and the progression that Edith Wharton described a century later in *The House of Mirth*. The protagonist first rejects a man who the reader is given to understand is suitable for her, then drifts as a house guest on extended visits through the establishments of the rich, where she is superficially welcomed, but made to know that she does not belong. The dashing men she seeks out wish only to use her; yet she has consciously made herself vulnerable to their irresponsibility. Eliza Wharton finally recognizes that the cause of her ruin "may be found in that unrestrained levity of disposi-

---

30. *American Lady's Preceptor*, 25–26; *Port Folio*, I (1809), 521. For the merger of reading history with Republican Motherhood, see John Adams to Abigail Adams 2d (Nabby), Aug. 13, 1783, Butterfield *et al.*, eds., *Book of Abigail and John*, 360.

tion, that fondness for dissipation and coquetry . . . the delusive dream of sensual gratification."[31] At the very end, she makes a moral choice that results in her death.

Although the tone of the narrative suggests that Eliza is young as well as emotionally immature, a closing footnote identifies her as thirty-seven years old at the time of her death. This detail points to the germ of fact at the core of the fiction. Hannah Foster's novel was indeed a history, loosely based on the life of a distant relative, Elizabeth Whitman.[32] But *The Coquette* only masquerades as history; in fact it is a novel that attempts to teach the reader not to read novels. It offers itself as a permissible indulgence in a mildly wicked form. Like others of its genre —*Clarissa, Charlotte Temple*—it offers sexual adventure, but blames the heroine for it. Eliza Wharton loses her control of reality because she misreads her novels.

If one variant of the attack on novel reading was the fear that novels taught women to trust their own passions, another variant was the criticism that fiction wasted women's time. It may be that the increase in leisure reading by women implies that women had increasing amounts of leisure time. But leisure does not happen, it is made. Nothing is more easily manipulated than one's use of time. Within broad limits, leisure is a matter of priorities. If women were in fact reading more, it may not mean that more leisure was *given* to them by increased urban services

31. Samuel Richardson, *Clarissa: Or the History of a Young Lady*, ed. John Angus Burell (New York, 1950); [Foster], *The Coquette*, 221–222.

32. Elizabeth Whitman and the poet Joel Barlow carried on an extended flirtation and correspondence while Barlow was contemplating marriage to another woman. The poet's biographers have trivialized the correspondents' references to each other as husband and wife, but these endearments may signify a physical relationship between the two. "O you are certainly the paragon of Husbands—" Whitman wrote Barlow on Feb. 16, 1779. "Were all married men like you, what a happy world for our Sex!" (BN 435, Baldwin Family Collection, Henry E. Huntington Library, San Marino, Calif.). After Barlow's marriage the letters dwindle. See James Woodress, *A Yankee's Odyssey: The Life of Joel Barlow* (Philadelphia, 1958), 63–64, and Elizabeth Whitman to Joel Barlow, Feb. 9, 16, 1770, Mar. 17, 29, 1770, Apr. 15, 1770, May 12, 1770, June 8, 1770, Baldwin Family Collection, Huntington Library. Caroline Healey Dall's account of the affair in *The Romance of the Association; or, One Last Glimpse of Charlotte Temple and Eliza Wharton: A Curiosity of Literature and Life* shields Whitman's reputation by using the fictional name Foster had used, but identifies the minister as Joseph Buckminster and the seducer as Pierpont Edwards. Dall complained that *The Coquette* smeared Whitman's name and represented the work of a "warm imagination . . . heated by the reading of Richardson's novel" (*The Romance of the Association* . . . [Cambridge, Mass., 1875], 68). For a defense of the men, see Charles Knowles Bolton, *The Elizabeth Whitman Mystery at the Old Bell Tavern in Danvers* (Peabody, Mass., 1912), and Woodress, *Yankee's Odyssey*, 64.

John Singleton Copley, *Mercy Otis Warren* (1763).
Courtesy Museum of Fine Arts, Boston; bequest of Winslow Warren.

Needlepoint embroidery by Mercy Otis Warren. Warren wrote privately of the difficulty of merging intellectual interests with traditional female responsibilities. She herself practiced elegant needlework, as this embroidered tabletop attests. Courtesy Pilgrim Society, Plymouth, Massachusetts. Photograph by Anthony J. Baker.

and industrial inventions, but that they had themselves rearranged their priorities and were *making* time to read. If so, that development would account for the shrill complaint that reading absorbed time that normally would be spent on household tasks and household production. When Mercy Otis Warren warned her niece against fiction, she set her caveat squarely in the context of the use of time in the domestic economy: "As your rank in life has not, nor perhaps ever will set you above an attention to the economy of domestic life; an acquired habit of continual industry will enable you to discharge the duties of prudence, decency and elegance in family affairs, and yet leave you leisure to improve your taste to cultivate your mind, and enlarge your understanding by reading, provided you throw away no part of your time."[33]

It could hardly be denied that "profound or abstruse learning" took long periods of time and concentrated attention—what one writer called "abstraction of mind"—which were thought to be "incompatible with . . . [women's] duties in life, which, though comparatively less important than those of men, are hourly recurring." American women, like British women, were supposed to work to benefit their husbands and families. In the explicitly titled *The Female Guide; or, Thoughts on the Education of That Sex, accomodated to the State of Society, Manners, and Government in the United States*, John Ogden deplored "the increasing luxurious stile of living in America" and complained that women were learning that "it is not genteel to work." He warned his female readers against "the pernicious consequences of that dangerous custom, of spending whole afternoons in company without any work. . . . Idle afternoons are proof of corrupt times, they make bad wives and gay daughters, they make families poor and a country wretched, by circulating scandal and folly, instead of industrious and useful arts, which make us rich and innocent."[34] Stating the popular case against learned women the better to answer it, Maria Edgeworth prepared a "Letter from a Gentleman to his friend, Upon the Birth of a Daughter." The essay, reprinted in America in 1810, cautioned, "I would not expect that my house affairs would be with haste dispatched by a Desdemona, weeping over some unvarnished tale, petrified with some history of horrors . . . at the very time when she should be . . . paying the butcher's bill."[35]

Comments like these were not metaphorical. They reveal that early modern homes were the site of enormous amounts of household production. The romanticization of the home in the nineteenth and twentieth centuries has tended to obscure the economic functions of the home and the housewife, but the steady drone of the spinning wheel and the loom persisted long after industrial development began. Even upper- and middle-class women who lived in cities and towns spent immense amounts of time at work. Elizabeth Drinker began her diary with an account of the work she did between 1757 and 1760, a list covering

33. Mercy Otis Warren to Rebecca Otis, n.d., 1776, Mercy Otis Warren Letterbook, Warren Papers, 57–58.

34. West, *Letters to a Young Lady*, 310; John Ogden, *The Female Guide; or, Thoughts on the Education of That Sex, accomodated to the State of Society, Manners, and Government in the United States* (Concord, N.H., 1793), 34, 39–41.

35. Edgeworth, *Letters for Literary Ladies*, 23–24.

nearly eight closely written pages. It includes frivolous gifts like braided watchstrings and pincushions, but it also included baby clothes, stockings, and shifts for herself. Long after the Revolution, when she was in her fifties—her children grown and married, her household staffed with both permanent and day-hired servants—she still produced many of the household necessities, "tireing . . . [her] eyes, cutting out Shirts and drawing threads." She measured her days by the rhythms of household production: "To day, like yesterday, only that instead of knitting I was mending stockings." Poorer women worked longer and harder on heavier materials; they made their own mattresses and bed ticking as well as their clothes. Poor relief was often furnished in terms of wool to spin. It seemed a commonsense assumption that women should be constantly busy.[36] A taste for literature—like a taste for dissipation—drew women's attention away from domestic work. In this context, reading of any sort was self-indulgent; it was an assertion of individual choice.

This emphasis on the efficient management of domestic responsibilities, and the notion that domestic work is a woman's *business*, has a curiously modern ring. Alex Inkeles's classic list of the characteristics of the modern personality mentions an acute sense of time and a need for efficiency in using it as leading traits. Mercy Otis Warren suggested this notion privately; Judith Sargent Murray spread it publicly in her writings. Both popularized the home as an efficient workplace as well as the locale of domestic production, a definition that foreshadows the home economics movement of the early twentieth century. Judith Sargent Murray's "new era in female history" was to be marked by women opposed "to every trivial and unworthy monopolizer of time." She spoke explicitly of *"female administration"* and of the impact efficient housekeepers could have. Her choice of words—"machine," "methodical," "economical"—conveys the sharp edge of her vision of the household. "It would be pleasant to observe the contrast between a family, the females of which were properly methodical, and economical in their distributions and expenditures of time, and one accustomed to leave everything to the moment of necessity. . . . The one is the habitation of tranquillity; it is a

36. Diary of Elizabeth Drinker, Mar. 13, 1798, Sept. 14, 1798. See also the detailed accounts of work kept by Ruth Henshaw of Leicester, Mass., beginning in 1801, Ruth Henshaw Bascom Diaries, Am. Antq. Soc. For poor relief furnished as wool for spinning, see Record Book, "Out of Doors Spinners Accounts, 1806–1807," Record Group 35.97, Philadelphia City Archives. Of the 256 recipients, all but a single male weaver were women, reflecting the common occupational segregation. For detailed description of women's work within the New England household, see Cott, *Bonds of Womanhood,* 19–62.

Bed rug made by Abigail Foote of Colchester, Connecticut. Abigail Foote's diary testified to the contributions to the family economy made by the work of young women. "Fix'd gown for Prude—Mend Mother's Riding-Hood—Spun short thread—Fix'd two gowns for Welsh's girls—Carded two—Spun linen—Worked on Cheese basket, Hatchel'd flax with Hannah, we did 51 lbs a-piece—Pleated and ironed—Read a sermon of Doddridge's. . . . Had two scholars from Mrs. Taylor's—I carded two pounds of whole wool and felt Nationaly" she wrote on the eve of the Battle of Lexington. Quoted in Thomas H. Woody, *Women's Education in the United States* (New York, 1929), I, 162.
Courtesy Historic Deerfield, Inc., Deerfield, Massachusetts.

Cover from *Universal Asylum and Columbian Magazine*, V (1790).
Courtesy The Library Company of Philadelphia.

well ordered community; it is a complicated machine, the component parts of which are so harmoniously organized, as to produce none but the most concordant sounds. . . . While the other . . . is a restoration of the reign of chaos."[37]

Mercy Otis Warren wrestled valiantly throughout her life with the problem of finding time for writing and reflection while raising four children and maintaining a large, elegant household. At intervals she reflected on these competing claims for female attention and recognized that the answers were not simple. Warren took these issues more seriously than virtually any other woman of her generation. Often the occasion for writing down her thoughts was the marriage or betrothal of a young woman relative or friend, when she would try to describe the new life her correspondent faced.

When she considered the domestic economy, Warren used the quasi-official term "department." She recognized that when a woman married she took on substantial economic responsibilities that resisted rearrangement. "Whatever delight we may have in the use of the pen," Mercy Warren wrote, "however eager we may be in the pursuit of knowledge . . . yet heaven has so ordained the lot of female life that every literary attention, must give place to family avocations." All reading except the Bible, she reported, "must" be postponed "till all matters of economy which belong to her department are promptly adjusted." Warren did not think these responsibilities could be evaded, though she did occasionally describe women as "confined to the narrow circle of domestic cares," and she did indulge herself in a bit of envy of unmarried women who were "free from those constant *interruptions* that necessarily occupy the mind of the wife, the mother and the mistress."

But for the long run Warren counseled a careful allocation of time that would permit the model woman to live in both the world of intellect and the world of domesticity. "A methodical and uniform plan of conduct, united with an industrious mind" would make a double life possible. She even permitted herself a deprecating comment on women who could not blend both worlds. She was scornful of those "who swim on the surface of pleasure," but she also pitied the woman who "is wholly immersed" in her household "and has *no higher ideas* than those which confine her to the narrow circle of domestic attention." Mercy Otis Warren's vision of the fully domestic woman was not unlike that of Mary Wollstonecraft,

37. Murray, *The Gleaner*, III, No. 87, 189, II, No. 35, 6, I, No. 3, 29–30.

who decried those who remained "immured in their families groping in the dark." Warren recognized that ordinary household dynamics encouraged this immersion. "We have one advantage peculiar to ourselves," she wrote bitterly. "We can conceal in the obscure retreat, by our own fireside, the neglect of those mental improvements to which the more domestic animal stands in little *need* of, as it is not necessary for her to leave the retired roof—whereas *man* is generally called out to a full display of his abilities." But if the woman who drowned her mind in domestic detail was shallow and shortsighted, the woman who had "both genius and taste for literary enquiry" but could not "chearfully leave the pursuit to attend to the daily cares of the prudent housewife" was also to be pitied. Even for Warren, literary pursuits were a form of luxury, and the woman who could not keep their attractions under tight rein was indulging in her own form of folly.[38]

The new attitudes toward housekeeping were reflected in satires in the popular press that suggested that housework was undervalued and should be modernized and made rational. These satires generally were written from the point of view of a woman who desperately seeks to maintain an orderly household, only to be outdone by a selfish, slovenly husband blind to the significance of her work. It may be that the satirical mode freed the writers to be less cautious than usual; certainly the sentiments expressed are sharp and often shrewd. When pursued energetically, housework was shown to be disruptive. "The rage for scouring and cleaning . . . is the vice of the ladies," wrote one satirist. "Mops, pails and brushes . . . Are scepters of control." Men in these caricatures are lazy; they do not care how much disorder they create or how much trouble they give their wives and servants. "The Drone" splatters ink, tracks mud in the house, stashes things on the mantelpiece, conveniently forgets his errands. In Francis Hopkinson's "Nitidia" the husband demolishes the parlor with his scientific experiments, and then expects his wife to prepare a formal dinner for his friends. "Nitidia" refers to her household as her "business" and suggests that it interferes with women's intellectual development; had women time for intellectual matters, surely they would put it to better use than men do. "You hear it echoed from every quarter—My wife cannot make verses, it is true; but she makes an excellent pudding. . . . she can't unravel the intricacies of political

---

38. Mercy Otis Warren to the daughter of a deceased friend, n.d., Mercy Otis Warren Letterbook, Warren Papers, 117; Mercy Otis Warren to Abigail Adams, Feb. 1774, *ibid.*, 145.

economy and federal government; but she can knit charming stockings—
and this they call praising a wife, and doing justice to her good character
—with much nonsense of the like kind."[39]

Critics thought that instead of reading fiction, women ought to be
reading something else (history) or doing something else (household production). But women seem to have persisted in their consumption of
fiction; their loyalty to the genre was not undermined.

Only Jane Austen sought to explain this loyalty. Her explanation appeared in 1818 in *Northanger Abbey*. Henry Tilney, his sister Catherine,
and their friend Miss Morland are out for a walk. Miss Morland con-
fesses her fondness for popular novels like *The Mysteries of Udolpho*.
She is aware that most people would consider history more suitable: "I
read it a little as a duty, but it tells me nothing that does not either vex or
weary me. The quarrels of popes and kings, with wars or pestilences, in
every page; the men all so good for nothing, and hardly any women at
all."[40]

The last phrase is the telling one. History promised to teach statecraft,
human nature, the management of political affairs. Even the farmer's
son, were he ambitious, might be persuaded that historical writing had
some personal significance for him. The instrumental argument by which
history was justified for boys was inappropriate for girls: women could
not be statesmen, they could not preside over legislative assemblies. Even
Catharine Macaulay's *History of England* had virtually no women as
principal actors, nor, for that matter, did Mercy Otis Warren's *History of
the American Revolution*. The best that could be offered girls as a justification for reading history was either the very distant promise that the
history they learned could ultimately be taught to their as yet unborn
sons, or the argument that history was attractive for its anecdotes and
example. If history were reduced to human interest, anecdote, and the
idiosyncrasies of individual behavior, it could easily be argued that fiction
presented the same material—perhaps better.

If a young woman, or her teacher, acted on the advice of Benjamin
Rush or Judith Sargent Murray and took to reading history, she would

39. "On Saturday and abused Cleanliness," *Connecticut Courant* (Hartford), Sept. 1,
1788; "The Drone," *Burlington Advt.*, Feb. 22, 1791; Francis Hopkinson, "Nitidia," ed.
Linda K. Kerber, *Signs*, IV (1978), 402–406.
40. Jane Austen, *Northanger Abbey and Persuasion*, ed. John Davie (London, 1971),
97–99.

find very little that was not vulnerable to Jane Austen's criticism. In the years of the early Republic, the only history about women consisted of assortments of biographical sketches, many lacking chronological order and usually lacking interpretative force. One of the most obvious uses of these compilations was made in the Philadelphia fund-raising broadside of 1780 which, as shown earlier, justified itself in part by reference to heroic women of biblical and historical times. Little was offered to explain the behavior of the women named in this list extending from Deborah to Catherine the Great. Other compilers could be more ambitious; the list in *The American Lady's Preceptor* was chronologically ordered and more coherently discussed: Cornelia, Boadicea, Margaret of Anjou, Catherine of Aragon, Anne Boleyn, Marie Antoinette. All except for Elizabeth Graeme Ferguson—who had been conveniently written about by a friend in a recent issue of the Philadelphia *Port Folio*—were European.[41]

Judith Sargent Murray's *Gleaner* essays, though they also marshaled scattered examples, were considerably more purposeful. Murray's vision of women's collective past was a history of strength and fortitude. "Courage," she wrote, "is by no means *exclusively* a masculine virtue." She admired the Spartan women for their "uncommon firmness." She believed women could be patriots, though she did think they displayed that patriotism in sacrifice rather than in legislation or fighting. Her interpretation of politics was mildly defensive: "If the triumphs and attainments of THE SEX, under the various oppressions with which they have struggled, have been thus splendid, how would they have been augmented, had not ignorant or interested men, after clipping their wings, contrived to erect around them almost insurmountable barriers." Murray tumbled her historical examples about, heedless of chronology: Charlotte Corday and Lady Jane Grey, Jane of Flanders and Margaret of Anjou, Portia, Julia, Aspasia, Volumnia, Mary Astell and Catharine Macaulay. To name them was not to provide an analytical history; her purpose was to use historical data as evidence against the "*idea of the incapability* of women."[42]

Women's history as a subject of study in America may be said to have begun with the late eighteenth-century search for a usable past, begun by

41. *The American Lady's Preceptor* had a subtitle: "A compilation of observations, essays, and poetical effusions, designed to direct the female mind in a course of pleasing and instructive reading." It was designed as a textbook for female academies: "No volume of selections has been published in this country especially designed for the reading of females."
42. Murray, *The Gleaner*, III, 192, 193, 197, 191.

compilers of "Ladies' Repositories," ladies' magazines, and textbooks for girls' schools. Much of their material came from British and European sources. When literary nationalists complained about the persistence of European reading materials in America, these women's books were among the offenders they had in mind. Long after political independence had been accomplished, women's reading remained a part of a transatlantic literary culture, of which cultural nationalists like Noah Webster were deeply skeptical. Books reflecting the European class-based social order would, it was feared, give young women a taste of such hierarchies and undermine the effort to build a democratic social order in America. In this sense, imported women's reading seemed unrepublican.

But there were no ready solutions to this problem, even for those who would agree that women ought to pay more attention to works speaking to the American experience. It would be nearly another generation before there were coherent histories of American women available for the female audience. Samuel L. Knapp's *Female Biography* did not appear until 1834, Lydia Maria Child's *Brief History of the Condition of Women* until 1845, Sarah Josepha Hale's *Woman's Record* until 1853. Elizabeth Ellet's great compilation of the activities of women during the Revolution appeared in 1850. Not until the 1850s did Benson Lossing begin the travels that culminated in his *Pictorial Field Book of the Revolution*, which included many accounts of women's deeds.[43]

In the years of the early Republic, very few histories could meet the demands of educators like Rush and Webster, yet refute Jane Austen's criticism that they treated "hardly any women at all" in their pages. When they were available, they were likely to be unsophisticated, even boring. But another sort of history was indeed widely available, one that met general approval and one in which there was no dearth of female heroes: women's confessional tracts, religious autobiographies, accounts of conversion experiences, even, occasionally, funeral sermons delivered in honor of a notable woman and published by her family or her minister. The appeal of these accounts had something in common with the novel,

---

43. Samuel L. Knapp, *Female Biography; containing Notices of Distinguished Women, in Different Nations and Ages* (New York, 1834); L. Maria Child, *Brief History of the Condition of Women . . .*, 2 vols. (Boston, 1845); Sarah Josepha Hale, *Woman's Record; or, Sketches of All Distinguished Women . . .* (New York, 1853); Elizabeth Fries Lummis Ellet, *Domestic History of the American Revolution* (New York, 1850); Benson J. Lossing, *The Pictorial Field Book of the Revolution*, 2 vols. (New York, 1859). The work of Child and Ellet is perceptively discussed in Susan Phinney Conrad, *Perish the Thought: Intellectual Women in Romantic America, 1830–1860* (New York, 1976), 103–122.

which itself often masqueraded as fictional confession. Among the standard ingredients was the struggle of the heroine against temptation. Her letters to parents and to friends might be included, giving the narrative the coloration of history and the shape of an epistolary novel. Her courtship—sometimes by one man, sometimes by several—was recounted. The saga usually culminated either in a conversion experience or in a triumphant deathbed scene, two public successes for which no woman needed to apologize.

The Christian Mourning with Hope is a good example of this genre. It begins with Samuel Worcester's sermon at the funeral of Eleanor Read Emerson in 1808 in Salem, Massachusetts. In this sermon, Mrs. Emerson appears as the model woman; the minister celebrates "the superior endowments of her mind; her quick and clear intelligence, her brilliant imagination, her animating vivacity, her ingenuous disposition, and her engaging social qualities. You knew how admirably she was formed . . . to diffuse a useful and benign influence around her."[44]

The sermon is followed by a lengthy memoir of Mrs. Emerson's life, extracts from her diary, and copies of her letters. While the funeral sermon is composed of glowing generalities, the historical materials introduce us to a woman who had not found her life simple or easy. Her health had been frail from childhood, but her mind was vigorous and her morale evidently high. When she was only fourteen she "commenced her beloved employment of school-keeping." Eleanor Read "kept" school steadily for the next twelve years; she was something of an entrepreneur, traveling to nine different Massachusetts towns in order to establish schools. She developed her own curriculum: reading, spelling, writing, grammar, composition, "religion," plain needlework, and public speaking. This last she considered a serious enterprise, though it was unusual in female schools; her purpose was "to rouse and improve the mind, to form the manners, give energy to the character, and perfect the pupil in the art of reading." She refused to teach painting and embroidery, thinking them "unnecessary." By the time of her death at the early age of thirty-one, she had taught "hundreds of young persons, whose minds she imbued with the rudiments of knowledge."[45]

44. Samuel Worcester, ed., *The Christian Mourning with Hope. A Sermon, Delivered at Beverly, Nov. 14, 1808, on occasion of the Death of Mrs. Eleanor Emerson, Late Consort of the Rev. Joseph Emerson . . . To which are Annexed Writings of Mrs. Emerson, with a Brief Sketch of her Life* (Boston, 1809), 20.

45. *Ibid.*, 27–28, 21.

Throughout her career Eleanor Read considered the state of her soul, attending revival meetings of all sorts, anxiously hoping to be saved. She chose the towns in which she set up schools in part because of her expectations of the ministers or churches there; she introduced "public prayer" in her schools even though she had reason to fear that school prayer "would be deemed ridiculous enthusiasm. . . . Here I began to hesitate. I searched the scriptures, to see, if the injunctions to women, not to speak in the church . . . would not excuse me. . . . But I found nothing. . . . how can I ever describe the conflict in my mind between pride and duty."[46]

Eleanor Read's world was a small one. Counseled to seek salt air for her health, she went to Salem, where she found the minister Samuel Worcester willing to be the patron for her school. In Salem she met Nancy Eaton, who was living with Worcester's family while she waited to marry another minister, Joseph Emerson. Nancy Eaton was fitting herself to become a minister's wife by living with and observing Worcester's family. The two women became close friends; after Nancy Eaton Emerson's death Eleanor Read married Joseph Emerson, and when Eleanor Read Emerson died, Worcester delivered her funeral sermon.

The two women "discoursed upon the importance of improving the female mind." It is clear that they were sensitive to the public argument about the limits of female intelligence. Eleanor Read reported their conclusions in her journal: "Let the man of real piety carefully examine the origin of the detested sentiment which leads him to consider learning and mental improvement as undesirable in a female. . . . will not the honest christian blush before his God for the unchristian and cruel degredation of the female mind? . . . We expatiated largely on the folly of multitudes of our unthinking sex."[47] Ironically, when Nancy Eaton Emerson died eight months after her marriage, Joseph Emerson blamed her death on the intensity of her studies. "Her bereaved husband is now convinced," wrote their friend Worcester, "that her education was not conducted upon the most judicious plan. While he entertains the same opinion of the capacity of females to understand everything, that man can understand, and also of the importance of improving their minds . . . He is fully of that opinion, that, if females wish to do the greatest possible good, they must not attempt to know every thing; but consent them-

46. Ibid., 49–50.
47. Ibid., 72.

selves to limit their attention to such pursuits, as are of the greatest moral and practical importance." Emerson thought that every hour that could be taken from "domestic pursuits" ought to be spent "in secret devotion, in religious conversation, in social worship," and in reading "a few of the best histories"—activities preferable to spending time "studying geometry, algebra, or natural philosophy."[48]

The memoir ends with a detailed account of Eleanor Read Emerson's deathbed, her farewells to family and friends, her eloquence in calling on relatives to repent, and, finally, her funeral and burial next to her friend Nancy Eaton Emerson.

When Rush and Webster told women to read history they were thinking of Livy and Tacitus, of Rollin and Macaulay. But the narrative of a life like that of Mrs. Emerson, while generally categorized as a devotional tract, was also a history dealing with themes central to the life experience of women of the post-Revolutionary generation. Eleanor Read, after all, was a girl of respectable family who developed a career in a relatively new sort of work. She did not merely "keep school"; she traveled alone to towns where she thought she could keep it most advantageously. She developed a curriculum of her own, exercising some originality in the process. She formed a very close female friendship, and she and her friend seriously considered whether it was appropriate to set bounds on female intellectuality. Under the trappings of a traditional devotional tract is a biography of an intense young woman who explored more widely than most of her peers the options open to her community and her generation. A book like this one must be classified as women's history as well as religious history.

The novel was the only other widely available form of narrative that tended to place women at the center. Women were determinedly present in the fictional "histories" of *Charlotte Temple* or *The Coquette* as they were not in the public histories written by Rollin or Macaulay. Even novels that did not name women in their titles—for example, Charles Brockden Brown's *Alcuin* and *Ormond*—often had women as central actors. Whether or not these characters came to a good end, the reader had the opportunity to observe women in physical or emotional crisis, to feel sympathy for heroines in the cautionary tales.

If a woman sought to learn how other women coped with reality, she had few printed resources other than fiction to which she might turn. The

48. *Ibid.*, 80n.

novel that claimed to be "founded on Fact" smudged the clear line between fact and fiction, and may well have seemed to its readers to fulfill some of the functions of narrative history.[49] The unrealistic elements could be discounted, the elements of truth sifted out. To deny women access to novels, as Jedidiah Strong had done, was to deny them access to a rich imagery of what women were and what they might hope to become.

49. See especially Eliza Foster Cushing's *Yorktown: An Historical Romance* (Boston, 1826), and *Saratoga; A Tale of the Revolution* (Boston, 1824). For a treatment of novels by and about women in the 19th century congruent with the interpretation offered here, see Mary Kelley, "The Sentimentalists: Promise and Betrayal in the Home," *Signs*, IV (1979), 434–446.

Chapter 9

THE REPUBLICAN MOTHER:

FEMALE POLITICAL IMAGINATION

IN THE EARLY REPUBLIC

The Spirit that prevails among Men of all degrees,
all ages and sex'es is the Spirit of Liberty.

                    —Abigail Adams, 1775

America Lamenting at the Tomb of Washington (early 19th century). Silk
embroidery. After Washington died, Columbia lived on. In many pictures made
after his death, Washington was the abstraction and Columbia the living being.
Courtesy Charles W. McAlpin Collection, Prints Division, The New York Public Library,
Astor, Lenox and Tilden Foundations.

WHEN WOMEN LOOKED BACK to the years of the Revolution, what did they remember? Several themes were repeated with great frequency. The war had been a nightmare. It had frightened people and disrupted lives. It had been a time when women had chosen political identities, prided themselves on their loyalism or on their patriotism, and performed services for the government of their choice. Women who had survived the war had been strong and courageous, but the Republic had offered only the most grudging response to their sacrifices, as Rachel Wells had discovered.

Americans did not choose to explore with much rigor the socially radical implications of their republican ideology. Only haltingly did a few develop the obvious antislavery implications of egalitarian rhetoric. Nor did they explore very deeply the implications of female citizenship; the Revolution and the Republic that followed were thought to be men's work. "To be an adept in the art of Government," Abigail Adams observed to her husband, "is a prerogative to which your Sex lay almost an exclusive claim."[1] Confiscation legislation provided the legal context in which the implications of female citizenship might have been developed but legislators and judges did not have a tabula rasa on which to begin and were unwilling to insist that all women be required to assume their own political—and therefore economic—identities. Instead women were left to invent their own political character. They devised their own interpretation of what the Revolution had meant to them as women, and they began to invent an ideology of citizenship that merged the domestic domain of the preindustrial woman with the new public ideology of individual responsibility and civic virtue. They did this in the face of severe ridicule, responding both to the anti-intellectual complaint that educating women served no practical purpose and the conservative complaint that women had no political significance.

Memories of the Revolution, as they appear in postwar fiction, suggest some of the lessons women drew from the wartime experience. An early exploration of women's political options appears in Mercy Otis Warren's verse play *The Ladies of Castile*, written only a year after the Peace of Paris and first published in a small volume of poems dedicated to George Washington in 1790. The play has received little critical attention. An introduction reveals that Warren wrote *The Ladies of Castile* at the urging of her son Winslow, who had apparently dared her to write a play with a non-American subject. She chose a setting from which she could draw ob-

---

1. Abigail Adams to John Adams, May 9, 1776, *Adams Family Correspondence*, I, 404.

vious analogies with the politics of her own time: "The history of Charles the fifth, the tyranny of his successors, and the exertions of the Spanish Cortes, will ever be interesting to an American ear, so long as they triumph in their independence, pride themselves in the principles that instigated their patriots, and glory in the characters of their heroes."[2]

The Ladies of Castile concerns two women of contrasting temperaments caught up in a revolutionary civil war: the soft and delicate Louisa, who introduces herself with the words, "I wander wilder'd and alone/ Like some poor banish'd fugitive . . . I yield to grief," and the determined Maria, wife of the leader of the rebellion, who announces in her opening scene, "Maria has a bolder part to act—/ I scorn to live upon ignoble terms." Like the White Queen in *Alice in Wonderland*, Louisa continually wrings her hands and mourns each turn of the political screw. She is torn by "warring passions" as her lover goes off to fight against her brother. She begs God for courage; she begs her father to spare her lover's life. But neither plea is answered, and, stunned by a false report of her lover's death, Louisa stabs herself.

If Louisa is Juliet, Maria has the strength of a virtuous Lady Macbeth. "Thou shoulds't have liv'd in mild and gentler times," she tells Louisa.

> But for myself—though famine, chains, and death
> Should all combine—nay, should Don Juan fall—
> Which Heav'n forbid—I ne'er will yield,
> Nor own myself a slave.

Maria prides herself on her strength; her husband says her "virtue's rais'd so far above . . . [the female] Sex." Even when she is worried for his safety, she feels within herself "a manly force of mind/Urging to deeds heroic and sublime." When *she* hears false news of her husband's death, she resolves, "I will avenge my lord . . . I never will despair." And after his actual death, she heroically rallies his troops.

> Behold, the virtuous citizens of Spain . . .
> Come, shew one sample of heroic worth,
> Ere ancient Spain, the glory of the west,
> Bends abject down . . .
> Secure the city—barricade the gates . . .

2. Warren, *Poems, Dramatic and Miscellaneous*, 100. See also Mercy Otis Warren to Winslow Warren, Sept. 1785, Mercy Otis Warren Letterbook, Warren Papers, 313–314, Mass. Hist. Soc.

I'll head the troops, and mount the prancing steed . . .
Not Semiramis' or Zenobia's fame
Outstrips the glory of Maria's name.[3]

For her virtue, there is happy reward at the end of the play.

The message of *The Ladies of Castile* is simple and obvious. Even in the exigencies of war, women must control themselves and their options. The Louisas of the world do not survive revolutions; the Marias—who take political positions, make their own judgment of the contending sides, risk their lives—emerge stronger and in control. "A soul, inspir'd by freedom's genial warmth," says Maria, "expands,—grows firm—and by resistance, strong."[4]

Mercy Otis Warren's introduction makes it clear that the civil war in Spain was to be taken as a metaphor for the Revolutionary civil war in America. A major lesson she had learned from it was that women who, like Louisa, ignored politics did so only at great risk. It is the Marias, whose souls grow strong by resistance, who take gritty political positions, who will survive and flourish under revolutionary conditions.[5]

As we have seen, similar suggestions about the significance of the Revolutionary experience appear in the works of Judith Sargent Murray and Charles Brockden Brown. Murray's Margaretta and Penelope Airy consciously develop self-confidence and self-respect. The novelist Brown imagined a more fully developed version of Murray's model woman for the heroine of *Ormond*, published in 1799. Constantia Dudley is eminently rational. When her father's fortune is embezzled, she sells "every superfluous garb and trinket," her music, and her books and supports the family by needlework, "her cheerfulness unimpaired." Constantia never flinches; she can take whatever ill fortune brings, from yellow fever to poverty so severe that her only alternative to starvation is cornmeal mush three times a day for three months. Through it all, she resists proposals of

---

3. Warren, *Poems, Dramatic and Miscellaneous*, 125–126, 144, 163–164.
4. *Ibid.*, 162.
5. In form and design, John Daly Burk's play *Female Patriotism* has some similarities to *The Ladies of Castile*. It too is written largely in blank verse and is set during a historic conflict that is taken to prefigure the American conflict with England. Joan has the companionship of Maria-like Mary of Anjou, who tells the dauphin that she is prepared to follow him to the field. Mary and Joan form a female community within a male military world: "In war, in camps,/Woman to woman is most necessary:/They sooth each other's fears and cares to rest,/By joint support, and mutual confidence" (Burk, *Female Patriotism*, act 4, sc. 4). Despite its title, however, Burk's play is not about female patriotism as a concept or a behavior, as is Warren's; it is, rather, about a single, miraculous female patriot.

marriage, because even in adversity she scorns becoming emotionally dependent without love.[6]

Everything Constantia does places her in sharp contrast to Helena Cleves, who is "endowed with every feminine and fascinating quality." Helena has had a genteel education; she can paint, and sing, and play the clavichord, but this fashionable gloss camouflages a lack of real mental accomplishment and self-discipline. "Exterior accomplishments" are sufficient so long as life holds no surprises, but when Helena meets disaster, she is unprepared to maintain her independence and her self-respect. She falls into economic dependence upon a "kinswoman"; she succumbs to the "specious but delusive" reasoning of Ormond and becomes his mistress. He takes advantage of Helena's dependence, all the while seeking in Constantia a rational woman worthy of his intelligence. Eventually, in despair, Helena kills herself.[7]

The argument that an appropriate education would steel girls to face adversity is related to the conviction that all citizens of a republic should be self-reliant. But this argument can be made independent of republican ideology. It may well represent the common sense of a revolutionary era in which the unexpected was very likely to happen, in which large numbers of people had in fact experienced reversals of fortune, physical dislocation, encounters with strangers. Constantia's friend Martinette de Beauvais had lived in Marseilles, Verona, Vienna, and Philadelphia. After disguising herself as a man and fighting in the American Revolution, she was one of the "hundreds" of women who took up arms for the French.[8] Constantia admires and empathizes with her friend. Nothing in the novel is clearer than the warning that if a woman is not ready to maintain her independence in a crisis, as Constantia and Martinette do, she risks sinking, like Helena, into prostitution and death.

Hannah Webster Foster paid no direct attention to the Revolution in her books, *The Boarding School* and *The Coquette*, but she seems to have assisted her daughters in the historical novels they wrote. Eliza Foster Cushing wrote two novels set in the war years with the obvious

6. Charles Brockden Brown, *Ormond*, ed. Ernest Marchand (New York, 1937 [orig. publ. 1799]), 19.

7. *Ibid.*, 98–99.

8. "It was obvious to suppose that a woman thus fearless and sagacious had not been inactive at a period like the present, which called forth talents and courage without distinction of sex, and had been particularly distinguished by female enterprise and heroism" (*ibid.*, 170).

titles *Saratoga; A Tale of the Revolution* and *Yorktown: An Historical Romance*. Each has a female character who complains about her exclusion from the main scene of action and who expresses her frustration at the constraints on her behavior. In *Saratoga*, Catherine Courtland, a self-proclaimed "daughter of America," is contrasted with her father, a soldier in Burgoyne's army who thinks women ought not to have political opinions, and with her weak and passive cousin Amelia, who is a loyalist because that course seems to her the path of least resistance. Catherine's father shrugs off her political conversations: "Go, go, you are an enthusiast, Kate. . . . Your fond, foolish sex have always some darling theme to rave about, and it is fortunate for us, that your fancies are only suffered to waste themselves in words." Catherine responds with both an acknowledgment and a criticism of the constraints placed on women: "I think, were we less limited, we should soon disprove the assertions of those who predict misrule and anarchy, as a necessary consequence of suffering us to exercise power."[9] By setting Catherine's self-reliant deportment against that of a female loyalist and her politics against that of a male loyalist, Eliza Cushing made it clear whom she thought her readers should admire. The Republic offered political roles only to men, but the talents of a Catherine would have been of far greater use to it than those of her hostile father.

Yorktown, despite its subtitle, was a gothic romance, its pages resonating with tangled mysteries of identity and parentage. Here the two central women are again drawn in contrast, but this time both are patriots. Helen, the young heroine, wishes she could help the patriot cause, but feels inhibited by social constraints. "Alas! unfortunate sex," she exclaims, "gifted with souls as lofty and aspiring as any which animate the lordly form of man; possessed of hearts, alive to every tender and exalted sentiment, and of spirits that can endure and dare what sterner man will often shrink from, yet limited to a narrow and subordinate sphere, trammelled by arbitrary custom, and scarcely permitted even the privilege of an independent word or thought!"[10]

In Maude Mausel, Cushing invented her first really original character. Maude is a middle-aged woman, perceived as old, who is never fully explained. Sometimes sinister, sometimes prophetic, she is treated by other characters as a witch. When she is asked if she is woman or fiend,

9. Cushing, *Saratoga*, I, 20, 221–224, 128–129.
10. Cushing, *Yorktown*, I, 229.

she replies, "It matters not. . . . I answer to the name of either, and sometimes do the work of both."[11] It is Maude, "the victim of passion," who alone can shake off the trammels of arbitrary custom that Helen finds so binding. It is Maude who infiltrates as a spy in the British camp, Maude who turns up, unannounced, in the ranks of rebel soldiers.[12] "You come to ask, why I am here," she says. "I answer, to fight for my country, as I have often done before—yes, often; and every ball which sped from my hand, was sure to drink the life-blood of a foe; nay, you cannot turn me from my purpose." But it is obvious that the author is ambivalent toward her creation. Maude's refusal to accept social constraints gains her the admiration only of the vulgar: " 'Well said, my brave old goody,' exclaimed a veteran, who stood beside her; 'I guess now if this here State of Virginy could send out a whole rigiment of sich 'are she tigers, there wouldn't long be sich a tarnal sight o' red coats swarming over their tobacco fields.' " Only the deviant woman could throw herself into the battle as Maude does: she is outside the boundaries of the respectable. But Maude also has the prophetic voice: "You have crushed my summer flowers beneath the corpses of your slain, drenched this verdant carpet with streams of human blood." War offers Maude a chance to redeem herself: without it she is only "the miserable victim of passion," with it she has occasion to demonstrate "the seeds of virtue . . . in her heart" by her service to the patriot cause.[13]

The relationship of these fictional heroines to the real women of the Revolutionary generation is complex. A pair of novels, written by a woman laden with the historically resonant name of Susan Anne Livingston Ridley Sedgwick, demonstrate how selective memory might work. In writing *Allen Prescott*, published in New York in 1834, and *Alida; or, Town and Country*, which appeared ten years later, Susan Sedgwick drew on the memories and experiences of her elderly aunt Susan Livingston Symmes, who had lived through the war. The novelist's inspiration figures in *Alida* as Alida Cargill, the elderly aunt of the heroine of the same name (which was one occasionally used in the Livingston family). What both Susans remembered about the war was its wastefulness of life and the terror experienced by civilians facing advancing troops. As a young girl, the aunt had in fact remained in her family home after the rest

---

11. *Ibid.,* 90.

12. *Ibid.,* II, 252.

13. *Ibid.,* I, 82–84, 94, II, 252. See also Cooper, *The Spy,* in which the role of the sybil is again given to a woman, Elizabeth Foster.

of the family had run, in the hope of maintaining her parents' claim to the property. Accompanied only by a neighbor's daughter, she stalwartly held her ground against a loyalist mob, although "frightend almost to Death": "She and I set with our Backs against the Cellar Wall and there remained untill the firing ceased. then we ventured upstairs, we looked more like death, than like human beings. aye my dear, it requires an abler pen than I wield, to describe the Panic, the Horror, and distress I underwent not to save a thousand Houses would I undergo the same again, I could not stand for hours after, on account of trembling."[14]

The elderly Susan Livingston Symmes, remembering this episode, emphasized her fright and her sense of helplessness. Her young relative transmuted this material into a story of a brave Alida standing her ground and saving her father's precious public papers by a clever ruse. The Revolutionary women whom Susan Sedgwick reconstructed out of her family's memories—like those of Murray, Brown, and Cushing—are Marias, not Louisas. They represent the way in which the daughters of the Revolutionary generation gave meaning to the events of their mothers' generation; they transmit the significance of the Revolution.[15]

Nurtured as she had been by the Revolution, what role was there for a Maria in the Republic? There were those who thought she was an aberration, acceptable only during crisis. Susan Livingston Symmes, for example, was always proud of her youthful bravery, but she regarded it as purely occasional and was critical of public roles of any sort for women. When her niece attended an Ohio ladies' academy that stressed elocution and public speaking, Susan demurred: "This I do not approve of for girls as old as Julia, in her 16th year, it requires a degree of self-possession that a Lady may as well be without, since our Sex is not destined for

---

14. Susan Livingston Symmes to Susan Sedgwick, Apr. 1, 1835, Ridley Papers, Box 5, Mass. Hist. Soc. The mob leader appears to have been a loyalist refugee named Steward, "a mean looking man" with a sad story. His children had been bound out to a patriot, who was now threatening to take them to Kentucky unless given "silk for a gown, a Negro wench, and one Hundred pounds in money," a ransom obviously far beyond the father's means. Steward had intended to seize the governor's daughter as a hostage for his own children's return, but he could not bring himself to do it. Susan did plead his case, ineffectively, to her father; Steward eventually retrieved his children through the assistance of an army officer.

15. The episode is fictionalized in [Susan Livingston Ridley Sedgwick], *Alida; or, Town and Country* (New York, 1844), 14–16. For another woman's proud memory of defying British soldiers, see [Frazier], "A Reminiscence," *PMHB*, XLVI (1922), 42–46: "The Captain, as he was going away [after pillaging the house] said, 'I had orders to take Mr. Frazer prisoner, and burn the house and barn, but these I give to you.' I replied I cannot thank you for what is my own, and if these were your orders you would not dare disobey them."

public-speakers."[16] Susan Ridley Sedgwick, the novelist, argued that the very success of the Revolution had made nurturing the "Maria" personality unnecessary. "It has indeed been observed by foreigners, with some surprise, that females here are remarkably exempt from the care of the public weal; that they either know nothing or care little about subjects connected with it," she wrote in *Allen Prescott*. Visitors usually accounted for this lack of involvement by commenting that American women were straitened by domesticity, "but there is a better reason," Sedgwick maintained. "Government here, though extending over all its protection and vigilance, is a guardian, not a spy. It does not rudely enter our houses, hearts, and consciences, . . . in codes of conscription, disabilities, and test-acts. . . . [Women] conceive themselves to have the best government in the world, because, in the main,—to use a female figure of speech—like a well made garment, it fits perfectly, and presses nowhere. But let this same garment give token of fracture, decay, or uneasy alteration, we should find their tongues move as quickly as their needles." So long as the male political order refrained from direct pressure on the family, her argument implied, Marias could be content to masquerade as Louisas.[17]

Sedgwick was writing in the 1830s, at a time when the ideology of domesticity had acquired unusual forcefulness in the upper classes to which she belonged. The abortive debate over women's political capacity prompted by the American and French revolutions was dormant in her time, though it was about to be reenergized in the course of the abolitionist campaign. But Sedgwick was wrong if she thought that retreat from political engagement had been simple for women or that their interest could be easily redirected. On the contrary, the heat of argument and the bitterness of satire at the turn of the century suggest that the woman question had indeed cut deep.

There were those who emerged from the Revolution comfortably able to accept a greater role for women in the public domain, ready to develop Condorcet's principle that republics were imperfect until they recognized the political claims of half of their people. Rachel Wells, Eliza Wilkinson,

---

16. Susan L. Symmes to Susan Ridley, June 11, 1806, Ridley Papers, Box 5.

17. [Susan Livingston Ridley Sedgwick], *Allen Prescott: or, the Fortunes of a New England Boy*, II (New York, 1834), 26–27. Yet Sedgwick could also acknowledge the psychological costs of the masquerade. Alida Frazier is a fine nurse and healer. Her creator observes: "Had she been a man, she would probably have founded a new school of medicine. . . . The bent of her genius, however, being restrained by her sex, she was obliged to follow, where she was well inclined to lead" ([Sedgwick], *Alida*, 22).

and Daniel Davis were among these individuals. The "aged matron" now known only as the "Female Advocate" wrote perhaps the most lucid analysis of the social order of the early Republic as it affected women, attacking contemporary refusals to include women in matters of church and public governance. She wished to function as a citizen, not as a subject. She complained that "men engross all the emoluments, offices, honors and merits of church and state." She conceded that St. Paul had counseled women to be silent in public—"if they would learn anything, let them ask their husbands at home"—but she pointed by contrast to St. Paul's own willingness to appoint women deaconesses. Women were not unsexed by taking part in community decisions: "What if they have no husbands, or what if their husbands . . . are not of the church; or what if, as is very common, the husband knows less of the scriptures than the wife? . . . the point . . . is carried much too far, in the exclusive male prerogative to teach, to censure, to govern without the voice of women, or the least regard to the judgment or assent of the other sex." The proper model for females, she thought, was the biblical Deborah, who lived actively in both the religious and the secular worlds. "Behold her wielding the sword with one hand, and the pen of wisdom with the other; her sitting at the council board, and there, by her superior talents, conducting the arduous affairs of military enterprise! Say now, shall woman be forever destined solely to the distaff and the needle, and never expand an idea beyond the walls of her house?"[18]

Other Americans had also made demands for the direct participation of women in public affairs: there is the well-known comment by Abigail Adams, which her husband jokingly turned away, that women ought to have the right to participate in the new system of government, for "all men would be tyrants if they could." All her life Abigail Adams was a shrewd commentator on the political scene, assuming as active an obligation to judge good and evil as if she were called on annually to vote. But she was known, of course, only in a circle that, though relatively large, remained private. In *Alcuin*, Charles Brockden Brown sneered at the "charming system of equality and independence" that denied women a part in the choice of their governors, but the circulation of his novel was small. St. George Tucker admitted that laws neither respected nor favored females, but he made the concession in a minor aside in a three-volume work. The women led by Esther De Berdt Reed and Sarah Bache through Philadelphia in 1780 to collect contributions for the American soldiers

18. *Female Advocate*, 6, 7–9, 22, 10.

encountered many who thought, with Anna Rawle, that "of all absurdities the ladies going about for money exceeded everything." The campaign did form the model for a score of postwar women's philanthropic groups, but it did not, it has to be said, provide a model of political action except by sacrifice.[19]

Expressions of a desire to play a frankly political role were regularly camouflaged in satire, a device that typically makes criticism less threatening and more palatable. Women continued to use satire as a tactic throughout the years of the early Republic, from the New Jersey "Humble Address of Ten Thousand Federal Maids," published in 1791, to the "Ladies Declaration of Independence," prepared at Sarah Pierce's famous school in Litchfield, Connecticut, on July 4, 1839.[20] Alongside the frivolous phrasing in the Litchfield Declaration is some earnest and serious comment on the unfilled promises of the Republic. Less than ten years later Elizabeth Cady Stanton would use the same technique.

"When in the Course of Human Events," the Litchfield Declaration began,

> it becomes necessary for the Ladies to dissolve those bonds by which they have been subjected to others, and to assume among the self styled Lords of Creation that separate and equal station to which the laws of nature and their *own talents* entitle them, a decent respect to the opinions of mankind requires, that they should declare the causes which impel them to the separation.
>
> We hold these truths to be self evident. That all *mankind* are created equal; that they are endowed with certain unalienable rights; that among these are life liberty and the pursuit of happiness.

The Litchfield women wished to change not governments but "social relations." They complained about men who invaded their tea parties: "They have plundered our pantries, ravaged our sideboards and destroyed our sweetmeats." But they defined social relations very broadly and also complained about men who refused "to pass Laws for the

19. Brown, *Alcuin*, 33; Anna Rawle to Rebecca Rawle Shoemaker, June 30, 1780, Rawle, "Laurel Hill," *PMHB*, XXXV (1911), 398; *The Sentiments of an American Woman* (Broadside), Philadelphia, June 10, 1780.

20. "The Humble Address of Ten Thousand Federal Maids," *Burlington Advt.*, Feb. 8, 1791; Miss Pierce's School Papers, 1839, Litchfield Historical Society, Litchfield, Conn. I am indebted to Prof. Annette Kar Baxter of Barnard College for discovering this document and sharing it with me.

accommodation of large numbers of Ladies unless they would relinquish the right of representation in the Legislature." "They have undervalued our talents, and disparaged our attainments; They have combined with each other, for the purpose of excluding us from all participation in Legislation and in the administration of Justice; From all offices of honor or emolument, From taking any part in public deliberations . . . For declaring themselves invested with power to act & legislate for us in all cases whatsoever."[21]

To accept an openly acknowledged role for women in the public sector was to invite extraordinary hostility and ridicule. Although neither political party took a consistent position on the matter, hostility to women's political participation seems to have been particularly acute in Federalist circles. It is no accident that it was a Republican periodical, for example, that first reprinted Mary Wollstonecraft's *Vindication*. The Federalist *Columbian Centinel* gave space to John Sylvester John Gardiner's antifeminist "Restorator" columns as well as Timothy Dwight's "Morpheus" essays; in other cities it seems to have been taken for granted that Federalist newspapers would be antifeminist. "It is said by one of the federalist papers," remarked the Republican *Register* of Salem, Massachusetts, that "'Women have no business to speak about politicks and that a woman meddling in politicks is like a monkey in a China ware shop, where he can't do any good but may do a great deal of mischief.' On our part we are of a contrary opinion, we can see no reason why, with the same evidence before them, they cannot judge on politicks or any other subject equally with men—On many subjects they certainly are better judges."[22]

Partisans were under no pressure to be consistent; but some arguments developed a life of their own, appearing and reappearing under different disguises. Among these the most persistent was the argument that linked female political autonomy to an unflattering masculinity. The tone of this antipolitical complaint was not unlike the anti-intellectualism directed against women, and indeed often appeared in conjunction with it. "From all we read, and all we observe, we are authorized in supposing that there is a *sex of soul*," wrote John Sylvester John Gardiner. "Women of masculine minds, have generally masculine manners. . . . Queen Elizabeth understood Latin and Greek, swore with the fluency of a sailor, and boxed the ears of her courtiers. . . . Mrs. Macaulay, the author of a dull

21. Miss Pierce's School Papers, 1839.
22. *Register* (Salem, Mass.), Oct. 4, 1802, Tapley, *Salem Imprints*, 118–119.

Philip Dawes, *A Society of Patriotic Ladies* (1775). Dawes's 1775 mezzotint offers the stereotype of the "patriotic lady" as necessarily ugly or foolish (note especially the two right foreground figures). A neglected child has come to grief under the table, attended only by a loyal dog, as the women attend to more pressing matters.
Courtesy The Library of Congress, Washington, D.C.

democratic history, at a tolerably advanced age, married a boy." A "mild, dove-like temper is so necessary to Female beauty, is so natural a part of the sex," reflected Parson Weems wistfully. "A masculine air in a woman frightens us."[23]

The fears seem similar, whether women put their minds to work on abstract problems or on political ones. A good example of this response appears in a letter written in 1790 by an unidentifiable Marylander who signed as Philanthropos. He was responding to another letter, now lost, that had appeared in the *Virginia Gazette* and had apparently offered a radical reading of the phrase "All mankind are born equal." Philanthropos thought the principle of equality could be "taken in too extensive a sense, and might tend to destroy those degrees of subordination which nature seems to point out," including the subordination of women to men. "However flattering the path of glory and ambition may be, a woman will have more commendation in being the mother of heroes, than in setting up, Amazon-like, for a heroine herself." The reasons he offered in support of the continued exclusion of women from "political bustle and anxiety" were of three sorts. Women, involved as they were with domestic cares, had no time for politics. Women were inept at politics; behind every queen lurked male advisers and guiding the well-known political vigor of Quaker women was a peculiar and distasteful view of the nature of the universe. But if women were inept, they were also somehow too effective. "A Female Orator, in haranging an Assembly, might like many crafty politicians, keep her *best argument* for last, and would then be sure of the victory—Men would be exposed to temptations too great for their strength, and those who could resist a bribe, offered in the common way, might reasonably yield to what it would be hardly possible for a *man* to refuse." Although the political woman was thus thought to be sexually aggressive, "famous" women of the past were, however, "generally deficient in those charms which it is the peculiar lot of the fair sex to excel in." Philanthropos ended with the familiar argument that as long as virtuous women had private opportunity to influence men and to "mould our minds," they ought not regret "their exclusion from the perplexity and tumult of a political life."[24]

In the next year, 1791, the *Burlington Advertiser* published a pair of semiserious satires in which women discuss the politics of excise taxes and national defense. Maria concedes that "the laws of Providence are

23. *Mercury and N.-E. Palladium*, Sept. 18, 1801.
24. *Va. Gaz. and Alexandria Advt.* (Alexandria), Apr. 22, 1790.

immutable: Man must do the rough work of society: Woman shines in the tender cares and elegant arts of domestic life." Roxana expresses a feminist impatience: "In fifty quarto volumes of ancient and modern history, you will not find fifty illustrious female names; heroes, statesmen, divines, philosophers, artists, are all of masculine gender. And pray what have they done during this long period of usurpation? . . . They have written ten thousand unintelligible books. . . . They have been cutting each other's throats all over the globe."[25] But even Roxana is made to slide into the now standard "Amazonian" vision; her brave new world is one in which female sexuality is unchecked and men are kept ignorant and servile—"the least defective males" reserved for sexual service. Once again, political autonomy seemed to lead straight to sexual radicalism for women and effeminacy for men.

Mary Wollstonecraft's own life story, once it was available in Godwin's memoir, could also be used to link political feminism to aggressive sexuality, as Timothy Dwight did in his bitter "Morpheus" essays. In an early dream sequence in "Morpheus," Wollstonecraft has arrived in America and sets out to teach its inhabitants wisdom.

> Women . . . are entitled to all the rights, and are capable of all the energies, of men. I do not mean merely mental energies. If any dispute remained on this subject, I have removed it entirely by displaying, in my immortal writings, all the mental energy of LOCKE and BACON. I intend bodily energies. They can naturally run as fast, leap as high, and as far, and wrestle, scuffle, and box, with as much success, as any of the . . . other sex.
>
> That is a mistake (said an old man just before her.)
>
> It is no mistake, (said the Female Philosopher.)
>
> . . . Why then, (said the senior again) are women always feebler than men?
>
> Because (said MARY) they are educated to be feeble; and by indulgence merely, and false philosophy, are made poor, puny, baby-faced dolls; instead of the *manly women*, they ought to be.
>
> *Manly women*! (cried the wag). Wheu! a manly woman is a hoyden, a non descript.
>
> Am I a hoyden? (interrupted MARY, with spirit)
>
> You used to be a strumpet.

25. *Burlington Advt.*, Feb. 1, 1791.

She tells him that she was not a strumpet but a sentimental lover, "too free to brook the restraints of marriage." Her interlocutor responds, "We call them strumpets here, Madam—no offence, I hope," and then argues that when a woman claims the rights of men and the character of a manly woman, she necessarily forgoes what he calls women's "own rights" to "refined consideration." The implication is that Wollstonecraft can be insulted with impunity. "Still, (said the senior) you ought to remember that she is a woman. *She* ought to remember it (said the young man.)" Thus political behavior, like abstract thought, continued to be specifically proscribed as a threat to sensual attractiveness. "*Cupid* is a timid, playful child, and is frightened at the helmet of Minerva," observed Maria Edgeworth.[26]

Only the Republican Mother was spared this hostility. In the years of the early Republic a consensus developed around the idea that a mother, committed to the service of her family and to the state, might serve a political purpose. Those who opposed women in politics had to meet the proposal that women could—and should—play a political role through the raising of a patriotic child. The Republican Mother was to encourage in her sons civic interest and participation. She was to educate her children and guide them in the paths of morality and virtue. But she was not to tell her male relatives for whom to vote. She was a citizen but not really a constituent.

Western political theory, even during the Enlightenment, had only occasionally contemplated the role of women in the civic culture. It had habitually considered women only in domestic relationships, only as wives and mothers. A political community that accepted women as political actors would have to eliminate the Rousseauistic assumption that the world of women is separate from the empire of men. The ideology of Republican Motherhood seemed to accomplish what the Enlightenment had not by identifying the intersection of the woman's private domain and the polis.

The notion that a mother can perform a political function represents the recognition that a citizen's political socialization takes place at an early age, that the family is a basic part of the system of political communication, and that patterns of family authority influence the general political culture. Yet most premodern political societies—and even some

---

26. "Morpheus," Pt. ii, No. 1, *Mercury and N.-E. Palladium*, Mar. 2, 1802; Edgeworth, *Letters for Literary Ladies*, 22. In Brown, *Alcuin*, 64, the absence of marriage is suggested as a primary feature of a utopian paradise of women.

fairly modern democracies—maintained unarticulated, but nevertheless very firm, social restrictions that isolated the female domestic world from politics. The willingness of the American woman to overcome this ancient separation brought her into the all-male political community.[27] In this sense, Republican Motherhood was a very important, even revolutionary, invention. It altered the female domain in which most women had always lived out their lives; it justified women's absorption and participation in the civic culture.[28]

Women had the major role in developing this formulation, women who had learned from the exigencies of the Revolution that the country needed Marias, not Louisas; Constantias, not Helenas. Those who shared the vision of the Republican Mother usually insisted upon better education, clearer recognition of women's economic contributions, and a strong political identification with the Republic. The idea could be pulled in both conservative and reform directions. It would be vulnerable to absorption in the domestic feminism of the Victorian period, to romanticization, even, in the "cult of true womanhood." It would be revived as a rallying point for twentieth-century Progressive women reformers, who saw their commitment to honest politics, efficient urban sanitation, and pure food and drug laws as an extension of their responsibilities as mothers. Yet despite its contradictory elements, this ideology was strong enough to rout Philanthropos and Morpheus by redefining female political behavior as valuable rather than abnormal, as a source of strength to the Republic rather than an embarrassment.

The triumph of Republican Motherhood also represented a stage in the process of women's political socialization. In recent years, political socialization has been viewed as a process in which an individual develops a definition of self as related to the state.[29] One of the intermediate stages in that process is called deference, in which a person expects

27. Gabriel A. Almond and Sidney Verba, *The Civic Culture: Political Attitudes and Democracy in Five Nations* (Princeton, N.J., 1963), 377–401.

28. Judith Jeffrey Howard finds a similar cluster of concerns in the ideal of the "patriotic mother" that was popular in Italy after the *Risorgimento*. In Italy, as in America, the notion of a mother who was political as well as domestic was a "Janus-faced" mediating device on which radicals and moderates could agree ("Women after the Italian Revolution" [paper delivered at the Conference on the Impact of Revolution and War on Women, Baruch College, City University of New York, 1978]). For a view that often contrasts with my own, see Joan Hoff Wilson, "The Illusion of Change: Women and the American Revolution," in Alfred F. Young, ed., *The American Revolution: Explorations in the History of American Radicalism* (Dekalb, Ill., 1976), 383–445.

29. See Almond and Verba, *Civic Culture*. The authors view politicization as a gradual process by which individuals cease to think of themselves as invariably acted *on* by the state,

to influence the political system, but only to a limited extent. Deference represents not a negation of citizenship, but an approach to full participation in the civic culture. The best description of this stage is Charles Sydnor's account of voting in Jefferson's Virginia. The Virginians freely chose their social superiors to office, but exercised no claim on office themselves.[30]

Deference was adopted and displayed by many women at a time when men were gradually abandoning that attitude; the politicization of women and men in America, as elsewhere, was out of phase. Women were still thinking of themselves as subjects while men were deferential citizens. As men then replaced the restrained, deferential democracy of the Republic with an aggressive, egalitarian democracy of a modern sort, women invented a restrained, deferential, but nonetheless political, role. The voters of colonial Virginia did not think themselves good enough to stand for election, but they chose legislators; the deferential women whom Judith Sargent Murray prescribed for the Republic did not vote, but they took pride in their ability to mold voting citizens. This hesitancy of American women to become political actors would persist. Are not the women of the postsuffrage twentieth century who did not use the vote to elect people like themselves similar to the deferential males of Jefferson's Virginia?

There was a direct relationship between the developing egalitarian democracy among men and the expectation of continued deferential behavior among women. Emile needs Sophie; the society in which he functions cannot exist without her. Just as planters claimed that democracy in the antebellum South rested on the economic base of slavery, so egalitarian society was said to rest on the moral base of deference among a class of people—women—who would devote their efforts to service: raising sons and disciplining husbands to be virtuous citizens of the Republic. The learned woman, who might very well wish to make choices as well as to influence attitudes, was a visible threat to this arrangement.

Republican Motherhood was a concept that legitimized a minimum of political sophistication and interest, and only of a most generalized sort. Skeptics could easily maintain that women should be content to perform this narrow political role permanently and ought not to wish for fuller

---

and end by thinking of themselves as *actors*, who force governments to respond to them. There are many stages along this continuum, and there is room for internal contradiction.

30. Sydnor, *Gentlemen Freeholders*.

Liberty and Washington, unknown artist (*ca.* 1800–1810).
Courtesy New York State Historical Association, Cooperstown.

participation. Women could be encouraged to contain their judgments as republicans within their homes and families rather than to bridge the world outside and the world within. In this sense, restricting women's politicization was one of a series of conservative choices that Americans made in the postwar years as they avoided the full implications of their own revolutionary radicalism. In America, responsibility for maintaining public virtue was channeled into domestic life. By these decisions Americans may well have been spared the agony of the French cycle of revolution and counterrevolution, which spilled more blood and produced a political system more retrogressive than had the American war. Nevertheless, the impact of many of these choices was to inhibit the resolution of matters of particular concern to women.

It has often been noted that an apparently apathetic population can become intensely political when real issues present themselves. But despite the increasing political sophistication of the male public, women were left with only the most primitive of political mechanisms: the personal or collective petition. That women made increasingly effective use of this option throughout the antebellum period does not negate the point that only a deferential political role was thought to be appropriate for them. The failure to establish an effective pension system for war widows suggests the limited responsiveness of legislators to women's real needs. Another index of the conservatism of the early Republic is the failure to give high priority to the liberalization of divorce. It is true that in Massachusetts and Connecticut, women made extensive use of the opportunity for divorce provided by colonial law, but most colonies did not have simple divorce codes, nor did any except Pennsylvania hurry to provide them after the Revolution.

When the war was over, Judith Sargent Murray predicted "a new era in female history." That new era remained to be created by women, fortified by their memories and myths of female strength during the trials of war, politicized by their resentment of male legislators slighting issues of greatest significance to women. But it could not be created until the inherent paradox of Republican Motherhood was resolved, until the world was not separated into a woman's realm of domesticity and nurture and a man's world of politics and intellect. The promises of the Republic had yet to be fulfilled; remembering the Revolution helped to keep confidence alive. "Yes, gentlemen," said Elizabeth Cady Stanton to the New York Legislature in 1854, "in republican America . . . we, the daughters of the revolutionary heroes of '76 demand at your hands the redress of our grievances—a revision of your State constitution—a new code of laws."[31] Stanton would wrestle throughout her own career with the contradictory demands of domesticity and civic activism. The ambivalent relationship between motherhood and citizenship would be one of the most lasting, and most paradoxical, legacies of the Revolutionary generation.

31. Elizabeth Cady Stanton, Susan B. Anthony, and Matilda Joslyn Gage, eds., *History of Woman Suffrage*, I (New York, 1881), 595.

A Note on Sources

"In offering this work to the public," wrote the first historian who sought to chronicle women's impact on the American Revolution, "it is due to the reader . . . to say something of the extreme difficulty which has been found in obtaining materials sufficiently reliable for a record designed to be strictly authentic." Elizabeth F. Ellet's comment of 1849 has not lost its force. Because it has been common to catalog women's letters and diaries under their husbands' names, women's manuscripts have often been submerged in family collections, and the size of the written record has often been underestimated. The letters of Ruth Barlow and Elisabeth Whitman, for example, are part of the Baldwin Family Papers at the Huntington Library, San Marino, California. The papers of Harriott Pinckney Horry are scattered in several Pinckney Family collections. The Hopkinson Family collection at the Historical Society of Pennsylvania was organized by a nineteenth-century archivist into eleven carefully chronological volumes of letters by men, followed by a miscellaneous twelfth volume marked "Letters from Ladies."

Undaunted by the enigmatic record, Mary Sumner Benson analyzed women's status in *Women in Eighteenth-Century America: A Study of Opinion and Social Usage* (New York, 1935); her book should be supplemented by Janet Wilson James's important dissertation, "Changing Ideas about Women in the United States, 1776–1825" (Ph.D. diss., Radcliffe College, 1954). Yet another twenty years elapsed before substantial historical attention was again directed at the role of women in the early Republic. This literature is succinctly reviewed in Barbara Sicherman, "Review Essay: American History," *Signs: Journal of Women in Culture and Society*, I (1975), 461–486, and in Mary Beth Norton, "Review Essay: American History," *ibid.*, V (1979), 324–337.

Among the more than two hundred manuscript collections consulted, the most useful for this book have been:

American Antiquarian Society, Worcester, Mass.: Abigail Adams Papers; Diary of Elizabeth Bancroft; Diary of Ruth Henshaw Bascom; Elijah Bigelow Papers; Mary Barker Farnum Diary; Sophia May Papers; Sarah Osborn Papers; Journal of Sally Ripley; Journal of Polly Rogers.

Special Collections, Columbia University: John Jay Papers.

Historical Society of Pennsylvania, Philadelphia: Elizabeth Sandwith Drinker Diary; Elizabeth Graeme Ferguson Correspondence (Gratz Collection); Samuel Rowlandson Fisher Diaries; Hopkinson Family Papers; Deborah Norris Logan Diary; Maria Dickinson Logan Papers; Meredith Family Papers; Pemberton Family Papers; Shippen Family Papers; Rebecca Shoemaker, Anna Rawle, and Margaret Rawle, Letters and Diaries.

Huntington Library, San Marino, Calif.: Baldwin Family Papers; Susan Johnson Journal; Martha Washington Letters.

Library Company of Philadelphia: Hannah Griffitts Papers; Correspondence of Benjamin Rush.

Library of Congress, Washington, D.C.: Elizabeth Jacquelin Ambler Papers; Cranch Family Papers; Pinckney Family Papers; Shaw Family Papers; Shippen Family Papers; Mercy Otis Warren Papers.

Massachusetts Historical Society, Boston: Adams Family Papers (available on microfilm); William Livingston Papers; Elizabeth Cranch Norton Diaries; Journal of Eliza Susan Quincy; Quincy-Howe Papers; Ridley Family Papers; Sedgwick Family Papers; Mercy Otis Warren Letterbook; Mercy Otis Warren Papers.

New-York Historical Society, New York City: Margaretta Ackerly Papers; Beekman Family Papers; Narrative of Helen Kortright Brasher; Aaron Burr Papers; Church Family Papers; John Jay Papers; John Tabor Kempe Papers; McDonald Papers (interviews with Westchester County survivors of the Revolution); Stocking Society Papers; Tryon County Papers; Williams Family Papers.

New York Public Library, New York City: Journal of Louisa Ackley; Susan Adams Papers; Journal of Henrietta Cornelia Bevier; Henry Callister Correspondence.

North Carolina Division of Archives and History, Raleigh, N.C.: Governor's Letterbooks; Iredell Family Correspondence; Johnson Family Collection; Little-Mordecai Collection; Pattie Mordecai Collection.

Sophia Smith Collection, Smith College, Northampton, Mass.: Letters and Diary of Mary Ann Archbold.

South Carolina Department of Archives and History, Columbia, S.C.: General Assembly Petitions.

South Carolina Historical Society, Charleston, S.C.: Charleston Poor House Journals; Commonplace Book of Ann Deas; Henry Laurens Papers; Manigault Family Papers; Middleton Family Papers; Eliza Lucas Pinckney Papers; Day Book of Harriott Pinckney; Pinckney Family Papers; Susannah Quince Papers; Rutledge Family Papers.

South Caroliniana Library, Columbia, S.C.: Izard Family Papers; Manigault Family Papers; Rebecca Motte Papers; Eliza Lucas Pinckney Papers; Sumter-Delage Papers; Eliza Wilkinson Papers.

Andrea Hinding, ed., *Women's History Sources: A Guide to Archives and Manuscript Collections in the United States,* 2 vols. (Ann Arbor, Mich., 1979) will greatly facilitate the work of future researchers.

The titles indexed in Charles Evans and Clifford K. Shipton, eds., *American Bibliography,* 14 vols. (Chicago, 1903–1955) and in Ralph R. Shaw and Richard H. Shoemaker, *American Bibliography: A Preliminary Checklist for 1801–1819,* 19 vols. (New York, 1958–1963) are being made available by the American Antiquarian Society in a Readex Microprint edition. *Early American Imprints: 1639–1800* (Worcester, Mass., 1956–1964) and *Early American Imprints, 2nd Series, 1801–1819* (Worcester, Mass., 1964–) include well over 300 titles by or about women published between 1750 and 1810. They include funeral sermons, memoirs, speeches, advice manuals, and fiction.

Periodicals varied in the extent to which they published material by and about women. The most useful for this book have been: *American Museum* (Philadelphia); *Baltimore Weekly Magazine*; *Boston Magazine*; *Independent Chronicle* (Boston); *Columbian Magazine, or Monthly Miscellany* (continued as the *Universal Asylum and Columbian Magazine*); *Weekly Magazine* (Philadelphia); *Evening Fireside* (Philadelphia); *Lady and Gentleman's Pocket Magazine of Literary and Polite Amusement* (New York); *Lady's Magazine* (Philadelphia); *Literary Magazine and American Register* (Philadelphia); *Massachusetts Mercury* (Boston); *Monthly Anthology* (Boston); *Mercury and New-England Palladium* (Boston); *New York Magazine*; *Philadelphia Minerva*; *Port Folio* (Philadelphia). An important guide to the periodicals is Eugene L. Huddleston, "Feminist Verse Satire in America: A Checklist, 1700–1800," *Bulletin of Bibliography*, XXXII (1975), 115–122.

A massive collection of the papers of the Continental Congress is available on microfilm as National Archives Microfilm Publication M-247. It includes many depositions and petitions by women, accounts of money owed to women, and records of slave women who fled with the British. These records are easier to search now that a computer index to them is available in the National Archives in Washington, D.C.

Historians of American law have paid relatively little attention to the difference in the impact of law on women from that on men. The work of Richard B. Morris is a rare exception to this generalization. His *Studies in the History of Early American Law* (New York, 1930), Section IV, is still useful although it probably paints too optimistic a picture of the advantages women gained when they moved from England to the colonies. See also Richard B. Morris, ed., *Select Cases of the Mayor's Court of New York City, 1674–1784* (Washington, D.C., 1935). Lawrence M. Friedman briefly discusses women's legal status in the early Republic in *A History of American Law* (New York, 1973), 179–186. For English precedent, see Frederick Pollock and Frederic William Maitland, *History of English Law before the Time of Edward I*, 2d ed. (Cambridge, 1968), I, 482–485, II, 399–406. Early American legal treatises are important guides to contemporary understanding of the law. Among the most thorough are Zephaniah Swift, *A System of the Laws of the State of Connecticut*, 2 vols. (Windham, Conn., 1795); Tapping Reeve, *The Law of Baron and Femme . . .* (New Haven, Conn., 1816); James Kent, *Commentaries on American Law*, 4 vols. (New York, 1826–1830). A succinct guide to early American court reports appears in Friedman, *History of American Law*, 282–292. See also William Jeffrey, Jr., "Early New England Court Records—A Bibliography of Published Materials," *American Journal of Legal History*, I (1957), 119–124, and David H. Flaherty, "A Select Guide to Manuscript Court Records of Colonial New England," *ibid.*, XI (1967), 107–126. State libraries often can provide checklists of their own legal materials.

A clear introduction to the work of Superior Courts at the end of the colonial period is John T. Farrell, ed., *The Superior Court Diary of William Samuel Johnson, 1772–1773* (Washington, D.C., 1942). It should be supplemented by Farrell, "The Administration of Justice in Connecticut about the Middle of the Eighteenth Century" (Ph.D. diss., Yale University, 1937). The most accessible introduction to equity in the early Republic is Henry William DeSaussure, *Re-*

ports of Cases Argued and Determined in the Court of Chancery in the State of South Carolina, from the Revolution, to [June 1817], 2 vols. (Philadelphia, 1854 [orig. publ. 1817]).

The availability of divorce varied greatly from state to state. See Nancy F. Cott, "Divorce and the Changing Status of Women in Eighteenth-Century Massachusetts," *William and Mary Quarterly,* 3d Ser., XXXIII (1976), 586–614; Thomas R. Meehan, " 'Not Made Out of Levity': Evolution of Divorce in Early Pennsylvania," *Pennsylvania Magazine of History and Biography,* XCII (1968), 441–464; Haywood Roebuck, "North Carolina Divorce and Alimony Petitions: 1813," *North Carolina Genealogical Society Journal,* I (1975), 75–90; James S. Van Ness, "On Untieing the Knot: The Maryland Legislature and Divorce Petitions," *Maryland Historical Magazine,* LXVII (1972), 171–175; William Nelson, ed., "The Early Marriage Laws of New Jersey and the Precedents on Which They Were Founded," in *Documents Relating to the Colonial History of the State of New Jersey (Archives of the State of New Jersey),* 1st Ser., XXII (Trenton, N.J., 1900), cxxiii–cxxvi.

The basic framework for discussing the iconography of the Republic has been established by E. McClung Fleming in two magisterial articles: "The American Image as Indian Princess, 1765–1783," *Winterthur Portfolio,* II (1965), 65–81; and "From Indian Princess to Greek Goddess: The American Image, 1783–1815," *ibid.,* III (1966), 37–66. Fleming traces the evolution of the personification of America from the seventeenth-century image of an "Indian Queen denoting the western hemisphere in the vigorous tradition of the far Continents, to an Indian Princess," who in turn is modified "from a dependent daughter to a free sister of Brittania." Basic guides include Clarence S. Brigham, *Paul Revere's Engravings* (Worcester, Mass., 1954); Lynn Glaser, comp., *Engraved America: Iconography of America through 1800* (Philadelphia, 1970); and Donald H. Cresswell, comp., *The American Revolution in Drawings and Prints: A Checklist of 1765–1790 Graphics in the Library of Congress* (Washington, D.C., 1975). For British prints, see Frederic George Stephens, *Catalogue of Prints and Drawings in the British Museum, Division I: Political and Personal Satires,* IV, V (London, 1883). Several catalogs from Bicentennial exhibits include female images and artifacts. See *A Rising People: The Founding of the United States, 1765 to 1789: A Celebration from the Collections of the American Philosophical Society, The Historical Society of Pennsylvania, The Library Company of Philadelphia* (Philadelphia, 1976); *Paul Revere's Boston* (Boston, 1975); and Lillian B. Miller et al., *"The Dye Is Now Cast": The Road to American Independence, 1774–1776* (Washington, D.C., 1975). In "From Liberty to Prosperity: Reflections upon the Role of Revolutionary Iconography in National Tradition," American Antiquarian Society, *Proceedings,* LXXXVI, part 2 (1976), 237–272, Michael Kammen traces the changing iconography of the image of Liberty. He argues that in the decade after 1796 the image of Liberty, once associated with emblems of republican rectitude and power such as the liberty pole and the eagle (and, I would add, emblems of intellect such as books and Minerva), was first accompanied and then replaced by images of prosperity, such as the cornucopia, fruit and grain, and the plow.

Clothing worn by women and the domestic items made and used by them, as well as portraits and engravings of women, are richly illustrated in Linda Grant De Pauw and Conover Hunt, *Remember the Ladies: Women in America, 1750–1815* (New York, 1976). Decorative and practical women's needlework is illustrated and placed in a historical context by Susan Burrows Swan, *Plain and Fancy: American Women and Their Needlework, 1700–1850* (New York, 1977).

Index

Ogden, John, 252
Oratory, 190 and n, 222, 275
Ormond, 271–272
Osgood, Daniel, 175
Otis, James, 13, 30–31, 80
Ott, Abigail, 86
Otto, Louis Guillaume, 181, 183

Palmer, Elizabeth, 80
Parker, Isaac, 147
Parker, Margaret, 53n
Parsons, Theophilus, 133, 134
Passion: attacks on, in fiction, 235, 239–245; in *La Nouvelle Héloïse*, 241–243; and republican ideals, 245
Patriotism: linked to motherhood, 11–12, 36, 84, 228, 235, 283; as exclusively male virtue, 24, 27, 35–36; Abigail Adams on female, 35, 36, 67; political activists redefine female, 104–105, 110, 269–271, 273, 274; as passive female virtue, 106, 110; linked to religious obligations, 110, 111, 113; Judith Sargent Murray on female, 259. *See also* Political behavior, women's; Republican Mother
Peale, Charles Willson, 75
Pease, Violet, 150
Pemberton, Mary, 95, 96
Pemberton, P[olly?], 96
Pendarvis, Mrs. (South Carolina loyalist), 129
Pennsylvania: hospitals in, 61; loyalists in, 86; property rights in, 145, 147; divorce in, 160, 181, 287. *See also* Philadelphia, Pennsylvania
Pensions: for war widows, 92, 287
Persian Letters, 19–20
Petitions, women's: as political device, 41, 85, 93–94, 99, 112, 162, 287
Philadelphia, Pennsylvania: patriot reoccupation of, 44, 51, 53, 65–66, 75; hospital in, 61; Continental Congress in, 61, 62, 79; Quaker community in, 63, 95–98; British occupation of, 63–64, 95; fundraising drive in, 99, 102–105; schools in, 210–212
"Philanthropos," 281
Philosophes: on political role of

women, 8, 15–16, 27, 105, 283. *See also* individual names
Pierce, Sarah, 202, 209, 214, 215, 278
Pinckney, Charles Cotesworth, 149
Pinckney, Eliza Lucas, 191–192
Pinckney, Harriott, 191
Plato, 26
Platt, Gerald M., 27
Pleasants, Mary, 96
Political behavior, women's: confined to domestic world, 7, 11–12, 36, 37, 76, 83–85, 276, 277, 278, 283, 287; compared to men's, 7–8, 73, 154; philosophes on, 8, 15–16, 105, 283; collective, 8, 41, 43–44, 67, 95–99, 102–104, 111, 112–113, 278; of *femes covert*, 9, 119–120, 123, 126–127, 129–130, 131, 133–136, 139, 159; role models for, 32, 104–105, 112, 206–207, 259, 277; in household economy, 37–45; petitions as mode of, 41, 85, 93–94, 112, 162, 287; and wartime activism, 54–60, 66–67, 73–74, 104–105, 110, 119, 269–271; tradition of deference in, 74, 78–80, 85; and religion, 110, 111, 113; J. Q. Adams on, 112; demands for public outlet for, 276–279; hostility toward, 279, 281–283. *See also* Patriotism; Republican Mother
Poor relief, 47, 142–143, 165, 170, 253
Port Folio, 247, 259
Pratt, Mary, 54 and n
Privy Council, of England, 160, 161, 181
Progressive movement, 284
Property and property rights: of married women, 9, 10, 120, 123, 141–142, 144–148; effect of, on women's political rights, 9, 36, 120; of loyalists' wives, 9, 50, 75, 123–134; petitions concerning women's, 54, 99, 127–129; of single women, 120; in prenuptial contracts, 141–142, 143; of widows, 141–142, 146–147; in Pennsylvania, 145, 147; and divorce, 167, 168–169, 170, 174, 180. *See also* Coverture; Dower rights